# THE ANCIENT HISTORIAN AND HIS MATERIALS

# THE ANCIENT HISTORIAN AND HIS MATERIALS

*Essays in honour of C. E. Stevens*
*on his seventieth birthday*

*edited by Barbara Levick*

1975

GREGG INTERNATIONAL

© GREGG INTERNATIONAL, D. C. Heath Ltd., 1975

ISBN 0 576 78240 8
Library of Congress Catalog Card Number 74-24315

Published in 1975 by GREGG INTERNATIONAL, D. C. Heath
Ltd., Westmead, Farnborough, Hants, England.

Typeset in Great Britain by
PREFACE LIMITED, Salisbury, Wilts
and printed in Great Britain by
REDWOOD BURN LIMITED,
Trowbridge and Esher

# Contents

# List of Abbreviations
(Modern Works Only)

| | |
|---|---|
| *AASOR* | *Annual of the American Schools of Oriental Research* |
| *ABSA* | *Annual of the British School at Athens* |
| *AE* | *L'Année Épigraphique* |
| *AHR* | *American Historical Review* |
| *AJP* | *American Journal of Philology* |
| *L'Ant. Class.* | *L'Antiquité Classique* |
| *Ath.* | *Athenaeum* |
| *BCH* | *Bulletin de Correspondance Hellénique* |
| *BJ* | *Bonner Jahrbücher* |
| *Brit.* | *Britannia* |
| *CAH* | *The Cambridge Ancient History* |
| *C et M* | *Classica et Medievalia* |
| *CIL* | *Corpus Inscriptionum Latinarum* |
| *CJ* | *Classical Journal* |
| *CP* | *Classical Philology* |
| *CQ* | *Classical Quarterly* |
| *CR* | *Classical Review* |
| *CREBM* | H. Mattingly, *Coins of the Roman Empire in the British Museum*, London 1923— |
| *EE* | *Ephemeris Epigraphica* |
| *EHR* | *English Historical Review* |
| *EJ²* | V. Ehrenberg and A. H. M. Jones, ed. *Documents illustrating the Reigns of Augustus and Tiberius*, ed. 2, Oxford 1955. |
| *FD* | *Fouilles de Delphes*, Paris 1909 |
| *G and R* | *Greece and Rome* |
| *GHI* | *Greek Historical Inscriptions* |

| | |
|---|---|
| GRBS | *Greek, Roman, and Byzantine Studies* |
| Herm. | *Hermes* |
| Hesp. | *Hesperia* |
| Hist. | *Historia* |
| IEJ | *Israel Exploration Journal* |
| ILLRP | A. Degrassi, ed., *Inscriptiones Latinae Liberae Reipublicae* |
| ILS | H. Dessau, ed., *Inscriptiones Latinae Selectae* |
| JRS | *Journal of Roman Studies* |
| Lat. | *Latomus* |
| MEFR | *Mélanges d'Archéologie et d'Histoire de l'École française de Rome* |
| MGH | *Monumenta Germaniae Historica* |
| NS | *Notizie degli Scavi di Antichità* |
| OCD | *Oxford Classical Dictionary* |
| OCT | Oxford Classical Text |
| PACA | *Proceedings of the African Classical Associations* |
| PBA | *Proceedings of the British Academy* |
| PBSR | *Papers of the British School at Rome* |
| Philol. | *Philologus* |
| PIR | *Prosopographia Imperii Romani* |
| PL | J. P. Migne, *Patrologia Latina* |
| RE | *Paulys Real-Encyclopädie der classischen Altertumswissenschaft* |
| REA | *Revue des Études anciennes* |
| Rev. Phil. | *Revue de Philologie* |
| RIC | H. Mattingly, E. A. Sydenham, etc., *The Roman Imperial Coinage*, London 1923–67 |
| RM | *Rheinisches Museum für Philologie* |
| RN | *Revue numismatique* |
| RR | R. Syme, *The Roman Revolution*, Oxford 1939 |
| SEG | *Supplementum Epigraphicum Graecum* |
| SIG | *Sylloge Inscriptionum Graecarum* |
| St. | Th. Mommsen, *Römisches Staatsrecht*, Leipzig 1887–88 |
| TAPA | *Transactions and Proceedings of the American Philological Association* |
| TG | *Tijdschrift voor Gescheidenis* |
| WS | *Wiener Studien* |
| YCS | *Yale Classical Studies* |
| ZDPV | *Zeitschrift des deutschen Palästina-Vereins* |
| ZfPE | *Zeitschrift für Papyrologie und Epigraphik* |

# A List of the Published Writings of Courtenay Edward Stevens

1932 'L'Archéologie romaine en Grande-Bretagne' *Association Guillaume Budé: Actes du Congrès de Nîmes*, Paris 1932, pp.165—171.

1933 *Sidonius Apollinaris and his Age*, Oxford 1933.

1934 'A Roman Inscription from Beltingham' *Archaeologia Aeliana* ser. 4 vol. 11, 1934, pp. 138—145.

1935 'Ramparts of Dorchester, Oxfordshire' *Antiquity* vol. 9, 1935, pp.217—218 (with G. S. Keeney).

1936 'The Coin of Arcadius from Heddon-on-the-Wall' *JRS* vol. 26, 1936, pp.71—73.
*Catalogue of Romano-British Pottery and other Items found on the Site of the Hall of the Institute, 20 Aldermanbury, London, E.C. 6.* [London 1936].

1937 'Gildas and the Civitates of Britain' *EHR* vol. 52, 1937, pp. 193—201.
'The Defences of Roman Dorchester' *Oxoniensia* vol. 2, 1937, pp. 41—73 (with A. H. A. Hogg).
'Un Établissement celtique à la Croix de Hengstberg, Commune de Walscheid, Sarrebourg (Moselle)' *Rev. Arch.* ser. 6 vol. 9, 1937, pp.26—37.

1938 'The Terminal Date of Caesar's Command in Gaul' *AJP* vol. 59, 1938, pp. 169—208.
'Existait-il à Évreux une Enceinte du Haut-Empire?' *REA* vol. 40, 1938, pp. 399—401.
'Magnus Maximus in British History' *Études celtiques* vol. 3, 1938, pp. 86—94.

1939 'The Fosse Way at Culkerton Wood' *Transactions of the Bristol and Gloucestershire Archaeological Society* vol. 61, 1939, pp.132—34.

1940 'The Frilford Site — a Postscript' *Oxoniensia* vol. 5, 1940, pp.166—67.

'L'Irlande et la Bretagne romaine' *Mélanges Radet, REA* vol. 42 (1940), pp. 671—81.

Review of the *Victoria History of the Counties of England, Oxfordshire*, vol. 1, ed. L. F. Salzman, London 1939, ibid. pp. 174—76 (with J. N. L. Myres).

1941 'Gildas Sapiens' *EHR* vol. 56, 1941, pp. 353—373.

'Agriculture and Rural Life in the Later Roman Empire' in the *Cambridge Economic History of Europe* vol. 1, Cambridge 1941 and (ed. 2) 1966.

'The British Sections of the Notitia Dignitatum' *Archaeological Journal* vol. 97, 1940 (published 1941), pp. 125—54.

'Earthworks on Hayes and West Wickham Commons' *Archaeologia Cantiana* vol. 54, 1941, pp. 28—34 (with A. H. A. Hogg and B. H. St. J. O'Neil).

1942 'The Land-Register of Arausio', *JRS* vol. 32, 1942, pp. 65—77 (with I. A. Richmond).

'Notes on Roman Chester' *Journ. of the Chester and N. Wales Archaeological Society* vol. 35, 1942, pp. 49—52.

1946 Translation of R. Lantier, 'Roman Gaul, 1940—44' *JRS* vol. 36, 1946, pp. 76—90.

1947 'A possible Conflict of Laws in Roman Britain' *JRS* vol. 37, 1947, pp. 132—34.

'55 B.C. and 54 B.C.' *Antiquity* vol. 21, 1947, pp. 3—9.

Translation of R. Lantier, 'Christian and Merovingian Gaul, 1940—44' *Antiquaries' Journ.* vol. 27, 1947, pp. 7—10.

1948 'The Building of Hadrian's Wall' *Archaeologia Aeliana* ser. 4 vol. 26, 1948, pp. 1—49.

1949 'A forgotten Specimen of Roman Sculpture from Hadrian's Wall' *Proceedings of the Society of Antiquaries of Newcastle-upon-Tyne* ser. 4 vol 11, 1949, pp. 264—268.

Review of R. Thomsen, *The Italic Regions from Augustus to the Lombard Invasions*, Copenhagen 1947, in *EHR* vol. 64, 1949, pp. 89—92.

1951 'Britain between the Invasions (B.C. 54—A.D. 43): A Study in Ancient Diplomacy' in *Aspects of Archaeology in Britain and Beyond, Essays presented to O. G. S. Crawford*, ed. W. F. Grimes, London 1951, pp. 332—344.

'The Will of Q. Veranius' *CR* N.S. vol. 1, 1951, pp. 4—7.

'Claudius and the Orcades' ibid., pp. 7—9.

'A Roman Author in north-west Britain' *Transactions of the Cumberland and Westmorland Antiquarian and Archaeological Society* N.S. vol. 50, 1951, pp. 70–79.

'The Decline and Fall of Roman Britain' *History Today* vol. 1, 1951, pp. 51–58.

1952  'The Roman Name of Ilchester', *Proceedings of the Somersetshire Archaeological and Natural History Society* vol. 96, 1951 (published 1952), pp. 188–92.

'A Lady of Quality from Roman Devon' *Report and Transactions of the Devon Association* vol. 84, 1952, pp. 172–177.

'A Roman Land-Settlement near Rochester' *Archaeologia Cantiana* vol. 65, 1952, pp. 150–159 (with D. M. Nightingale).

'Crossing the Rubicon' *History Today* vol. 2 (1952), pp. 373–8.

'The "Bellum Gallicum" as a Work of Propaganda' *Lat.* vol. 11, 1952, pp. 3–18, 165–79.

1953  'Britain and the Lex Pompeia Licinia' *Lat.* vol. 12, 1953, pp. 14–21.

1955  'A.D. 476: The End of the Roman Empire' *History Today* vol. 5, 1955, pp. 401–406.

'Hadrian and Hadrian's Wall' *Lat.* vol. 14, 1955, pp. 384–403.

1956  'Some Thoughts on "Second Carausius" *Numismatic Chronicle* ser. 6 vol. 16, 1956, pp.346–349.

1957  'Roman Gaul' in *France, Government and Society,* edd. J. M. Wallace-Hadrill and J. McManners, London 1957 and (ed. 2) 1970, pp. 19–34.

'Marcus, Gratian, Constantine' *Ath.* N. S. vol. 35, 1957, pp. 316–347.

'Nero – forgetting the Fiddler' *The Listener* vol. 57, 1957, pp. 673–74.

1958  'African Corn-Fields: a Review' *Antiquity* vol. 32, 1958, pp. 25–29.

1959  'Julius Caesar's Elephant' *History Today* vol. 9, 1959, pp. 626–7.

1960  Review of *Roman and Native in North Britain*, by I. A. Richmond, London 1958, in *Antiquity* vol. 34, 1960, pp. 309–11.

1963  'The "Plotting" of B.C. 66/65' *Lat.* vol. 22, 1963, pp. 397–435.

1965  'How Britain was different' *The Listener* vol. 73, 1965, pp. 591–593.

1966   *The Building of Hadrian's Wall,* [ed. 2] Kendal 1966.
'The social and economic Aspects of rural Settlement' in
*Rural Settlement in Roman Britain* (Council for British
Archaeology, Research Report no. 7), ed. C. Thomas,
London 1966, pp. 100—128.

1967   'Progress Report on Britain' in *Roman Frontier Studies,*
[ed. S. Applebaum] Tel Aviv 1967, pp. 34—37.

1968   Review of N. K. Chadwick, *The Druids,* Cardiff 1966, in
*EHR* vol. 83, 1968, pp. 108—111.

1971   'Constantine the Great and the Christian Capital,
A.D. 324—527' in *Byzantium: an Introduction,* ed.
P. Whitting, Oxford 1971, pp. 1—13.

# Introductory Note

Let us make no bones about it: his cleverness first and foremost is what makes C. E. Stevens so eminently *Festschrift*-worthy. The adjective, slowly and reflectively said, is one of his highest terms of praise, and that is only fitting in a man whose mental agility, supported by a superb memory, is the characteristic that strikes at once. Stevens can tackle a problem familiar to students for years, take a new look at old pieces of the jig-saw, rearrange them, bring in others that nobody had ever suspected to be relevant, and come up with a picture that is at once fresh and convincing, because three dimensional. That is, as all good theories should, it allows the spectator to go through and beyond it to the solution of other problems.

Every friend, colleague, and former pupil will have his favourite 'crash-winner' (I use Stevens' own exultant term). My own, perhaps because it was the first I met, is Augustus blackmailed by the man who 'revealed' the conspiracy of Murena to him. The Princeps showed uncommon gratitude to Castricius (Suet., *Div. Aug.* 56) and within the decade he was providing exceptionally attractive equestrian posts for Castricius Myriotalenti filius (*ILS* 2676). No wonder Livy never dared write the history of those years (for that, in Stevens' view, is the reason for the gap in Livy's history at this point — and in the works that were based on his). Or, more recently, Claudius repairing to an out of season holiday resort to issue the imperial edict that enfranchised the Anuani (*ILS* 206): a snub to the senate, which in conservative constitutional theory was supposed to control Italy (Tac., *Ann.* 13.4.3), and one which he aggravated by issuing the edict on the Ides of March. These

1

unpublished items exemplify Stevens' methods; although at first they appear trivial, they throw a flood of light on the conspiracy of Murena (a ruthless frame-up) and on the policies of Claudius (Caesarian and hard on the senate). From items accessible to all I commend Stevens' detaching of the true course of events in Gaul during Caesar's governorship from Caesar's disingenuous account of them in the *Commentarii* (*Lat.* vols 11–12, 1952–53); or his exploitation of the elephant that Caesar is said to have had with him in Britain (Polyaenus 8.23.5) as part of a campaign against Cn. Domitius Ahenobarbus, and as a model for the Emperor Claudius (Dio 60.21.2), who in taking several of the beasts to Britain is shown once again as an admiring follower of the first of the Caesars (*History Today* vol. 9, 1959).

Caesar and Augustus, two of the cleverest politicians that Rome produced, are fit subjects for C. E. Stevens. The date and subject of the first article call to mind how he spent his war years (1943–46): it was the creating of 'black' propaganda against Hitler's Germany that made him so adept an analyst of misrepresentation: practice in embedding the vital lie in a mass of genuine information fostered the skill to detect the lies embedded in the works of Cicero and Caesar; the *Latomus* article was the most obvious and immediate product of those years. Nor was the necessary study of Hitler's own methods wasted. Successful attainment of power was at least one thing that he had in common with Augustus, and the proper parallels between the two 'crooks' were not lost on Stevens.

The war years were an interruption, coming when Stevens had already been established with a Fellowship by special election at Magdalen since 1933, although, as he himself puts it, he had waited longer for a job than had been thought possible. After taking his First in Greats in 1928 as a scholar of New College he held an open award at Oriel College: the Robinson Exhibition. There within two years he wrote his B. Litt. thesis and published it in 1933: *Sidonius Apollinaris and his Age*.

The subject indicated the direction that Stevens was to take: the provinces of Gaul and in particular of Britain have not ceased to occupy him since. He held a university senior studentship in 1930/31 and on the recommendation of Maurice Bowra ('He'll have to be sent out or thrown out; I like him; let's send him out') he went as Craven Fellow (1931–33) to Belfast to study Celtic land tenure, teaching himself Irish for the purpose. Gaul and Britain have carried him on into the later

Empire, to Gildas and (in his Ford lecture of 1971) Giraldus Cambrensis. It is here too, on what may seem an unpromising wicket and before spectators used (in spite of Ian Richmond's performances) to the game more staidly played, that Stevens has made some of his most brilliant strokes. Who else in the legitimate course of argument could have quoted St. Mark's Gospel in an article on Hadrian's Wall, thereby winning a bet with Sir Mortimer Wheeler? Roman Britain and its archaeology are not our main concern here, but the two branches of scholarship to which Stevens has devoted himself (each enough to occupy a full career) have interacted. Stevens' approach to the problems that faced the Gracchi and to the measures that they and later reformers took to deal with them has been influenced and facilitated by his knowledge of systems of land tenure in other societies and of the conditions that govern Mediterranean farming; his chapter on that subject in the *Cambridge Economic History* is not to be missed.

We began with cleverness, but that is common enough and need serve no serious purpose. Stevens has put into his theories the hard work they deserve and he has never shrunk from the laborious minutiae of scholarship, in the library or in the field. His volume on *The Building of Hadrian's Wall* (1961) is sufficient proof of that. This means that he has never cheated. However unfamiliar a passage that he brings in evidence, however paradoxical his interpretation of a familiar one may seem to conventional critics, they have to take serious account of it. Further: the pains that Stevens takes over his ideas enhance their natural elegance, and they take on an aesthetic value that is independent of their merits as hypotheses. That is not to say that they are to be treated as finished works. They change and evolve from season to season or from decade to decade, yet remaining unmistakably his own. There is consistency through the whole body of the work at any time, too; given Stevens' view of the Gracchi, one pupil remarked, his view of Caesar follows, and his view of Augustus and Claudius.

A scholar must transmit his views, on paper or orally. For this second way, something more than a gift for clear exposition is required, and Stevens possesses it in the highest degree: warmth of personality and a generous concern for his fellow enquirers. These qualities, together with his infinite capacity for work, even for the humblest drudgery, undertaken for his pupils, made him more than a splendid performer on the lecture platform; not merely what he himself would claim, 'a careful tutor' and a wily opponent of his pupils' examiners (he proved a judicious and discerning examiner himself); they made him a great teacher.

The periods of history that Stevens had studied as an undergraduate had not been the most popular ones, and before the war his researches took him out of the mainstream of Greek and Roman History; so that when he went back to Magdalen in 1946 to assume the tutorial fellowship that Michael Parker had given up, he had, in his own words, to 'make it up as he went along'. It was as well, because, as he also says, 'the cleverest things I have done have been done in tutorials'; the flow of ideas was prodigious — and prodigal. Pupils who have turned professional know how much they benefited; their debts will be obvious to readers of this volume, where they are duly acknowledged. But debts are not always acknowledged, or even conscious. That is nothing to Stevens; quoting his old tutor, R. G. Collingwood, he would say that when scholars complain that an idea of theirs is being used by someone else it is because it is the only idea they will ever have. 'Anybody can have what's in my head. There are plenty more where that came from.'

His Rhys Research Fellowship (1965) would have given him more time for his own work; this he resigned prematurely, and some of his friends think that he has spent too much of his time in teaching — all those certainly who have seen the framed timetable that stood on his desk to record the term when pupils from 13 colleges took up 72 hours of his week.

Yet Stevens' achievements as a teacher — better, as a person — are immeasurable. He is honoured after all for his individual outlook on the subject to which — 'because it is fun' — he has devoted himself, wherever that outlook has manifested itself. For Stevens has made no school, as he belongs to none. One quality in any case could not be imitated: the originality that makes him, as one contributor to this book puts it, 'ask the right questions'; another is the emphasis he puts on 'gutting the source' — getting the last ounce of meaning from a writer, a stone, written or unwritten, a coin. That requires a third quality: a sensitivity to the continuity of history and to its reverberations (this is where Stevens' memory serves him so well); an awareness that something of this kind has happened before; an ability to recognise patterns, to compare or connect events far removed one from the other. That sensitivity extends, as of course it should, to modern times. An instance from Gaul will suffice. What effect did taking the wrong side in 49 B.C.

have on Massilia? A long-standing one indeed, according to Stevens. Three years later it lost territory to the colony of Arelate, and Marseille can still claim to be under-represented on the Conseil Départemental.

And so this volume is no dutiful tribute, but an offering joyfully made by friends. Three former pupils of Stevens, George Forrest, David Stockton, and Peter Cuff, were in at the beginning and gave much help, encouragement, and advice. At a later stage Christopher Grayson and John Davies were equally generous, the last no pupil, but with no less good will for that. The volume grew as one contributor suggested another, but only a few of the honorand's many and distinguished pupils could be approached, for want of space; natural growth had arbitrarily to be checked; even in Ancient History we are a token sample, and one whole group had to be excluded from a volume that is a tribute to Stevens the ancient historian rather than Stevens the archaeologist — if they can be kept distinct.

The theme of the book imposed itself on us as we reflected on Stevens' qualities as a historian and his preoccupation with 'gutting the source', but it (and probably the title too) was actually suggested by Tim Ashplant, a pupil who has moved from Ancient to Modern History.

Not only personal friends should be thanked. We owe a debt of gratitude to Gregg International for backing our enterprise and, in particular, to their editor Miss A. E. Harroway, who has taken unstinting pains with it right from the start. And this editor would like to thank the contributors, who have submitted with cheerfulness and patience to the ruthless paring that has been necessary to keep the book to the planned size and price. That is a point that should be made publicly in fairness to their work; essays, like travellers, naturally come in different sizes, but I have been a Procrustes with a bed too short for most.

Indeed, the range and diversity of the contributions to this volume reflect to some extent the range of Ancient History itself: political and military history, historiography, prosopography, social and economic history, the history of religion are all touched on; and the techniques illustrated are correspondingly diverse. Literary sources are duly gutted, inscriptions and coins squeezed for all they are worth; topography and the results of archaeological surveys pressed into service, and the fruitfulness of analogy at least indicated.

The ancient historian lacks the full resource of primary and ephemeral evidence that is at the disposal of students of modern and especially of the most recent history. Hence one salient feature of the discipline: the ancient historian is preoccupied with the work of his distant precursors in the ancient world itself, men who had either witnessed what they were writing about or had already processed the primary (or secondary) sources that they held relevant. It is of the first importance to probe what they wrote, their purpose in writing, and their credentials as writers of history. Then comes the evaluation of such contemporary evidence as does survive (for reasons not usually relevant to historians). Finally comes the problem of placing the two kinds of evidence (not that they can be satisfactorily distinguished: consider the *Commentarii* or the *Res Gestae Divi Augusti*) into a convincing relation one with the other, an activity never to be undertaken without the first two; and they themselves are not always feasible in isolation.

For that reason alone the historians would have been well represented in the volume, though the greatest of them is dealt with only obliquely. Against the claim of Pausanias that two fifth-century monuments commemorated a victory of Argives and Athenians over the Spartans at Oinoe in the Argolid A. Andrewes sets his own inspection of the site and the silence of Thucydides (and other sources). Without being named, Thucydides is the object of a shaft launched by Aristotle in the course of his comparison between poetry and history; so G. E. M. de Ste. Croix, who shields the historian from what he regards as an unjustified attack. With Christopher Grayson's essay on Xenophon we come to an inferior continuator of Thucydides; but that is just Mr Grayson's point: do we understand Xenophon correctly when we take him to be attempting to write history at all?

Caesar did not claim to be a historian but Cicero said that his work made the efforts of later writers superfluous. Not so. The *Commentarii* were the product of a propagandist of genius, the man who, as P. J. Cuff shows, had as general and politician, the heir of Marius, long prepared the position he was to fight from in 49 B.C. Professor Wightman's essay raises another and precise problem of genres: were the *Commentarii* distinct from the *Ephemeris* that survived to the fourth century as potential material for Protadius' history and, if so, how did they differ from it? There is an additional perspective for us here: the limitations and oversights of a historian writing in late antiquity, a prisoner in the continuum of his culture. The theme is touched on by other contributors.

In the ancient historian's second field of operations the apparent immediacy of much poetry makes it fair game — and a perpetual source of controversy. How much information can any given poet legitimately be expected to yield a historian? George Forrest and Colin Hardie consider aspects of the work of two great poets of antiquity. Mr Forrest, dealing with Aristophanes' attitude towards the Athenian Empire, returns to a familiar problem, the political stance of Aristophanes (or was he 'just' a comic poet?). Virgil's attitude towards Octavian is Mr Hardie's subject; he finds conflict between commentators on the *Eclogues* and a contemporary historian, none other than Virgil's patron Pollio, whose work has been transmitted to us through Appian.

It is not easy, then, for the ancient historian to do without his ancient predecessors. Peter Garnsey and John Percival demonstrate areas in which it may be done. Mr Garnsey's evidence is purely epigraphic; his essay examines criteria for assigning to the class of freedmen men whose descendants acquired distinction in the towns of Italy, offering an estimate of their relative numbers. From the Albertini Tablets, fragmentary though they are, emerges the shape of land-holding in fifth-century north Africa, with some features traceable back to the early Empire.

Like Professor Andrewes, S. Applebaum brings topography into play, but combines it with contemporary Jewish evidence and the testimony of the historian Josephus to elucidate the attitude of Jews to city life in the Hellenistic period. D. L. Stockton seeks a new explanation for Rome's persecution of the Christians from evidence that is familiar and nicely conflicting: pagan literary sources, historical and semi-official, and legal documents are set against the account of Jewish-Christian relations given in *Acts* and the apologies of later Christian writers.

With a group of essays centring on Tacitus we are in the third arena of the ancient historian's endeavour. Not surprisingly: the quantity of materials available make it easy to use them and his work for mutual illumination, and the writer's outlook and methods (which are examined by Professor Yavetz) make it imperative that we should. A. R. Birley critically examines the biography of Agricola, correcting bias and filling in gaps. One piece of evidence, an inscription hitherto unpublished, is what J. H. D'Arms mainly brings into play to elucidate an episode from the *Annals*, the abortive intervention of C. Cassius Longinus in disturbances at Puteoli; his subject is well complemented by Mr Garnsey's. One essay, the editor's, invokes numismatic evidence; historian and coins alike are fitted as harmoniously as possible into a pre-existing conceptual background, as a tiny instance of the indivisibility of history.

Dr Percival's essay ends on a questioning note (how, if at all, is the field pattern of the Albertini Tablets related to the open field system of the Middle Ages?). So does our whole volume. John Morris finds in India and the Middle East practices that may throw light on problems of western archaeology and history — one of them a problem posed by the absence of evidence. Like Dr Percival, Mr Morris points out new ways forward. We have only to ask the right questions, questions not necessarily posed by the European evidence. On the importance of asking the right questions R. G. Collingwood, as Mr Morris says, was explicit, and his pupil C. E. Stevens, unlike another historian of Gaul, Protadius, has always understood it. It is appropriate that an essay on that theme should close a volume composed in honour of a man ever ready to ask new questions, and so many of those manifestly the right ones.


B. M. Levick

# 1

# Could there have been a Battle at Oinoe?

My studies have diverged widely from those of my old friend since our school days, and that was convenient enough when we shared the Ancient History teaching of our two Colleges and each could stick to his own side of the fence, Greek or Roman; but it is a handicap on this occasion, when I would prefer to offer him something more closely related to his own interests. But he has never disdained military history and he always liked a puzzle. For this one he would surely find a solution more positive and much more ingenious than my own, and I look forward to hearing it.

The battle of Oinoe in the Argolid is still intermittently in the news. Though N. G. L. Hammond found no room for it on the crowded canvas of his single volume (*History of Greece*, ed. 2., Oxford 1967, pp. 292–3), it duly appears in R.A. Tomlinson's *Argos and the Argolid*, London 1972, p. 112; and it has its small niche in R. Meiggs' account of the Pente-kontaetia (*The Athenian Empire*, Oxford 1972, p. 96), earning an appendix in that powerful work because it is notoriously a problem (pp. 469–72). Gomme (*Commentary*, vol. 1, p. 370, n. 1) called it 'elusive', and it more than ever eludes me.

One half of the problem has been very liberally discussed, the odd fact that Pausanias refers to two fifth-century com-memorations of Oinoe, a painting in the Stoa Poikile (1.15.1) and a group of statues at Delphi (10.10.3), whereas there is no trace of it in Thucydides or in any source other than Pausanias. For the intricate questions here involved I refer to the full and courageous treatment by L. H. Jeffery in *ABSA*, vol. 60, 1965, pp. 41–57, with the comments of Meiggs. My concern is with

9

the topographical problem, which deserves more attention than it has received.[1]

The approximate site of Oinoe is not in doubt. Pausanias (2.25.1−3) takes us out of Argos by the gate towards the Deiras, past a double temple not precisely located, after which we proceed for an undefined distance and cross the river-torrent called Charadros (cf.Thuc.5.60.6), and there is Oinoe. Above it is Mt Artemision, with a temple of Artemis on its peak; and the springs of the Inachos are on this mountain. There he leaves us, but the route is taken up again at 8.6.4−6, where he speaks of the two passes over from the Argolid into the territory of Mantineia. The narrower of these two ways, called Prinos, runs διὰ τοῦ Ἀρτεμισίου, and for this he refers us back to his earlier mention of the mountain, the temple and statue of Artemis, and the sources of the Inachos − clearly to 2.25.3, though the statue was not actually mentioned there. While the river bed and the path run side by side, the Inachos is the Argive border with Mantineia, but then the water turns away from the path into Argive territory, and that is why the poets call the river Argive.

That is clear enough. To reach Oinoe from Argos we must go up the valley of the Xerias, and though Pausanias does not measure the intervals we must go some distance up it before it becomes plausible to say that Artemision is above Oinoe. The valley is narrow and its sides steep, and it is unlikely that there was ever any settlement there before the point, some 11−12 km. up the defile, where a tributary enters the valley from the north and it broadens out a little: see Ernst Meyer, *RE* vol. 17, cols. 2237−40, Oinoe 8. Even there, as Tomlinson remarks (p. 38), there is little cultivable land and the population can hardly have been much thicker in antiquity than it is now. After that, Pausanias' reference in 8.6.6 to the Inachos, whatever one may make of the detail,[2] at least ensures that his path crossed the north face of Artemision: that means, as Meyer argued, that the ancient route was not the lower one south of the peak through Tourníkion, but one that went directly up from Oinoe, west and a little north, to the neighbourhood of the pleasant modern village of Karyá, then west across the mountain to come down to Nestáni (formerly Tsipianá), above the southern end of the Argon Pedion (Paus.8.7.1) east of Mantinea.

Into this framework we have to fit a battle. It had better not be too large, for if it occurred we have to account for Thucydides' silence about it, and the easiest way to do that is to suppose that the event made a big impression at the time, victories over the Spartan army being always rare, but that thereafter it was overshadowed by the major engagements of the First Peloponnesian War with their more important con- sequences (so, e.g., Meiggs p. 472). All the same, it must be large enough to warrant a painting and a sizeable group of statues. The painting, Pausanias says, showed the Athenians drawn up against the Spartans at Oinoe in the Argolid, not the height of the battle but its beginning, ἐς χεῖρας ἔτι συνιόντες: the phrase hardly gives us an estimate of the numbers involved, but it sounds like more than a mere skirmish, and within the Stoa this battle had to compete with some large-scale events. The Argives have got left out here, but they were the dedicators of statues by Hypatodoros and Aristogeiton of the Seven against Thebes made, as the Argives themselves say, from the victory won over the Spartans in Argive Oinoe by αὐτοί τε καὶ Ἀθηναίων ἐπίκουροι. Pausanias adds, as his own guess, that the group of the Epigonoi also dedicated here by the Argives commemorated the same event.[3]

That is quite a weight of commemoration, and one's first reaction must be that there is hardly enough level ground, at any site possible for Oinoe, to stage a battle of suitable dimensions; but the painting demands a battle and one must do one's best to provide one. It is a slight difficulty that the Spartans came by a high path whose use by a military force is not attested for any other occasion; but Agis in 418, for instance, took most of his troops from Phleiasia into the Argolid by a difficult and unexpected route to avoid the Argive army at Nemea (Thuc.5.58.3—4), and our Spartans could equally have a good reason for choosing the mountain route rather than the familiar road down past Hysiai and Lerna. The obvious possibility is that the operation involved some sort of surprise. It is more of a difficulty that their next move, if they had not been met at Oinoe, would take them through a long and narrow defile which no army would be eager to enter.[4] For the regular Spartan army it would have been almost essential to seize the bare and broken mountain above, a considerable undertaking; so if this was to be their route we had best suppose that they had reason to expect that no opposition would be offered till they were through the defile, but that again suggests surprise, and the clandestine movement of a small picked force. They would then emerge just north of the Larisa, the citadel of Argos, and very close to the city walls. The use of this back door suggests an attempt on the city itself, but that could hardly be by open assault: someone had contracted to let them in, and there were usually Spartan sympathisers among the Argive aristocracy who might have done this.[5] Every feature of the enterprise seems to call for secrecy and a small force, wholly unsuitable for Pausanias' painting.

This may be the place to mention the late fourth-century inscription of an Argive thiasos (Hiller, *Hist.Gr.Epigramme*, no.85), which has been brought into the story. This was first published by W. Vollgraff in *BCH* vol. 32, 1908, p. 236ff., in an article hopefully entitled 'Praxitèle le jeune.' A fuller and better text, largely agreed by Vollgraff, was given by R. Herzog in *Philol.* vol 71, 1912, pp. 1—23 (his article was called 'Auf den Spuren der Telesilla', but we need not pursue her here, or the younger Praxiteles). Two hexameters dedicate to Leto statues of Apollo and Artemis by divine command, then the thiasos describes its procedure:

ἐβδεμάται μέσαι θυσίαν ἄγομες κατὰ μῆνας

ἐξ οὗ Πλείσταρχον ηὑκ[τ]ωρ ἐξήλασε Ἀπόλλων.

For Vollgraff and for most critics this was Pleistarchos the brother of Kassandros, and the event was to be fitted into the interventions of the Diadochoi in the Peloponnese at the end of the fourth century. Herzog however discovered here the Spartan king Pleistarchos son of Leonidas, for whom no other action is recorded and who died, evidently without male issue, in 459/8 (Diod.13.75.1); and he identified the event as the battle of Oinoe. It is one of the curiosities of Greek studies that Beloch (*Gr.Gesch.* vol. 2[2], 1, p. 165, 2, pp. 206—9), while rejecting Pausanias' testimony about the Stoa Poikile (the picture was of Oinophyta) and casting considerable doubt on his testimony about the statue-group at Delphi (the connection with Oinoe was pure conjecture), nevertheless acclaimed Herzog's conjecture as 'sehr ansprechend' and gave the battle of Oinoe a place in his Pentekontaetia. Since then the inscription has earned an ambiguous reference in a footnote of Gomme's (above), but has not to my knowledge surfaced elsewhere. It hardly needs saying that the repulse (or rather expulsion?) of Pleistarchos by night cannot be fitted together with the painting in the Poikile; the thiasos more probably celebrated an event nearer to the time of its inscription. It is true that we know of no suitable event in the career of the Macedonian Pleistarchos, but he is a less shadowy figure than the son of Leonidas, and is recorded to have played a part in the history of his time.

To return up the valley to Oinoe, we have further to ask how the Argives and their Athenian allies came to be there, ready to receive the Spartans when they come down. If the Spartan operation was a plot, it had been given away, and very likely the fact that the Spartans had started from the Arcadian side had been signalled to the Argives. If we are then to have a battle, the Spartans must come down the valley, which they would hardly have done if they could see the allied forces drawn up against them. An ambush would fit better than a regular hoplite battle, but we can allow that much fighting, after which the Spartan survivors presumably scuttled back up the mountain while the Argives and Athenians went back to Argos to celebrate their glorious victory.

To account for an engagement in this remote and unlikely spot we have to reduce its scale below what is required for the monuments which are supposed to celebrate it, and doubt inevitably creeps in, as it has crept into Miss Jeffery's last paragraph. To reassure herself about the unwelcome silence of Thucydides she concludes with the question 'yet could the antiquarian, or oral, sources used by Pausanias really have been wrong in both cases?' Beloch contrived to accept that Pausanias was wrong; and while not many of us could sustain life for long on those bare heights of scepticism which Beloch inhabited, with Miss Jeffery's help we may scramble up that far after him.

She faced two artistic problems, of which the more serious is the anomaly at this date of the public display of a painting of a real contemporary battle against Greeks. C. Robert, *Die Marathonschlacht in der Poikile*, Halle a. S. 1895, p. 43, rolled out the list of known historical paintings before the date of the Poikile: Miss Jeffery (p.50) goes over the catalogue more coolly, pointing out that it contains no case of a battle of Greek against Greek and noting in the tragedians a 'normal convention of introducing the contemporary and topical obliquely in terms of the antique.' Her answer is that the painting really showed a mythological subject, Theseus' recovery of the unburied bodies of the Seven from Thebes, the subject also of Aeschylus' *Eleusinioi*. Since Pausanias took the Athenians' adversaries to be Spartans not Thebans, this involves the assumption that the two sides were not labelled, or had lost their labels, yet it was somehow nevertheless known that the painting commemorated Oinoe. This sounds forced, as she says, and one might also complain that no reason has been advanced, why Athens should commemorate Oinoe with a painting of this particular episode in her heroic past; the best that could be said is that this is an episode in which there is a link between Athens and Argos, but a Spartan enemy is really needed. Her hands, and those of other critics, would be happily freed if Pausanias were merely wrong about the connection with Oinoe. Meiggs (p. 472) does not meet her main argument directly, and his explanation, that 'at the time a victory on land over Sparta was an amazing achievement', will only work if there was an achievement that might amaze.[6]

Miss Jeffrey's other problem is that the Argives, with their own very flourishing contemporary school of sculpture, should have employed two Theban artists[7] to make their dedication for Oinoe (pp. 49–50). It is indeed a problem, and her answer is that the Argive troops who fought at Tanagra stayed on and also fought at Oinophyta, and in the course of that campaign looted a group of the Seven which had originally been commissioned and set up by the Thebans for some quite other purpose; and that the Argives appropriated this for their own dedication at Delphi (pp. 50, 56 with n. 60). That is bold and attractive, but also paradoxical, for booty taken in the campaign of Oinophyta should commemorate Oinophyta and not some quite other occasion. The inscription, though it presumably told Pausanias that the dedicators were the Argives and gave him the names of the sculptors, did not say what these Seven commemorated; that came, he says, from Argive informants. Pausanias might have misunderstood them. Oinoe is again an embarrassment: if we could get rid of it but adopt the rest of Miss Jeffrey's hypothesis, the monument could commemorate Oinophyta[8] and we should have dealt with the anomaly of the Theban sculptors.

We must therefore ask again what the chances are that Pausanias' attributions were wrong. He speaks with placid assurance about the subject of the painting in the Poikile, with no doubtful 'as the Athenians say' or any suggestion that he is using his own judgement, and one would guess that he is here simply repeating what he was told, in writing or orally. The battle took his fancy, for some reason, as witness his personal attribution of the Epigonoi at Delphi to the same occasion, and his interest in it might have helped him to misunderstand informants who in fact told him that the dedication of the Seven was for Oinophyta. If Oinoe is a fraud, or reckless exaggeration of some quite minor scuffle, the fault should lie with an Athenian source which did not know the country in the way most Argives would. It would help if we could find a reason why some Athenian transferred a painting of (say) Theseus' exploit to a battle at Oinoe,[9] but that is not essential. The reason may lie in something we know nothing about, or there may have been no good reason: as Wade-Gery liked to point out in such cases, error may be irrational.

The essential point is the unsatisfactory nature of the evidence. Pausanias' statements about two fifth-century monuments are the only positive items, and each creates considerable difficulty in itself. Gomme (ibid.) noted that Pausanias 'writes as though the battle were well known,[10] which to us it notoriously is not. Much historical literature known to Pausanias is lost to us, but much remains, Thucydides included, and the silence of that whole tradition has always been a trouble to those who seek a real context for Oinoe. I have not even mentioned the difficulty of finding such a context, or of the question which troubled Miss Jeffery (p. 53ff.), how the Athenian troops came to be in the Argolid in the first place. These difficulties form another element of doubt; but my basic trouble is that I do not believe there is room for the battle on the ground.

I thus find it easier to suppose that Pausanias was somehow wrongly informed. It may seem harsh to try to deprive the historians of the Pentekontaetia of one of their regular exercises in speculation, and I do not for a moment suppose that I shall have succeeded in doing so. But if the argument is to continue, the speculators must think a little harder what sort of battle they want to install at the foot of Mt Artemision.

## Notes

[1] I have to confess that my only visit to the site was as long ago as 1937; but my recollections and notes seem to tally with such maps and descriptions as are available, and Prof. R. A. Tomlinson very kindly confirms the main topographical point. Since no one else has thought this aspect worth investigation, I may perhaps be allowed to rush in. Warm thanks are due to L. H. Jeffery and R. Meiggs, who read a first draft and offered helpful criticism, which was restrained and civilised of them but does not of course implicate them in my conclusion.

[2] It all depends which stream he took to be 'the' Inachos, and

where exactly the ancient path ran. The main part of this border was presumably along the crest of the ridge which runs north from the western shoulder of Artemision.

[3] For the Epigonoi see W. G. Forrest, *CQ* N.S., vol. 10, 1960, p. 227.

[4] The only alternative available is to suppose that at some stage they meant to cross the mountains to the north or north-east and come down into the valley of the Inachos, which is more open, as Tomlinson tentatively suggests to me; and G. Fougères (*Mantinée et l'Arcadie orientale*, Paris 1898, p. 412 n.4) contemplated cutting the whole knot by emending Oinoe to Orneai. The latter is a dangerously drastic solution: with the former we should have to think up a reason why the Spartans did not in the first place take the more northerly pass, Pausanias' Klimax (8.6.4), which comes down directly into the Inachos valley; and still more, why the Spartans ever came down to the floor of the Xerias valley at Oinoe.

[5] For this period, see Forrest (n.3) pp. 226–9.

[6] His supposition that 'Oenoe was added after the other paintings' removes one discrepancy, the unsuitability of the subject in an otherwise 'Cimonian' context (cf. Jeffery p. 42), but not the basic difficulty.

[7] The Theban origin and the date of the sculptors has long been certain: see Jeffery p. 49.

[8] The actual identification of 'Oinoe' with Oinophyta (H. E. Stier, *Eine Grosstat der attischen Geschichte*, Stuttgart 1934) is not tenable: see Jeffery p. 56, n.59.

[9] It might help if the picture showed a nymph Oinoe (Robert p. 7) with her name written in and still visible; but not much, for the connection of the Seven with Argive Oinoe (Paus. 2.25.1) is not so conspicuous that the false inference would come easily.

[10] That makes it all the more striking, as Stier remarked (n. 8, p. 34), that Pausanias does not mention the battle when he comes to the site of Oinoe at 2.25.

A. Andrewes,
New College,
Oxford.

# 2

# Aristophanes and the Athenian Empire

My old tutor has a taste for propaganda, black or white, soft or hard, for making it and for breaking it, so I hope that he will bear with an attempt to see if any lurks in an area somewhat alien to his own — the plays of Aristophanes.

Aristophanes must be a valuable guide to Athenian political behaviour — when Plato, who was in some ways no fool, wished to instruct Dionysius of Syracuse in the subject he sent him, not a copy of Solon's laws, not a text of Thucydides, but a collection of the comedies. But, it is felt, a writer so politically aware must have had political views of his own and must have used his twice-yearly opportunity at the Lenaea and Dionysia to propagate those views. So we have had Aristophanes the 'Conservative', Aristophanes the 'Cimonian democrat', Aristophanes the 'champion of the country against the town', Aristophanes the 'campaigner for peace' — and many other things.

But in a quietly devastating note in CR vol. 52, 1938, pp. 97 – 109, the late Professor Gomme questioned earlier insights into Aristophanes' politics and the principle on which they were based. For him Aristophanes was a poet and a dramatist, nothing more. His purpose was to create convincing characters and put them in amusing situations, an artist pure and simple — not a politician.

However, to show that previous political interpretations were wrong was not to rule out the possibility of a new interpretation which might be right, and, in his attack on the principle as such, Gomme made two mistakes. Firstly he argued that Aristophanes, though commenting frequently on political issues, was not commenting seriously, he was making jokes. But from the fact that someone is not commenting seriously it does not follow that he is not commenting with serious intentions. Secondly he argued that since matters with which Aristophanes concerned himself were topical and often trivial it was wrong to think that he was interested in broad questions of political principle. But it is precisely with topical and often trivial matters that most politicians concern themselves most of the time. We call them radicals or conservatives because their responses seem overall to fall into a radical or conservative pattern, not because they regularly expound radical or conservative doctrine. In Aristophanes there may be no such pattern. But it is legitimate to ask if there is one, perhaps even possible to find it.

Before we ask, however (and I shall not get around to asking here), there is some essential groundwork. First, we must find out as much as we can about the political context in which each play was written, rehearsed and performed, so that we read the *Knights*, say, with only the last months of 425 and the spring of 424 in mind, not 411 or even 423. Secondly, we must not jump directly from a decision on the poet's attitude on a specific issue in a given year to the generalization 'Therefore he was a conservative', but rather look first at what he may have to say about the same issue in other plays, remembering, of course, that a man's views can change over forty years and that even if they stay the same his reaction to any particular manifestation of a problem may differ from what it was to another manifestation of the same problem. We must not argue 'He was in favour of peace in 411, *therefore* he was in favour of peace in 425'. But if we find independent evidence that he was in favour of peace in 425, in 421, in 411 and perhaps elsewhere, we can conclude that on one major question he sided consistently with the Athenian right-wing. If that question was integral, vital to right-wing thinking, the wider generalisation would follow. If it was not, then we must wait until we have established a similar attitude on other issues before making it.

It might be objected that to establish a political pattern would still not prove that Aristophanes was expressing his views in order to persuade as well as to amuse. Indeed it would not — but it would make it very much more likely and I should be ready to assume that he was. Conscience would prick only if I found myself forgetting the qualification 'as well as to amuse'. He need not have been a comedian and nothing more. But he was first and foremost a comedian. More than that, he was a competing comedian and in order to win a prize he had to make jokes which a majority of his audience thought were funny or could be made to think were funny. Nevertheless, a very great comedian in a very competitive business made the *Great Dictator* and *Modern Times*.

So much for principle. The object of this paper is to look at Aristophanes' thoughts on one issue, the relationship between Athens and the other members of her alliance — a hesitant second step in the programme suggested above.[1] I begin with some quotations from Gilbert Murray.[2] 'One Athenian . . . flinched from no danger and counted no cost . . . It (the *Babylonians*) seems to have been a thoroughgoing attack on the whole policy of the "Tyrant City" towards its Allies'. Again, 'In this attack on Cleon in the *Knights*, while he piles up the list of Cleon's iniquities, one feels that most of the suffering they cause falls on the Allies'. Or again of the *Wasps*, ' "Squeeze the Allies still harder" argued the war-party "or else there will not be enough to feed the people!" "Rubbish" says Aristophanes. "Feeding the people is a trifle. It is your wretched war and your rapacious ways of collecting revenue that use up all the funds." At least that is what he would say if he were perfectly serious.'

What Aristophanes 'would say' — he does not say it. What 'one feels' — again there is no explicit reference in the text. It is only in the *Babylonians*, the lost play of 426, that it is held that Aristophanes is openly attacking the Athenian *demos*' cruelty towards its subjects. Here we have a valiant defence of the allied cities against Athenian extortion and brutality — or here we should have had it if the play had survived.

It becomes important to reconstruct the *Babylonians*. But, fortunately, no need to do it afresh[3] Briefly, the name of the play was the *Babylonians* and this implies that the chorus was composed of Babylonians who were, according to Hesychius, represented as branded slaves working in a mill. On the standard view these slaves represented the allied cities. But the evidence for this is no more than the Hesychius passage, an explanation of the proverbial phrase, Σαμίων ὁ δῆμός ἐστιν · ὡς πολυγράμματος which occurred in the play. 'This must be the people of Samos, all covered with letters', a reference to the branding of the Samians after their unsuccessful revolt from Athens in 440. A character in the play, Hesychius says, seeing the slaves and ἐπαπορῶν, not knowing what to make of them, produces this desciption. Plutarch in his *Pericles* 26 has a variant to ἐπαπορῶν. For him the saying is a puzzle, a riddle, ἠνίχθαι. Can this really mean that the chorus in the mill was openly described as, or known to be allied cities? Surely not. Their identity to the observer is a puzzle. The Babylonians appear, all covered with letters, and he makes a guess, a wild, comic guess at their identity. It is tempting to think that fragment 88, the one word Ἰστριανὰ comes from the same context. The people of Istros had the habit (Hesychius s.v.) of tattooing themselves. 'Are they Samians?' 'No.' 'Are the letters Istrian then?' 'No.' Another wrong guess — and it is to be noted that Istros was not an ally of Athens. Be that as it may, what we have is a joke, in rather bad taste, at the expense of, not in favour of the Samians.

Now this is a vital point. Σαμίων ὁ δῆμος is the crossroads. If it is implied by these words in the text of the play that the chorus represented allied cities or that Plutarch's or Hesychius' comments suggest this identification, then in 426 Aristophanes was presenting his audience with the idea that their allies, or at least the Samians,[4] were no better off than slaves. If it is not implied, and I emphatically believe that it is not, then there is not a tittle of evidence in other fragments of the *Babylonians* or in references to it that gives any hint that Aristophanes held such a view.

The other fragments are unrevealing. One of them, frg. 65, describes a man in fetters carrying a shield. Murray comments 'How could the Allies fight effectively for Athens when they were in fetters?' How indeed, but where are the Allies in the Greek? ἀνὴρ πεδήτης ἰτέαν ἐνημμένος. In another, frg. 82, there is mention, says Murray, of someone — 'was it an Athenian soldier?' — killing some islander's yoke of oxen because he wanted the beef. Well, was it an Athenian soldier? and, where is the islander in the Greek? ἢ βοιδαρίων τις ἀπέκτεινε ζεῦγος χολίκων ἐπιθυμῶν. One could go on; enough to say that there is nowhere a whisper of an islander or an ally.

Nevertheless the Allies were involved in the play somehow. We have Aristophanes' word for it in the *Acharnians* of 425. At line 502 he refers to Cleon's prosecution of him after the *Babylonians* for maligning the city while Allies were present. A scholiast fills in the detail; the play had poked fun at the magistrates of Athens and especially at Cleon. Moreover, in the parabasis, at lines 634ff., Aristophanes sets out to give an account of his earlier work and the benefits it had brought to

Athens. 'I deserve your gratitude because I have stopped you from being deceived ξενικοῖσι λόγοις! In days gone by you were taken in all the time by ambassadors ἀπὸ τῶν πόλεων (line 636) who flattered you and got their way. But I showed them up for what they were and so did you a good turn — and incidentally I have also done you a good turn τοὺς δήμους ἐν ταῖς πόλεσιν δείξας ὡς δημοκρατοῦνται (line 642), a line which I leave untranslated for the moment. As a result of this they now come ἐκ τῶν πόλεων (line 643) bringing you the tribute, eager to hear this splendid poet.'

It has been thought that the ξενικοὶ λόγοι were the honeyed words of Gorgias of Leontinoi on his embassy to Athens in 427. But this is impossible. The πόλεις of lines 642 and 643 can only be the member states of Athens' league; the πόλεις of line 636 must then be the same. If so, Aristophanes is claiming that on the one hand he attacked allied embassies, on the other that he did something (in line 642) which deserved Athenian and allied gratitude. Many have seen the answer in taking δημοκρατοῦνται in other than its normal sense, 'living under a democracy'. The *demos* which exercises the *kratos* is the Athenian *demos* — a perfectly legitimate comic distortion of the meaning of the word, and one which nicely solves the problem of allied gratitude — Aristophanes has attacked the harshness of the Athenian *demos* towards its subjects and the Allies love him for it (thus, e.g., Rogers and Starkie). It is not a serious objection that nothing in the text would direct the hearer to this interpretation — the actor could easily make it plain. But it is serious that in finding a link with what follows we lose any proper link with what has gone before and raise the nasty question — why should the Athenian *demos* be grateful for being attacked? Sensing this difficulty Norwood proposed a modification, that Aristophanes need not have been attacking Athenian behaviour, but only expounding it, perhaps even praising it. This is not impossible; one difficulty is removed. But we still lack an easy sequence of thought and, I feel, the line loses some of the punch which we expect from its position (and its consequences). A third interpretation would also have it that Aristophanes' purpose was exposition, not, however, of Athens' treatment of the Allies, but of the democratic system itself, a solemn lecture on the mechanics of democratic government. The Russian S. Y. Luria[5] has argued that Aristophanes, by revealing to the Allies how the Cleisthenic deme system worked, so impressed them that they came scurrying to Athens with the tribute to keep such a good thing going on. On a collective farm, maybe, but not in Ancient Greece.

An alternative then that will make sense, a version proposed by Gomme[6] without argument. That we take δημοκρατοῦνται in its normal sense of 'living under a democracy' i.e. one's own democracy. 'I took the lid off allied democracy.' This fits perfectly with what has gone before – 'I showed you how crooked allied embassies were and I showed you how awful the democracies were from which they came.' But at first sight it does not fit with what follows – allied as well as Athenian gratitude.

To see why it does we must digress a moment on the question of Athenian relations with the Allies. When we talk about Athens and the Allies we tend to see one small circle marked 'Athens' and one large one marked 'Allies'. That, of course, is wrong. We should think of one large one marked Athens and then a whole host of smaller ones marked Chios, Seriphos, Paros etc. Each of these, we easily forget, was a state on its own, a miniature Athens, each with its own problems, each with its own politicians, its own Cleon or Nicias. As a result the relationship was not a simple one, Athens – Allies, or even Athens – individual Ally. It was a relationship between this class at Athens and that class in Miletos, between this individual Milesian and that Athenian.

Luria's article, in spite of a note of Stalinist conformity, was an important step in the right direction. An even more important step was Mr de Ste. Croix's brilliant study of the Athenian Empire in *Hist.* vol. 3, 1954, pp. 1–41. Luria is principally concerned with the relationship demos/demos oligoi/oligoi viewed from Athens, de Ste. Croix with the same from the allies' standpoint. We must go further on Luria's lines and analyse in even greater detail the attitude of different groups in Athens to the question of the treatment of their subjects.

Before doing so, one other important point. Both Luria and de Ste. Croix are supporters of the Athenian *demos* and its *arche*. I share their view, but what matters is not whether we in the end decide in favour of this party or that – it is that we should recognise that there were two or more parties. Some may want to refute de Ste. Croix. They must remember that it can only be done by arguing in his terms.

The first thing we must get quite clear is that no one in

Athens with the possible exception of a few cranks ever wanted to get rid of the empire, to set the Allies free. It would have been economic and political suicide for Athens to do so. The empire was there and that was that. As Pericles says in Thuc. 2.63, τὸ ἄρχειν ᾧπερ ἄπαντες ἀγάλλεσθε. But there could be arguments on how to administer it and it is here that differences could arise, how to administer, who was to administer and in whose interests. For not all took pleasure in the empire for the same reasons.

The very poor approved because it meant cash for payment to the jurors, for festivals, buildings and the maintenance of the fleet; the business man because it brought trade to the Piraeus and profits to his pocket; the civil servant because it meant lucrative jobs abroad as *episkopoi* and so on. The very rich approved because their status as Athenians gave them excellent opportunities for financial exploitation.

Indeed this last aspect is enjoyably illustrated by a little story about Thucydides, son of Melesias, Pericles' opponent of the 440's. He, we are told, the man who appears time and again as a great champion of allied liberty, a high-minded opponent of Pericles' misuse of the tribute, he went to Aegina when ostracised and there revealed his *philarguria*. He indulged in moneylending and threw the Aeginetans out of their homes for debt. A malicious anecdote in a doubtful source, but, true or false, it is a good illustration of the sort of opening that wealthy Athenians now had.[7]

These economic differences would certainly lead to different attitudes to questions of imperial control and exploitation, but it is not a simple connection. There is the added complication of political feeling and social sentiment which could often coincide with economic interest but might just as often clash.

The natural sympathy of rich for rich and poor for poor, of aristocrat for aristocrat and democrat for democrat certainly existed. It is stated bluntly enough by the PsXen. *Ath. Pol.* at 1.14, οἱ χρηστοὶ . . . τοὺς χρηστοὺς . . . σῴζουσι, and even more bluntly by the oligarch Phrynichos at Thuc. 8.48. 'The *demos* in the allied states actually regards the Athenian *demos* as its *kataphyge* against oligarchic oppression.' But wealth and class are by no means the whole story and de Ste. Croix's simple rule, oligarch loved oligarch and hated the empire, democrat loved democrat and loved the empire, can only lead to trouble if too rigidly applied. Herodotus the aristocrat from subject Halicarnassus moved easily into the circle of Thucydides, son of

23

Melesias, but this did not lead him to a hatred of Athens or even, I suspect, of her ἀρχή.[8]

Where, then, did Aristophanes stand? There are a few passages in other plays that have some bearing on his attitude. Firstly, he assumes throughout as did all Athenians that the ἀρχή exists and will exist; not only that, but that it should exist, that Athenians have a complete and absolute right to rule. Indeed it is openly stated in *Wasps* 711 — the Athenians received rewards worthy of their land and what they did at Marathon. Secondly, it is taken for granted throughout that the tribute was part of the natural order of things. The most important passage is *Wasps* 656ff. where Aristophanes through Bdelycleon propounds a splendid new scheme for imperial control. The tribute in future should go to the citizens of Athens not into demagogues' pockets. In place of the existing system, each subject city should keep twenty Athenians in a state of ease by direct *ad hominem* distribution. Again, in the *Acharnians* parabasis, Aristophanes rests his claim to Athenian gratitude on the fact that the tribute is paid on the nail. As simple as that, and there is no sign here of a sensitive conservative soul shrinking from the exploitation of the Allies. Far from it.

Empire and tribute then are accepted. What Aristophanes is criticising is something specific. It is that the profits of empire go not into Athenians' pockets but into those of the demagogues, particularly of Cleon. Just as in the *Acharnians* he is concerned to expose inefficiency in the government, so in the *Babylonians* we may infer that he was complaining about corruption in the government. In other words Aristophanes never claims to be defending the Allies against the Athenian *demos*. He does claim, loud and long, that he is defending the Allies *and* the Athenian *demos* against Cleon and his like. These are his own words at *Peace* 759 ff. 'I held on, fighting on your behalf and on that of the islanders.' At *Knights* 801 the Sausage-seller accuses Cleon: 'you plunder the cities, you take bribes from the cities, but the *demos* through the mists of war can't see the dirty tricks you're up to', and at the very end of the play the discomfited Cleon is to be exposed to the delighted view of 'the Allies whom he has injured'. There is no need to multiply examples.

Now there certainly are some passages where the poet does suggest that Athenians as a whole should or could have been gentler with their dependants. To take one example: *Peace*

935f. The people are to become gentle, like lambs in their ways and much softer with the Allies. But when these are taken against the background sketched above they lose their general significance. That background is specific. Cleon and his like are the enemies.

Well, we know that the Athenian *demos* seemed to think that it did not need to be defended against Cleon. Why should we imagine that the Allies or rather all Allies were any more anxious to be defended? Aristophanes merely exaggerates a sectional championship into a general one. But there is more to it.

What exactly will have happened? Suppose the story of Thucydides, son of Melesias, and his moneylending were true. What might the Aeginetans do? They would send an embassy to Athens to complain. When Methone wanted to be excused its arrears of tribute what did it do? It sent an embassy to Athens. The Mytilineans sent one in 427 to plead for mercy.[9] But how did they go about it? By concocting as good a speech as they could to deliver in the assembly. But only the very naïve would have relied on a speech alone. Many will already have had friends among Athenian politicians, many more will have known who was likely to be sympathetic — or have known who might be bought. The Aeginetans would, of course, have made straight for Thucydides' enemy Pericles (after making sure that they hadn't accidentally chosen an old friend of the Alcmaeonids or an old wrestling partner of Melesias as one of their representatives). The Mytileneans went straight to Diodotus (whether he received any of the money that Thucydides says they were lavishly distributing is an open question[10]).

And what about the audience in the assembly? How would they react? They would judge, I should guess, on four grounds, on what the ambassadors said (was it a case or not?), on how they said it (did they call Athens ἰοστέφανοι often enough?), on who they were (an ἀνὴρ παχὺς from Chalcidice or a known friend of the *demos* from Methone?), but as much as anything by who rose to speak for or against them when they had finished, Cleon, Nicias, Diodotus, Hyperbolus, who? And so they voted.

But in this assembly there were a few who decided in part on different grounds, young men in the main, and all of the upper class, young men who had learned from the sophists about the realities of politics, who knew that flattery was a mere trick of rhetoric, who felt like the opponents of Cleon in the Mytilene debate that nothing could match their δεξιότης, their ξύνεσις,

25

who watched their more ordinary fellows, the φαυλότεροι τῶν ἀνθρώπων, vote to excuse Methone from its tribute with a sneer for their gullibility.

One of these young men was Thucydides the historian. De Ste. Croix's onslaught on Thucydides' analysis of the Athenian Empire was perhaps a little severe. Nevertheless no one would deny, I think, that the historian's judgement has taken a nasty knock. But de Ste. Croix's explanation of the contrast between Thucydidean assessment and Thucydidean fact is to my mind rather less satisfactory. He sees it simply as a result of Thucydides' oligarchic inclinations. That this bias helped to distort the picture is obviously true, but it is not the whole story. Sophistic cynicism also played its part. 'All government exploits its subjects and no one likes to be exploited. Ergo the Athenians exploit their subjects' (and of course in fact they did) 'and the subjects cannot like it'. This is the abstract principle stated abstractly by the Old Oligarch — Thucydides does not state it though he comes near to making Pericles and Cleon state it for him — τυραννίδα ἔχετε τὴν ἀρχήν. Well, there was some evidence that some Allies did indeed dislike Athenian rule. So the principle must be right. But there could be no evidence that any Allies thought otherwise. A revolt against Athens, a speech against Athens, these were incontrovertible signs of discontent. But there was no sign of contentment that could not be explained away as the result of fear or of craven flattery. An Athenian who spoke of the harsh realities of power must be telling the truth; but one who spoke of defending the Allies, of protecting their interests — what could that be but sentimental eyewash or a result of bribery? It is always nice to have a theory that will explain everything. Thucydides' theory did. It is just a pity that it was a false theory.

It is also a pity, because it means that he tells us nothing of the kind of things that might have been said on the other side. And consequently, we know virtually nothing of them. The general tone can be picked up from Lysias' *Epitaphius*, Plato's *Menexenus*, Isocrates' *Panegyricus* and *Panathenaicus*, but a bit off-key — John Wayne and the Green Berets at his and their worst. For genuine noises what do we have?

We have an oath or two, sworn by Athenians. For example to the Samians after their revolt of 440. 'I shall do and advise and say only what is good for the people of Samos . . .' Did the men who swore that oath have their tongues in their cheeks, all of them? Or did one or two have a tear in their eye? We have

Aristophanes, the embassies that sang of λιπαραί and ἰοστέφανοι Ἀθῆναι. Where were their tongues . . or tears? Was Ion's gift of Chian wine base flattery or genuine gratitude? Was Athens' protection of her allies in Euripides' mind when he wrote the *Heracleidae* and the *Supplices*?[11] And how do we explain some of the things Herodotus said?

But at best this is a sorry collection to let us see what an Athenian 'White-Man's Burden' looked like to those that carried it, or to those who liked having it carried for them. Only enough to remind us that some saw it as a burden and some liked it to be carried.

And so at last we are back to line 642 of the *Acharnians* and to the *Babylonians*. But by now it must be clear what I think we are to make of it, and of them.

Dionysus had come to Athens. I don't know why — had some eastern cult just been introduced? — and with him a crew of odd Babylonian attendants — why not? Herodotus had just hit the market.[12] But Cleon and his like did not approve of new-fangled cults; they stood for the pure old Athens, for the Marathon tradition, forgetting that Pan had then been a newcomer. Cleon went for Dionysus like a proto-Pentheus and Cleon no doubt suffered, as Lamachus was to suffer in next year's *Acharnians* — and Pentheus somewhat later. But meanwhile another interest, the Allies, and their embassies. One cannot tell whether they came in as part of the main plot, to denounce Dionysus for example — one can imagine a nice embassy from Naxos — or in a passing scene like the opening of the *Acharnians*, an assembly that waded through a mire of allied nonsense before it reached the issue (young artists — Aristophanes was 19 or so — have a tendency to use their good tricks more than once).

Either way, Aristophanes had insulted Cleon and had said rude things about some particular friends of his among the Allies who had come a long way in the hope of hearing nicer things than this. Aristophanes was prosecuted. But the prosecution failed. Aristophanes sat back and purred — nineteen years old remember. A bit frightened by the glimpse of authority — the *Acharnians* of the next year is a cautious play — but encouraged by the success of acquittal, more encouraged by letters that poured in from Naxos and Siphnos and the rest. 'If only all Athenians were like you,' they said. 'Why did we send that filthy man who said he had Cleon in his pocket instead of someone who has you or Diodotus in his pocket to talk for us? Don't worry, we're not disloyal, but next time we have a problem you will see, won't you, that we are properly treated'. And Aristophanes wrote back. 'Of course, my dear chap; my uncle knew your father.'

All this is not pure frivolity. The sad thing is that we have only the tiniest peak of the upper-class iceberg in our view. But we do know how Aristophanes summed it all up. 'I showed up those ambassadors, those friends of Cleon, for what they were, flatterers, pure and simple. And so you have saved yourselves a lot of money — you turned down a dozen embassies this year. What's more, you mustn't think that the Allies are upset by this. All my correspondence shows that they are delighted to have responsible government at last. There may be a few more reasonable embassies next year of a rather different kind. Naturally you won't turn them down. In the meantime, they've paid their tribute willingly.'

To put it in perspective. De Ste. Croix thinks that the Athenian Empire was a good thing, others think it was a bad thing, others waver in between. But all must agree that Athens' control was something like America's control of Western Europe, or Russia's of Eastern Europe; nothing like Britain's grip on her colonies or Rome's on her provinces. A firm control, but not readily defined. It comes back again to personalities, Imre Nagy or Janos Kadar against Kruschev; Heath or Wilson against Nixon; de Gaulle against — well, 'moi contre le monde'.

Meanwhile, there is Thucydides, Malcolm Muggeridge, sniping on the sidelines. And where is Aristophanes? — I don't know. I only know that he's in there in the thick of it, 'flinching from no danger and counting no cost' — but only because there was no danger to flinch from, no cost to pay. For all we know the *Babylonians* won the prize.

## Notes

[1] First step (on his attitude to the war), *The Phoenix*, vol. 17, 1963, pp. 1–12.

[2] *Aristophanes*, Oxford 1933, pp. 25, 47, 75.

[3] See G. Norwood, *CP* vol. 25, 1930, p. 1 ff.

[4] Nothing justifies an extension to other allies.

[5] *Vyestnik Drevnii Istorii*, 1947, pp. 15 ff.

[6] *Historical Commentary on Thucydides* on 4.88.2.

[7] On the life of Thucydides, H. T. Wade-Gery, *Essays*, Oxford

1958, pp. 252, n.2, and 262.

8  I shall argue this elsewhere.

9  R. Meiggs and D. Lewis, *GHI*, Oxford 1969, no. 65; Thuc. 3.50.3.

10  Thuc. 3.49.3.

11  So Luria suggests (loc. cit.). See especially *Heracleidae* 755—65.

12  Mr. Fornara will forgive me if I retain the usual date for publication (see *JHS* vol. 91, 1971, pp. 25—34).


W. G. Forrest,
Wadham College,
Oxford

# 3

# Did Xenophon intend to
# write History?

Xenophon as a historian stands condemned. His intellectual honesty is impugned as his abilities are questioned. For the history of the first half of the fourth century he is frequently ignored in favour of the unknown author of the *Hellenica Oxyrhynchia* fragments, in favour of parochial *Atthides*, hardly less fragmentary, in favour of orators, the bias of whose speeches is at the same time universally recognised, and also in favour of Ephorus, intuitively read between the lines of a third-rate first-century hack, Diodorus.[1]

I have no defence to offer; nor should I venture here any ingenious thesis of systematic misrepresentation. Such is the undisputed prerogative of that master of the art to whom this essay is with affection, and respect, dedicated. Instead I shall ask the simple question: did Xenophon intend to write history? There are I believe serious grounds for doubting this.

Criticism of the *Hellenica* as a historical work is general and well-known. The major faults are omissions (of minor details, as the patronymics of four of the seven generals at 6.3.2, but also of important and well-known historical events, as the Second Athenian Confederacy or Epaminondas' presence at Leuctra), elliptic writing ($εἰδότες\ τὸ\ πρᾶγμα\ ἐφ'\ ὃ\ ἀπεστάλκεσαν$ at 5.4.9 precedes the lacuna), delayed order (as Agesilaos' reaction to, and involvement in the aftermath of, Phoebidas' seizure of the Cadmeia, which is most revealingly noted at 5.4.13), and inaccuracies (in so far as these can be checked from the other sources, as for example that the Thebans were for provoking war with Phocis and made the alliance with Athens at 3.5.7 whereas the

Boeotians as a whole are indicated both by *Hell. Oxy.* 18(13) and the inscription, Tod *GHI* 101). Full examples can be found in most commentators. A more interesting criticism, recently well analysed by Soulis,[2] is the fictional character of Xenophon's way of writing: the presentation of information in personalised terms, the addition of literary frills or psychological observations, the introduction of anecdotes as if they were fairy-tales, constant reference to the truth or falsity of prophecies, interruption of narrative for comment upon it, use of vague terms of exaggeration, the generally anecdotal structure of the narrative, and the totally fictitious character and content of many speeches.

Criticism of Xenophon's historicity on these three grounds (broadly of omissions, inaccuracies, and fictional presentation) is valid and could be pressed further. I shall not do that here. It is however important to recognise that it was in *explaining* these weaknesses that critics found Xenophon's bias and attacked his intellectual capabilities (respectively his slipshod memory, his use of untrustworthy sources, his inadequate research, and his lack of dedication). But these interpretations are very much harder to sustain than the basic criticisms. Thus, for example, it is difficult to maintain that Xenophon carefully avoided mention of the Second Athenian Confederacy in order not to embarrass Sparta or in order to avoid praising Athens when the Confederacy was a well-known contemporary fact and must anyway be assumed for the activity of Athens in the 370's as described in the *Hellenica* itself. Furthermore, did not Thucydides equally omit significant events: the Peace of Callias, and Persian affairs? Is an incomplete final sentence the sole acceptable evidence of unfinished composition? Turning to the criticisms of lack of research and inaccuracy on the other hand we can point to many examples of careful composition in Xenophon. Clearly it is wrong to suppose all omissions and faults can be explained by a single line of interpretation, but to multiply interpretations of bias and connect them to an ingenious reconstruction of Xenophon's life and composition is as plainly absurd as the premiss that a *single* reconstruction may be found to accommodate *all* bias.

However the point that I wish to stress here is that these interpretations need not be justified at the outset. They are, it is true, needed to explain *historical* weaknesses in the *Hellenica*; but this assumption, that the work is historical, remains to be justified.

It is impossible of course to overlook the form of the *Hellenica*: a narrative account of Greek history, in roughly chronological order, apparently a straight continuation of Thucydides' account, and itself also anticipating further continuation: τὰ δὲ μετὰ ταῦτα ἴσως ἄλλῳ μελήσει (7.5.27, the concluding phrase). However this is far from enough to establish that Xenophon's work was meant to be history, or even that it was meant to be as historical as Thucydides'.

The continuation from the end of Thucydides to Xenophon's *Hellenica* is awkward. Discrepancies have been noted in style, in chronology, in cross- and backward-references. They need not be repeated here,[3] but add up to the conclusion that the 'continuation' is *purely* formal. If the most striking discrepancy, the syntactical break between the last sentence of Thucydides and the first of Xenophon, is pressed as it should be, it becomes possible to doubt whether Xenophon's work even formally was a continuation of Thucydides'. Possibly more attractive than the explanation that a sentence has been lost from either work, is that Xenophon may have rewritten someone else's continuation of Thucydides. Candidates are not hard to find: Cratippos' *Hellenica* and, if this was not the same work, the Oxyrhynchus *Hellenica* were both written early in the fourth century and there may have been others. Xenophon's *Hellenica* might therefore on this argument be regarded as much a rehearsal of a recognised literary theme (and later Theopompos repeated the exercise) as a continuation of an uncompleted history.

Further, whatever the relation of the *beginning* of Xenophon's *Hellenica* to Thucydides' history, there is good reason to dissociate the bulk of it from this beginning. Scholars have offered a bewildering array of possible reconstructions of the composition of the work, and little consensus exists. Virtually all however would agree on a break of some significance after 2.3.9. The most objective criterion available, that of statistical style analysis, has shown further that a considerable interval elapsed between the writing of this first part and that of the remainder.[4] For a number of other reasons I should place the first part in the early 380's (or late 390's) and believe that the remainder was written, with interruptions for certain other works,[5] in the last years of Xenophon's life in the 350's.[6] This particular position is not perhaps so vital, as once the major break at 2.3.9 is recognised then it ceases to be possible to regard the *Hellenica* as a work conceived as a (historical) unity.

If Xenophon wrote with some idea of continuing Thucydides, a position that I feel should not be entirely abandoned, he nevertheless adjusted considerably his predecessor's whole perspective. Thucydides at 5.26.1 clearly marked what he considered to be the end of his account of the war: the dismantling of the Long Walls. Xenophon went on beyond this point (reached at *Hell.* 2.2.23) to add another few months before ending the war at 2.3.9. But more importantly Xenophon's extension was deliberate, as is clear from his marking the earlier point as where people *thought* that peace (or rather freedom) had come. This is heavy irony, as the subsequent events, described in Xenophon's *Hellenica*, but already obvious by the later 390's, would clearly show. The very end of the *Hellenica* can be compared here. The battle of Mantinea solved no problems, settled no differences, yet Xenophon concluded by inviting further continuation. To Xenophon might therefore I believe be ascribed the view that the affairs of Greece formed a continuum. This might be seen further as a reaction to the belief of Thucydides that events, as his Peloponnesian War, could be isolated as past histories. However, that Xenophon had a view about history, albeit a valid and interesting one, does not imply that he intended to write it.

Stronger in Xenophon than the idea of the continuity of the Greek struggle is the pessimism that accompanied such a realisation. Mantinea solved no problems, indeed Greece was more unsettled after the battle than before it (7.5.27). In other words, Xenophon's *Hellenica* has progressed from the idealisation of City-state conflict, from the virtues brought out on the battlefield, from the great men of his narrative, into an unsatisfactory reality. I feel it can be no accident that precisely the same approach can be found in the conclusions to other works of Xenophon. The *Anabasis* ends (at 7.8) with a somewhat sordid, and unrelated, campaign to win Xenophon a fortune: contrast his earlier idealistic dream to found a colony on the shores of the Black Sea,[7] or his assertion of sharing all he possessed with his men,[8] or even his pious and careful dedication to Artemis.[9] In the final part of the *Cyropedia* (8.8) the glorious (and idealised) past of Persia is contrasted with its despicable present. Again the fourteenth, and plausibly the last proper, chapter of the *Lacedaemoniorum Respublica* contains critical comment on the real situation in Sparta, despite the excellence of the system described in the earlier theoretical chapters. Both these latter passages are of course notorious hunting grounds for those who seek changes in Xenophon's political attitudes, and who either regard the passages as spurious or as 'palinodes'.[10] At the expense of much further argument, I shall simply note here that each passage represents a *different* change of opinion by Xenophon on a *different* subject: the moral fibre of Persia and the effectiveness of the Lycurgan régime. More impressive is the fact that all four books cited end with pessimistic evaluation of realities in contrast to earlier (theoretical) potentialities. This conclusion must throw doubt upon the historical intent behind the works concerned: is this simply less obvious in the *Hellenica* because of its form and subject-matter than in say the *Lac. Resp.* or *Cyropedia*?

Apart from form and subject-matter some indication of Xenophon's historical intent in the *Hellenica* might also be sought in conscious reference to historical method or aim. There are however no passages which on examination show this, and certainly none comparable with Thucydides' statements at 1.22 or 2.35.2, for example.

Three passages can be considered. In the first, 7.2.1, Xenophon writes in detail about Phlius, 'for if one of the great powers does some fine and noble action all historians write about it; but it seems to me that if a state which is only a small one has done numbers of great and glorious things, there is all the more reason for letting people know about them.'[11] These statements are all vague; no great states or historians are mentioned or even indicated. The remark is simply to introduce a digression on something 'fine and noble' — on how the Phliasians adhered to their alliance and remained loyal to their friends.[12]

In the second passage, 2.3.56, Xenophon gives Theramenes' last words — the joke about a libation to his prosecutor Critias. This Xenophon says is 'not worthy of note', but then goes on to use it to make an observation about Theramenes' character, that even at death he did not cease being φρόνιμος or lose his sense of humour. We might infer that this observation was therefore more properly 'worthy of note'. I suspect however a literary device to introduce Xenophon's comment on Theramenes (which he wished to make for other reasons). It is clear that this passage (2.3.56) cannot be used to show that Xenophon had any historical criterion in mind.

4.8.1 is the last, and also most explicit, of the three passages. After his mainland narrative has reached 388/7, Xenophon turns to events overseas that have happened in the meantime and describes his method of selection: 'I shall pass over those actions that are not worth mentioning, dealing only with what deserves to be remembered'. What follows however hardly gives due space to matters of historical importance. Instead we read of Derkyllidas and the loyalty of Abydos, of Thibron's lack of discipline, of the contrasted fates of Thrasyboulos and Anaxibios (a moral fable), of Teleutias' control of his troops (balance and contrast to the earlier Thibron episode). These details moreover greatly overshadow in the *Hellenica* the battle of Cnidus and negotiations with Persia, to mention only the most obvious significant historical events of the period.

In historical terms these three passages are excessively general, irrelevant or simple-minded elaboration of the immediate context.[13] However they do hang together in referring to what was worth mention, and in each case properly describe what Xenophon has done — namely to concentrate on *moral* points. I think it is perverse to insist upon a *historical* reference for 'worthy of mention' and then to criticise Xenophon for not living up to his own statement of intent.

Other intrusions by Xenophon into his narrative follow the same pattern as these passages that explicitly refer to his method. Apart from simple references to the date of writing (as 6.4.37 Tisiphonus still ruling) or to the fact of a digression (as 6.1.19 or 7.2.1), Xenophon invariably intervenes in order to point a lesson. Thus, often, he praises or criticises a military stratagem: 7.2.27—8 Iphicrates' rowing practice; 6.5.51 Iphicrates' delayed entry into the Peloponnese; 7.5.8 Epaminondas' camp; 3.4.16—18 observations on the morale at the Ephesus games; 4.3.16 the uniqueness of the battle of Coronea. Xenophon may also comment directly on individuals: 7.5.8 Epaminondas; 4.8.31 Thrasyboulos; or 2.3.56 Theramenes, as already discussed above. Similarly he may pass a moral judgement on events being described: 5.4.1 the downfall of Sparta attributed to ἀσέβεια; 5.4.24 the unjustness of Sphodrias' trial. These passages could be supplemented by many more. It is by contrast extremely difficult to find an explicit *historical* judgement in Xenophon's *Hellenica* that it not itself some sort of moralistic comment. In 4.8.24 Teleutias (campaigning against Athens and Persia) captures Philocrates (an Athenian sent to help Euagoras against Persia); Xenophon brings out this very contradiction. Similarly, 7.5.26—27, the statement that Mantinea solved no problems, cannot but be read as a comment on the futility of the Peloponnesian struggles.

One seeks in vain evidence of concern on Xenophon's part for a properly historical approach equally to chronology, to causation, or to motivation. The vagaries of his chronology are notorious: the vacuous connections (μετὰ δὲ ταῦτα, etc.); the lack of absolute dates; the superficiality of the Thucydidean system imposed on the first part;[14] the confusion of frequent flashbacks. Causation and motivation on the other hand were complicated subjects for all Greek writers of this period. Thucydides shows signs of changed positions on the latter, motivation, in his growing recognition of the relevance of the individual to his original city-state calculus;[15] and the theory was being closely studied by fourth-century philosophers.[16] In allowing a greater part for individuals in the *Hellenica* Xenophon certainly goes further than Thucydides. It is difficult however to feel that the motives and characters of Xenophon's individuals ever form an integral part of his historical narrative. On causation Xenophon can be more seriously criticised for presenting pretexts and for ignoring real causes: thus at 6.3.1 he describes the Athenian initiative for peace in a way that contrasts with the sort of planning for the mastery of Greece ascribed to the Thebans at 7.1.33. More often however he simply juxtaposes events, and in the later books especially falls back on divine intervention.[17]

Again I shall not pursue these points further here.[18] The historical criticisms are valid. My argument however is that they do not amount to any sound reason for considering that the *Hellenica* was written as history. Equally I have shown in this part that there is no positive evidence of historical intent behind the work. Its form and subject-matter amount only to a superficial indication; there are no explicit statements of intent, or of method; there is no evidence of concern for a historical approach to causation or motivation.

The traditional critical approach of Xenophon is therefore misguided as it assumes, wrongly, that Xenophon's *Hellenica* was written as history. In fact by collecting the elements of non-historicity contained in this traditional criticism a very plausible and more positive account of the work emerges: the strong fictional element in an ostensible historical form; the concentration upon Xenophon's personal interests, upon military strategem, anecdote, and above all moral judgement; the positive advocacy of a particular way of life and attitude to politics.

If regarded as primarily didactic, the *Hellenica* fits well into the context of Xenophon's other works. This interpretation can further be fully supported by references in them. At *Anab.* 5.8.26 Xenophon defines what is worth remembering as the good *rather than* the bad. The vocabulary and the sentiment recall the three passages from the *Hellenica* considered above: 7.2.1, 2.3.56, 4.8.1. More explicitly didactic is the purpose of the *Agesilaos* (10.2): καλὸν ἄν μοι δοκεῖ ἡ 'Αγησιλάου ἀρετὴ παράδειγμα γενέσθαι τοῖς ἀνδραγαθίαν ἀσκεῖν βουλομένοις. The *Agesilaos* was an admitted encomium[19], but much of Agesilaos' career is also described in the *Hellenica*, and often word for word with the *Agesilaos*. Xenophon's views on education should be pursued in *Memorabilia*, where Socrates is represented by Xenophon as standing to teach καλοκἀγαθία at *Mem.*1.2.12. The uniqueness of Sparta (we read elsewhere) lay in the fact that she was the only Greek state to make καλοκἀγαθία a public duty: μόνη δημοσίᾳ ἐπιτηδεύουσα τὴν καλοκἀγαθίαν (*Lac. Resp.* 10.1)

I do not think this view of Xenophon is necessarily very far from the position reached at present by modern critics of his supposedly historical writings. To take three examples: Soulis[20] constantly and successfully criticises Xenophon's historical abilities; he wonders briefly[21] whether Xenophon should be regarded as a historian at all; but then slips back into the traditional view of Xenophon's 'hypocrisy', called by Soulis, because of Xenophon's lack of consistency and patency, 'simple-minded'. Breitenbach[22] has pursued the idea that Xenophon was primarily interested in leadership in the *Anabasis*, the *Agesilaos*, and the *Cyropedia*; the thesis should now, I suggest, be extended to the *Hellenica* and be broadened to wider issues. Finally Nussbaum has[23] subjected the *Anabasis* to a detailed analysis of social organisation and of leadership, in theory and practice; not surprisingly he finds the work most suitable for such study, but he fails[24] to make the further point, not a great one, that this was what Xenophon wrote it as.

My position need not be tied down to regarding the *Hellenica* as didactic and *not in any sense* historical. There is room for uncertainty as to what in the early fourth century counts as historical. The border-line between real and unreal, fact and fiction, was confused; that fact is most clearly seen in the biographical developments of the early part of the century (and Xenophon wrote biography);[25] it is no less true of philosophical writing (the notorious Socratics, of which Xenophon was of course one); and of the pseudo-history of rhetoric (Isocrates, but again no less Xenophon). There was at this period considerable uncertainty about the function of history, and individual writers went different ways. Thucydides' approach has gained modern recognition, but was not necessarily acceptable to (nor understood by ?) his contemporaries. The number of different 'histories' that were written to continue his account well illustrates the uncertainty. Ephorus and Theopompus show the predominantly moralistic approach that was ultimately established.

Theopompus abandoned his *Hellenica* at the battle of Cnidus and turned to Philip of Macedon. We might ask why, and one answer could well be that Theopompus recognised the historical importance of Philip. However, this does not explain his failure to complete the *Hellenica*, and, secondly, it is clear from the fragments that Theopompus' interest in Philip, his fascination for Philip, was not historical but moral. Whether Philip be hero or anti-hero,[26] he clearly presented a more interesting subject than the continued bickering of Greek states. As Xenophon had written this, in the long run, went nowhere. If history is approached from a moralistic angle, it is clearly important to find suitable subjects (παραδείγματα). This was what Theopompus found, and preferred, in Philip. It remains therefore briefly to consider here Xenophon's παραδείγματα, and to criticise his use of them. I can do little more however than indicate the shape of the problem.

First must be isolated the central themes in Xenophon's teaching. These I take to be Panhellenism (in the sense of a war against Persia to encourage some sort of unity between the states of Greece and closely akin, in effect, to Isocrates' final position) and the Peloponnesian way of life (distinct from the Spartan, which was only for Spartiates, but equally distinct from the politically charged outlook of most non-neutral city-states). Alongside these elements can be added instruction on military matters, and general moral issues (piety, observance of law, continence). These themes are deployed in the general παράδειγμα Xenophon chose — the Spartan alternative to Thucydides' Athenian Empire. The inadequacy in reality of this παράδειγμα explains much that is omitted from the *Hellenica* as also its extraordinary unevenness. But criticism should now follow, and I do not wish to give the impression of not being critical.

First Xenophon can be faulted on his understanding of some military details, especially Theban tactics.[27] Second I find naïve his view that in inter-state politics all depended upon the καλοκἀγαθία of state leaders (the same criticism of course applies to the parallel philosopher-kings of Plato). Third his social outlook was unbelievably insular and one-sided, and his judgement in practice blinded by personal feelings.[28] Finally I do not consider as at all realistic the Panhellenic ideal that rested on a campaign against the barbarian.

Such judgement naturally must be subjective, but I cannot accept Xenophon's use of his παράδειγμα any more than I can approve the distortion of history that has resulted. The final problem however remains: how are we to use Xenophon's *Hellenica* as historical evidence? I suggest that we can rely on it only marginally more happily than we resort to his *Cyropedia* for early Persian history or to the *Agesilaos* for Spartan policy. Issues touching the central didactic themes have been distorted considerably where we can check them. For example Agesilaos' plan to march ἀνωτάτω in Asia Minor is transposed to the end of his campaign there and left unfinished.[29] In this case the reason for distortion could be a wish to leave open the possibility of a Panhellenic crusade, or it could be an attempt to conceal the extent of Agesilaos' failure, or it could be a literary device to contrast the potential of a united Greece with the unprofitable reality of disunion. No simple key exists to resolve such distortions, and the negative conclusion seems inevitable: given a fundamental break with historical fact in the total concept of the work there is no real reason to suppose any particular part of it accurate. Our estimation of Xenophon's imaginative powers may perhaps limit the extent of the fictitious element, but it cannot define it.

I should like to end by citing a passage from the treatise 'On Hunting' (*Cyneg.*13.7). Doubts have been raised about the authorship of the whole, but this passage is certainly contemporary with Xenophon and I should like to believe it was in fact written by him. It is a conscious reflection of Thucydides 1.22; the author defends his account and explains his aim: 'My aim in writing has been to produce sound work that will make men not wiseacres (σοφιστικούς) but wise and good (σοφοὺς καὶ ἀγαθούς). For I wish my work not to *seem* useful (alas χρήσιμα rather than ὠφέλιμα), but to be so, that it may stand for all time unrefuted (ἀνεξέλεγκτα ᾖ εἰς ἀεί)'.[30] If one accepts that Xenophon's *Hellenica* continued, but perverted, the purpose of Thucydides' histories, then this passage is confirmation. Moreover it points to precisely the reason for Xenophon's being read and liked in antiquity, and indeed right down to modern attempts to suppose him to be a Thucydides-type historian,[31] which he most certainly was not. In the first century of this era Dio Chrysostom wrote that 'Xenophon, and he alone of the ancients, can satisfy all the requirements of a man in public life'.[32]

## Notes

[1] M. I. Finley, *Greek Historians*, Cambridge 1959, p. 14; J. Hatzfeld, *Helléniques*, Paris 1949, vol. 1, p. 18; E. M. Soulis, *Xenophon and Thucydides*, Athens 1972, p. 189.

[2] Soulis, op. cit., pp. 32–8.

[3] The most readable recent discussion is in W. P. Henry, *Greek Historical Writing*, Chicago 1967, chs. 1 and 2.

[4] Statistics based on subconscious elements of style must be distinguished from other subjective criteria (humour or moralising) and from conscious variation in style (synonyms, for example). See especially W. Dittenberger, *Herm.* vol. 16, 1881, pp. 330–33, but with some caution J. Hatzfeld, *Rev. Phil.* vol. 4, 1930, pp. 113–27, 209–26, and M. MacLaren, *AJP* vol. 55, 1934, pp. 121–39, 249–62.

[5] Thus the *Agesilaos* was probably written at some point in the drafting of *Hellenica* 4.4–5, as comparison of parallel passages and narrative styles shows.

[6] The planks in this argument are briefly: that references to the 350's occur only in the later books (as 6.4.37, Tisiphonus' rule being c.358–355); that the stylistic development over the later books is gradual; that the late writing of the *Hellenica* fits better into what can independently be reconstructed of the date and order of Xenophon's writings and of the circumstances of his life.

[7] *Anab.*5.6.15–16, and note also 6.4.1–8.

[8] *Anab.*7.3.20; 6.4.39; 7.41–42; 8.1–3.

[9] *Anab.*5.3.7–13.

[10] See conveniently, though with different conclusions, E. N.

Tigerstedt, *The Legend of Sparta in Classical Antiquity*, vol. 1, Stockholm, etc., 1965, n. 530 (pp. 462—64).

[11] Penguin translation.

[12] Cf.7.3.1.

[13] Taken seriously they have been used as evidence of deliberate misrepresentation: thus Soulis, op. cit., p. 18.

[14] Henry, op. cit., pp. 39—45.

[15] H. D. Westlake, *Individuals in Thucydides*, Cambridge 1968, especially pp. 308—19, with G. E. M. de Ste. Croix, *The Origins of the Peloponnesian War*, Oxford 1972, I.ii and especially pp. 16—25.

[16] Cf. Aristotle's *Nic. Ethics.*

[17] 4.4.12; 7.5.12; 5.26.

[18] For motivation see recently Westlake, *Essays*, Manchester and N.Y. 1969, ch. 13.

[19] 1.1 and 10.3.

[20] As cited in n. 1 above.

[21] P.94.

[22] H. R. Breitenbach, *Historiographische Anschauungsformen Xenophons*, Freiburg i.d. Schweiz 1950, and further in *RE* vol. 9A, s.v. Xenophon.

[23] G. B. Nussbaum, *The Ten Thousand*, Leiden 1967.

[24] Especially on pp. 12—13.

[25] See A. Momigliano, *The Development of Greek Biography*, Cambridge, Mass., 1971, pp. 43—64.

[26] See W. R. Connor in *GRBS* vol. 8, 1967, pp. 133—54. I am inclined to agree that Theopompus was impressed by the material success that accompanied Philip's (morally) dubious methods.

[27] See the recent studies by G. L. Cawkwell on Cunaxa, in the Penguin *Anabasis*, Harmondsworth 1972, Introduction, pp. 36—43, and on Leuctra, in *CQ* vol. 22, 1972, pp. 260—63.

[28] Xenophon insists *passim* on the importance of friendship (*Anab.*1.9.20ff.; 7.7.42; *Hell.*7.2) and all but cites φιλεταιρία as a justification for some of Agesilaos' more questionable actions (*Ages.*2.21, contrast Isoc. 5.86—7 and *Epist.* 9.12—13).

[29] The plan which Xenophon notes at 4.1.41 should rather be placed at 3.4.29 in view of *Hell. Oxy.* 22 (17) 4 and Isoc. 4.144.

[30] Loeb translation. On the question of authorship, see E. Marchant, *Loeb Xenophon* vol. 7, pp. xxxvi—xliii, and Breitenbach, *RE* 1A, col. 1913 f., against D. J. Mosley, *OCD*², s.v. Xenophon, and J. Luccioni, *Idées politiques et sociales de Xénophon*, 1948, pp. 23—6.

[31] With Thucydides the modern historian tends to find much in common; the identification of historical aims is however to be suspected, as I have attempted to show in *CQ* vol 22, 1972, pp. 62–73.

[32] Dio Chrys.18.14 (Loeb translation).

C. H. Grayson,
Council of Europe,
Strasbourg
(formerly New College, Oxford).

# 4

## Aristotle on History and Poetry
## (Poetics 9, 1451[a]36–[b]11)[1]

In a famous passage in the *Poetics*, chapter 9 (1451[a]36–[b]11), Aristotle disparages history (ἰστορία) in comparison with poetry (ποίησις). He begins by stating that 'the function of a poet is to describe not what has happened (τὰ γενόμενα) but the kind of thing that might happen,[2] and what is possible according to probability or necessity' (οἷα ἂν γένοιτο, καὶ τὰ δυνατὰ κατὰ τὸ εἰκὸς ἢ τὸ ἀναγκαῖον). He goes on to say that the distinction between historian and poet (ἱστορικός and ποιητής) resides not in the one writing prose and other verse (for the work of Herodotus, he says, if put into verse, would still be history) but 'in the fact that the one [history] describes what has happened, the other [poetry] what might happen'. The conclusion he proceeds to draw is that 'poetry is something more philosophic and more worthwhile (σπουδαιότερον) than history, because poetry deals rather with universals, history with particulars' (ἡ μὲν γὰρ ποίησις μᾶλλον τὰ καθόλου, ἡ δ' ἱστορία τὰ καθ' ἕκαστον λέγει). And Aristotle goes on to explain what he means by 'universals' and 'particulars': universal statements are about what a particular kind of man will say or do 'according to probability or necessity'; particular statements are about 'what Alcibiades did or had done to him'.

This passage is perfectly explicit and unqualified, and it is wrong to seek to explain it away, for example by dragging in *Poet.* 23, 1459[a]21–4, where Aristotle refers to 'our usual histories (ἱστορίας τὰς συνήθεις),[3] which have to set forth not one action but one period, and all that happened during that period concerning one or more persons, however disconnected the several events may have been'. This passage leaves open the

45

possibility that there may be histories of a different, less usual, kind. Some may also think here of another passage in *Poetics* 9 (1451$^b$ 29—33), where Aristotle mentions that a poet who takes his subject from actual history is none the less a poet for that, 'since there is nothing to prevent some historic occurrences from being such as happen in the probable and possible order of things, and it is in that aspect of them that he is their poet'. But even if we take into account the possibility that in Aristotle's mind there was more than one kind of history, and that some historical events might be conceived as illustrating the possible, the probable, even the necessary, we are left with a definite assertion, in the passage in *Poetics* 9 with which we began, about the relationship of poetry in general and history in general: poetry is more philosophic and more worthwhile than history. I fancy that most people would agree with a recent statement: 'To us this seems a very strange conclusion, but it is entirely consistent with Aristotle's view-point. In real life any chain of events is influenced by chance and accident. But the poet can and should represent an ideal sequence of events, the events as they would occur according to the general rules governing human behaviour'.[4] And an article on Aristotle's use of the word ἱστορία expresses a view which I think most Aristotelians would hold: that in so far as ἱστορία in Aristotle can sometimes mean 'knowledge' rather than (as usual) 'history', or 'research', 'enquiry', it refers to knowledge of particular facts only, not qualifying in Aristotle's eyes as a proper science, ἐπιστήμη.[5]

My purpose here is to argue that although our *Poetics* passage is indeed consistent with views expressed by Arisotle when he is speaking loosely, yet if we take account of a number of important but much-neglected passages in which Aristotle defines his terms with more than usual care, we must admit that his disparagement of history is not entirely justified on his own principles, at any rate in so far as it refers to the historian whom he is likely to have had most in mind when describing history as 'what Alcibiades did or had done to him': namely, Thucydides. This will involve our taking notice of a concept which appears on numerous occasions in Aristotle but is too often ignored altogether, or given scant attention, by philosophers: τὸ ὡς ἐπὶ τὸ πολύ, which I shall consistently translate 'the as a general rule'. ('The usual', 'normal', 'habitual' would often represent the meaning well enough, but the awkward phrase I have deliberately chosen provides the nearest parallel I can think of in English to the rather curious Greek expression, which in its substantival form — not just ὡς ἐπὶ τὸ πολύ, which is common enough[6] — I have not encountered outside the works of Aristotle.) It is a main aim of this essay to stimulate discussion of the rôle played by τὸ ὡς ἐπὶ τὸ πολύ in Aristotle's thought, a question which seems to me to need a thorough investigation, by someone interested in Aristotle as a scientist and not merely as a philosopher. In the major works on Aristotle which I have consulted, I have found nothing more than passing remarks on this subject.[7]

The distinction drawn in *Poetics* 9, between 'the universal', τὰ καθόλου, and 'the particular', τὰ καθ᾽ ἕκαστον, is used by Aristotle in different connections and in different senses.[8] If we neglect the passages concerned with τὸ ὡς ἐπὶ τὸ πολύ, we can easily suppose it to be a fundamental element in Aristotle's thought that full scientific knowledge, ἐπιστήμη,[9] is only of 'the universal',[10] and of 'the necessary', τὸ ἐξ ἀνάγκης,[11] something that 'cannot be other than what it is'.[12] These two ideas, 'the universal' and 'the necessary', are closely connected, as are those of 'the particular' and 'the accidental' or 'the contingent', for universal attributes are defined as those which belong necessarily (ἐξ ἀνάγκης) to their subjects,[13] and the universal is also defined as 'the always and everywhere', τὸ ἀεὶ καὶ πανταχοῦ,[14] and is contrasted with 'the accidental' or 'the contingent', τὸ συμβεβηκός,[15] which is commonly found opposed to 'the necessary'. At least, that is the way in which Aristotle's thought on the subject of ἐπιστήμη is commonly conceived and presented — and when it is so conceived, it can be used as part of the justification for the statement in *Poetics* 9 which we are considering, placing poetry above history: whether or not Aristotle is right in the way he characterises poetry and history respectively, what he says will at least be consistent with his general philosophical position. In fact, however, the conception of ἐπιστήμη as being appropriate only to 'the universal' and 'the necessary' oversimplifies and seriously misrepresents the main stream of Aristotle's thinking. Even in *Poetics* 9 it will be noticed that the 'universal' statements of poetry are defined as being what will happen not merely *necessarily* but also *probably* (κατὰ τὸ εἰκός). It is at this point that we must seriously consider Aristotle's concept of τὸ ὡς ἐπὶ τὸ πολύ, 'the as a general rule', the usual, the normal, the habitual. This appears very frequently: it can be found at least in the *De Interpretatione*, in the *Analytics* both *Prior* and *Posterior*, in the *Topics*, the *Physics, Metaphysics* Δ, E, and K, the *De Generatione et Corruptione*, the *Generation of Animals*, the *Parts of Animals*, the *Ethics*, and the *Rhetoric*.

At the end of *Metaphysics* Δ (a book consisting almost entirely of definitions)[16] Aristotle employs a classification which is not the twofold one we have noticed already, into attributes which are either necessary or accidental (ἐξ ἀνάγκης or συμβεβηκός), but threefold: he adds to the other two 'the as a general rule'. In the next book of the *Metaphysics*[17] the same threefold classification appears, and here it is specifically recognised that full scientific knowledge is possible not only of 'the always' but also of 'the as a general rule' (ἐπιστήμη πᾶσα ἢ τοῦ ἀεὶ ἢ τοῦ ὡς ἐπὶ τὸ πολύ, 1027ᵃ20–1). And Aristotle adds an example: it is true as a general rule that honey-water (τό μελίκρατον) is useful for a patient suffering from fever. In *Metaphysics* K he is equally explicit, and again ἐπιστήμη πᾶσα is either of what exists always or of 'the as a general rule'.[18]

In discussing the presentation of arguments, in the *Topics*,[19] Aristotle again distinguishes three types of events, not only those occurring of necessity or 'as it may chance to happen' (ὁπότερ' ἔτυχεν,[20] a synonym for τὸ συμβεβηκός), but also those which occur 'as a general rule'; and elsewhere in the *Topics*,[21] as on one occasion in the *Posterior Analytics*,[22] he draws the same distinction, adding in each case to the words ὡς ἐπί τὸ πολύ the explanatory phrase 'and in most cases' (καί ἐν τοῖς πλείστοις). On another occasion in the *Posterior Analytics* Aristotle also introduces this threefold distinction, asserting that there can be no ἐπιστήμη by demonstration of chance conjunctions, for these exist neither by necessity nor as a general rule, and demonstration (ἀπόδειξις) is concerned with one or other of these two.[23]

Aristotle also makes use of the same threefold classification at several points in *Physics* 2.[24] First (5, 196ᵇ 10–21, especially 10–13) he emphasises that chance (ἡ τύχη) cannot be said to be the cause either of things which always happen in the same way (τὰ ἀεὶ ὡσαύτως γινόμενα) or of 'the as a general rule', nor can the effect of chance be identified with any of the things that come about either by necessity and always (ἐξ ἀνάγκης καὶ ἀεί) or as a general rule. We can account for what exists always or as a general rule, whereas chance is in a different category (197ᵃ18–20). In another passage (7, 198ᵇ 5–6), on the causes of motion, he is prepared to speak of a result

48

following either 'without qualification' (ἁπλῶς) or 'as a general rule' under the heading of 'necessity' (ἀνάγκη). And a little later (8, 198ᵇ 34–6) he speaks of natural things like teeth as coming about in a particular way either always or 'as a general rule', distinguishing them from things which arise 'by chance or spontaneously' (ἀπὸ τύχης καὶ τοῦ αὐτομάτου).²⁵ Düring cites this passage as introducing the concept of 'das statistisch Normale',²⁶ and he makes an apposite reference to *De Caelo* 3.2, 301ᵃ 5–9, where Aristotle says that the nature (φύσις) of things is 'that which most of them possess for most of the time' (οἵαν ἔχει τὰ πλείω καὶ τὸν πλείω χρόνον). There are several other passages which also need to be cited in this connection. *De Gen. An.* 1.19.727ᵇ 29–30 asserts that 'it is what occurs as a general rule that is most in accord with the course of nature' (μάλιστα κατὰ φύσιν); and 4.7, 777ᵃ 18–21, ends with an identification of what is according to nature with 'the as a general rule' (τὸ κατὰ φύσιν ἐστι τὸ ὡς ἐπὶ τὸ πολύ). According to *De Part. An.* 3.2, 663ᵇ 27–9, 'in studying nature we must consider the majority of cases, for it is what occurs in every case (ἐν τῷ παντί) or as a general rule that is in accord with nature' (κατὰ φύσιν). In *Rhet.* 1.10, 1369ᵃ 35–ᵇ 2, things that happen by nature (φύσει) are said to occur either always or as a general rule.²⁷ In the *Prior Analytics* 1.3, 25ᵇ 14–15, Aristotle again identifies 'the as a general rule' and the natural (together defining 'the possible') by using the words ὅσα δὲ τῷ ὡς ἐπὶ τὸ πολὺ καὶ τῷ πεφυκέναι λέγεται ἐνδέχεσθαι, καθ' ὃν τρόπον διορίζομεν τὸ ἐνδεχόμενον. In a rather difficult passage in *De Gen. An.* 4.4, 770ᵇ 9–13, he speaks of monstrosities as occurring contrary to nature 'as she is as a general rule', distinguished from 'the nature which is always and by necessity'; such unnatural occurrences, he says, are to be found only within the category of 'the as a general rule', of things which might have been otherwise.

In an important passage near the beginning of the *Nicomachean Ethics* Aristotle shows his acumen as a scientist by pointing out that in discussing some topics we are obliged to begin with τὰ ὡς ἐπὶ τὸ πολύ and must then come to conclusions of the same order: an educated man is one who strives for that degree of precision in each branch of knowledge which the nature of the subject admits.²⁸

In several contexts in the *Analytics* Aristotle employs the concept of 'the as a general rule'.²⁹ The most interesting, perhaps, is *Anal. Post.* 2.12, 96ᵃ 8–19 (especially 8–11, 15), where

Aristotle opposes what is 'as a general rule' to the universal (τὸ καθόλου), defined as what happens 'always and in every case'.[30] There are some other passages making use of the notion of 'the as a general rule' which do not need to be mentioned separately.[31]

It is time to explain the relevance of Aristotle's concept of 'the as a general rule' for the passage in *Poetics* with which we began. I am going to argue first that Aristotle, in writing that passage, must surely have had in mind precisely the historian whom many people might wish to exempt from his strictures about history dealing only with particulars: namely, Thucydides. I shall also argue that Thucydides dealt very much with 'the as a general rule' and with behaviour that was characteristic of human nature, Aristotle, on his own principles, ought not to have given 'what Alcibiades did or had done to him' as an illustration of the essential character of history.

When Aristotle chose that illustration, he must at least have had Thucydides in mind among others, and indeed was probably thinking mainly of Thucydides, who was the prime source of information about the earlier years in which Alcibiades played an important part on the political stage. Many scholars have found it puzzling that whereas Aristotle makes numerous references to Herodotus[32] (whom he calls ὁ μυθολόγος, the story-teller[33]), and also makes use of his work without naming him, he never once mentions Thucydides — or, for that matter, other historians who were much read in his day, such as Xenophon, Ephorus, Theopompus, and Aristotle's relative Callisthenes, or even the early Atthidographers whose works he undoubtedly used: Hellanicus, Cleidemus and Androtion. I believe nevertheless that Aristotle had certainly read Thucydides.[34] Alcibiades of course plays a very important rôle in Books 5, 6, and 8 of Thucydides, who describes his activities over a period of some ten years, from 421 to 411; and anyone referring to 'what Alcibiades did or had done to him' is far more likely to have had that period primarily in his mind than the remaining seven years of Alcibiades' life (nearly half of them spent in exile), the main authorities for which, in Aristotle's day, will have been Xenophon's *Hellenica* and the Oxyrhynchus historian whose continuation of Thucydides is nowadays seen to have been a main source for Ephorus.[35] There is not a very great deal about Alcibiades in Xenophon's *Hellenica*, and it seems unlikely that the Oxyrhynchus historian can have had much more to say.

We are left, then, with the probability that in his selection of a characteristic example of history Aristotle chose to speak of events the main source for which in his day (as in ours) can only have been Thucydides, the one historian who, in the opinion of most of us, is least open to the charge of merely relating particular events and failing to deal with universals, with 'what might happen'. I have discussed Thucydides at length elsewhere[36] and have argued that one of the dominant ideas in his work is the consistency of human behaviour, and the belief that by studying precisely how human nature has worked in a great number of actual cases one can form a good general idea of it and then proceed to deduce what is likely to happen in a particular situation with which one is confronted. Thucydides understood, as much as anyone, that the course of events is always liable to be disturbed by sheer chance (τύχη),[37] by the unpredictable and incalculable (ὁ παράλογος, τὸ ἀστάθμητον);[38] but he nevertheless realised that the study of past events can give understanding of how men are *likely to behave*, and can therefore provide a useful guide to action in the present. The constancy of human nature ensures that *patterns of behaviour will tend to recur*. This is the origin and the justification of Thucydides' claim (1.22.4) that his own History will be 'useful' and 'a possession for ever'. One of the most remarkable features of Thucydides' work is that its 'lessons' (if such a term is permissible) are implicit in the narrative and do not need to be spelt out in the History in general terms. As one of the greatest of English philosophers said of him, 'Digressions for instruction's cause, and other such open conveyances of precepts, (which is the philosopher's part), he never useth; as having so clearly set before men's eyes the ways and events of good and evil counsels, that the narrative itself doth secretly instruct the reader, and more effectually than can possibly be done by precept'.[39]

My conclusion about the interpretation of our *Poetics* passage is as follows. We have seen that the rigid dichotomy which Aristotle sometimes establishes, as in *Poetics* 9, 1451[b]6–9, between the universal and the particular (as elsewhere between the necessary and the contingent or accidental) is often replaced by a three-term distinction, with 'the as a general rule' appearing in the middle; and when this occurs, 'the as a general rule' is closer to the universal and the necessary than to the particular or contingent, in that it too is conceived as an appropriate subject of ἐπιστήμη. Now in *Poetics* 9, 1451[b]8–9, Aristotle surprisingly defines the universal in terms of *probability* as well as necessity; and this surely entitles us to complain that on his own principles the distinction he ought to have drawn here was his threefold one, between, on the one hand, the universal *or 'the as a general rule'* (which may indeed be concerned with probabilities), and on the other hand, the particular. If this is so, then, especially if we may take Aristotle to be thinking in the first place of Thucydides, he ought not to have written off history as dealing only with particulars, even if it does partly concern itself with 'what Alcibiades did or had done to him'. The poet, according to Aristotle, speaks of 'what is possible according to probability or necessity'. But what the poet actually *says* is concerned with a particular action: if we are to derive ἐπιστήμη from it, in Aristotle's sense, we have to take the further step of recognising the general (the universal or the necessary) in the particular. Is there any essential difference in what we make of the History of Thucydides? I believe not, once we are allowed to introduce the concept of τὸ ὡς ἐπὶ τὸ πολύ and take account of the fact that that is precisely what Thucydides often offers us. Even on Aristotle's own premises, therefore, it is possible to think that his disparagement of history in the *Poetics* is not fully justified.

I prefer the explanation I have given of the *Poetics* passage to that of Pippidi, who in an interesting article published in 1948 argued that Aristotle, when he wrote the passage we are considering, was not thinking of Thucydides *as a historian*.[40] Pippidi would thus exempt the work of Thucydides from Aristotle's strictures, but only by (so to speak) transferring Thucydides from the Faculty of History, where he surely belongs, to that of Political Philosophy.

I would emphasise, in conclusion, that in *Poetics* 9 history is not absolutely disparaged: it is merely said to be less philosophic and worthwhile than poetry. To reinforce this observation it is well to recall the fact that Aristotle himself wrote a very considerable amount of what we should call historical work, even if he doubtless produced some of it with the help of pupils. First, if we may take the *Athenaion Politeia* as a characteristic example of the 158 *Politeiai* (constitutions of individual states) with which Aristotle is credited,[41] then each of these works will have begun with an account of how the constitution in question reached the form it had in Aristotle's day. He would have been entitled to say of these works that here he was not writing a mere narrative of random events, about 'what so-and-so did or had done to him', but was describing the life processes of creatures, a series of human societies:[42] this, he might have said, was what he had in mind when he referred to ordinary histories as 'our usual histories' in *Poetics* 23.[43] Aristotle was also responsible for the *List of Victors at the Pythian Games*, the compilation of which by Aristotle himself and his relative Callisthenes is proved beyond doubt by a Delphic inscription;[44] the *List of Olympic Victors*,[45] the genuineness of which, accepted in antiquity, is made highly probable by the certainty that Aristotle compiled a similar Pythian list; the *Didaskaliai* and *Nikai Dionysiakai*, which were also victor-lists;[46] the *Nomima* or *Nomima Barbarika*;[47] the *Dikaiomata* or *Dikaiomata Poleon*;[48] and perhaps the *Hypomnemata*, which may well have been (like the *Nomoi*, in no less than 24 Books) a joint work of Aristotle and Theophrastus, although ultimately published in the name of the latter.[49] The existence of such works is a sufficient refutation of the view that is to be found in some modern works, that Aristotle was merely a philosopher and so must not be treated seriously as a historian.[50] He evidently saw research into historical facts as a necessary condition, though not of course a sufficient condition, of full scientific knowledge of human society.[51]

I am very glad to have this opportunity of paying tribute to 'Tom Brown' Stevens, whose teaching of the 'Greats' pupils in Magdalen and New College whom we shared for nearly twenty years, from 1953 to 1972, was both devoted and inspiring.

### Notes

[1] I wish to acknowledge some useful criticisms of the draft of this essay, by G. E. L. Owen and by two other philosophers who were once my pupils in Ancient History: Edward Hussey and Terence Irwin. If I have not made the best use of their comments, the fault is entirely mine.

[2] Others might perhaps translate 'could happen' or 'would happen'.

[3] I accept the MS text συνήθεις and rather prefer the MS εἶναι to Bywater's emendation, θεῖναι. I need only refer to Raymond Weil, *Aristotle et l'histoire: Essai sur la 'Politique'*, Paris 1960, pp. 163–76, especially 170–3. As for other readings and their translations, it should be sufficient to refer to two standard

works: Ingram Bywater, *Aristotle on the Art of Poetry*, Oxford 1909, pp. 70—3, 305—6; and G. F. Else, *Aristotle's Poetics: The Argument*, Cambridge, Mass., 1957, pp. 569—79.

[4] G. E. R. Lloyd, *Aristotle: The Growth and Structure of his Thought*, Cambridge 1968, p. 276.

[5] Pierre Louis, 'Le mot 'ΙΣΤΟΡΙΑ chez Aristote' *Rev. de Phil.*, ser. 2, vol. 29, 1955, pp. 39—44, especially 44 and n. 1.

[6] See e.g. Thuc. 2.13.3; 6.46.4; Plato, *Polit.* 294e; Isocr. 12. 165; 15.271; and many other examples, including of course some in Aristotle himself, e.g. *Hist. An.* 7.3, 583$^b$ 3,8; *Eth. Nic.* 3.1, 1110$^a$ 31—2; 8.13. 1161$^a$ 27; *Rhet.* 1.12, 1369$^a$ 34; *Pol.* 4.4, 1291$^b$ 9—10.

[7] See e.g. J.M. Le Blond, *Logique et méthode chez Aristote*, ed. 2, Paris 1970, p. 79 ('la curieuse notion du ὡς ἐπὶ τὸ πολύ, qui joue un rôle assez notable dans les recherches d'Aristote'); Ingemar Düring, *Aristoteles. Darstellung und Interpretation seines Denkens*, Heidelberg 1966, as cited in n. 26 below. In some other well-known books on Aristotle I have found nothing relevant. The only treatment of the subject at length that I have been able to discover is the able article by J. Barnes, 'Aristotle's Theory of Demonstration' *Phronesis* vol. 14, 1969, pp. 123—51 (especially 133—7), which came to my notice only when this essay was completed and overdue.

[8] See e.g. *De Interpret.* 7, 17$^a$ 38—$^b$ 1, and other passages cited by H. Bonitz, *Index Aristotelicus*, Berlin 1870 and Graz 1955, p. 356$^b$ 32—8.

[9] Only in *Metaph.* M 10, 1087$^a$ 10—25 (a very difficult passage) does Aristotle expressly qualify this, to apply to knowledge δυνάμει rather than ἐνεργείᾳ.

[10] E.g. *Anal. Post.* 1.31, 87$^b$ 37—9; 33, 88$^b$ 30—1; *Eth. Nic.* 6.6, 1140$^b$ 31—2 (cf. 10.9, 1180$^b$ 15—16: τοῦ κοινοῦ); *De Anima* 2.5, 417$^b$ 22—3; *Metaph.* B 6, 1003$^a$ 14—15; K 1, 1059$^b$ 26; 2, 1060$^b$ 20—1 (τῶν καθόλου καὶ τοῦ τοιουδί); M 9, 1086$^b$ 5—6; 10, 1086$^b$ 33.

[11] E.g. *Eth. Nic.* 6.3, 1139$^b$ 22—3; 6, 1140$^b$ 31—2. Cf. *Anal. Post.* 1.33, 88$^b$ 31.

[12] E.g. *Anal. Post.* 1.2, 71$^b$ 15—16; 4, 73$^a$ 21; 6, 74$^b$ 6; 33, 88$^b$ 30—2 ('the necessary cannot be otherwise').

[13] *Anal. Post.* 1.4, 73$^b$ 26—9. On the exceptionally strict sense of καθόλου here, see W. D. Ross, *Aristotle's Prior and Posterior Analytics,* Oxford 1949, pp. 522—3.

[14] *Anal. Post.* 1.31, 87$^b$ 32—3; cf. 2.12, 96$^a$ 8—9 (ἀεί . . . καὶ ἐπὶ παντός), 15 (καὶ ἐπὶ παντὶ καὶ ἀεί).

[15] As in *Metaph.* Δ 9, 1017$^b$35−18$^a$2. Aristotle's fullest definition of τὸ συμβεβηκός is in *Top.* 1.5, 102$^b$4−26.

[16] *Metaph.* Δ 30, 1025$^a$14−21 (especially 14−15, 20−1). Most people seem prepared to accept this book as Aristotelian, even if it could originally have been a separate work.

[17] *Metaph.* E 2, 1026$^b$24−37 (especially 31−3, 35−7), 1027$^a$8−26 (especially 8−11, 15−17, 19−24, 25−6). Whether this book is actually by Aristotle is disputed. Many scholars have accepted it; and those who have seen in it the hand of a redactor have usually accepted the material as Aristotelian, even if it has been rearranged by someone else — e.g. Andronicus, in the opinion of Düring, op, cit. (n. 7), pp. 587−9, 592−3.

[18] *Metaph.* K 8, 1064$^b$30−65$^a$6 (especially 1064$^b$32−6, 1065$^a$1−3, 3−6).

[19] *Top.* 2.6, 112$^b$1−18 (especially 1−2, 14−15).

[20] Cf. ὅπως ἔτυχεν in *Metaph.* K 8, 1064$^b$36; ἀπὸ τύχης in *Anal. Post.* 1.30, 87$^b$19−27; *Phys.* 2.7, 198$^b$36−9$^a$2.

[21] *Top.* 5.1, 129$^a$6−13.

[22] *Anal. Post.* 1.14, 79$^a$17−28.

[23] *Anal. Post.* 1.30, 87$^b$19−27.

[24] *Phys.* 2.5, 196$^b$10−21 (especially 10−13); 7, 198$^b$5−6; 8, 198$^b$34−6.

[25] Cf. *De Caelo* 1.12, 283$^a$31$^b$−2; *De Gen. et Corr.* 2.6, 333$^b$4−7.

[26] Düring, op. cit. (n. 7), p. 239, n. 372. Cf. pp. 331 and n. 262, 491 and n. 381 ('die statistische Wahrheit die gute Wahrheit ist').

[27] Cf. *De Gen. et Corr.* 2.6, 333$^b$4−7.

[28] *Eth. Nic.* 1.1 (3), 1094$^b$19−27.

[29] *Anal. Prior.* 1.3, 25$^b$14−15; 13, 32$^b$4−10 (where it is the opposite of τὸ ἀναγκαῖον and ἐξ ἀνάγκης); 27, 43$^b$32−6; *Anal. Post.* 1.14, 79$^a$17−22; 30, 87$^b$19−27 (especially 20−1, 25−7: here τὸ ὡς ἐπὶ τὸ πολύ is distinguished both from what is ἀναγκαῖον and from τὸ ἀπὸ τύχης).

[30] Aristotle is very emphatic: he has ἀεί . . . καὶ ἐπὶ παντός twice (lines 8−9, 14) and in line 15 τοῦτο γάρ ἐστι τὸ καθόλον, τὸ ἐπὶ παντὶ καὶ ἀεί.

[31] E.g. *De Interpret.* 9, 19$^a$18−22; *Rhet.* 1.2, 1356$^b$15−17, 1357$^a$22−32; 2.19, 1392$^b$31−2; *Hist. An.* 6.17, 571$^a$26−7.

[32] Not only in the *Ath. Pol.* (14.4), but also in the *Poet.*, *Rhet.*, *Eth. Eud.*, *Hist. An.*, and *De Gen. An.*: see Weil, op. cit. (n. 3), p. 313, n. 20, repeating the list in Bonitz, op. cit. (n. 8),

p. 320. Add *Hist. An.* 8.18, 601$^b$1, where most MSS have 'Hesiod'.

[33] Arist., *Gen. An.* 3.5, 756$^b$6—7. Perhaps he was thinking of such statements as the one in Her. 3.101.2, that the semen of Ethiopians is black, which he contradicts in *Gen. An.* 2.2, 736$^a$10—13.

[34] I base this belief not so much on possible parallels such as those listed by Weil, op. cit. (n. 3), p. 312, n. 4 (e.g. between *Ath. Pol.* 18.4 and Thuc. 6.58.2), as on the close verbal correspondence of certain passages dealing with the events of 411 (which of course Aristotle had more reason to study when writing the *Ath. Pol.* than anything else in Thucydides), in particular (a) the references to Euboea in *Ath. Pol.* 33.1 (lines 28—9 OCT) and Thuc. 8. 96.2; 95.7; (b) *Ath. Pol.* 32.2 and Thuc. 8.68 (where the names occur in the same order and the description corresponds); (c) the characterisation of the government of the Five Thousand in *Ath. Pol.* 33.2 and Thuc. 8.97.2; and (d) the 100 years in *Ath. Pol.* 32.2 (line 12 OCT) and Thuc. 8.68.4 (lines 27 ff. OCT); and most of all on the appearance in Arist., *Pol.* 5.4, 1304$^b$10—15, of the Thucydidean picture of the revolution of the Four Hundred, so very different from Aristotle's account in *Ath. Pol.* 29—33. (I shall argue elsewhere that the latter account reflects a change of opinion, influenced very probably by the *Apology* of Antiphon and the *Atthis* of Androtion.)

[35] The best account of Alcibiades is by J. Hatzfeld, *Alcibiade*, ed. 2, Paris 1951.

[36] In *The Origins of the Peloponnesian War*, London 1972, pp. 5—33. When I wrote that book I had not read A. Parry, 'The Language of Thucydides' Description of the Plague' *Bull. of the [London Univ.] Inst. of Class. Stud.* vol. 16, 1969, pp. 106—18, who makes some useful points against the exaggerated claims of Cochrane, Weidauer, and others concerning Thucydides' intellectual debt to the Hippocratic writers and his employment of the medical vocabulary of the age, but is himself guilty of indefensible exaggeration of the views he attacks — as when, in his last sentence, he actually accuses his opponents of trying to persuade us that Thucydides saw the great Plague of Athens as 'a thing subject to rational human control'! It is on the basis of exaggerations of this sort that Parry feels able to go to the opposite pole and pretend that Thucydides did not intend his work to have any practical usefulness — a point of which I think I have sufficiently refuted in my op. cit., pp. 29—33.

37 See my op. cit., p. 31, n. 57.
38 See my op. cit., pp. 30–1, with 25 and n. 52.
39 Thomas Hobbes, as cited in my op. cit., p. 28.
40 D. M. Pippidi, 'Aristote et Thucydide: En marge du chapitre IX de la *Poétique*' in *Mélanges ... offerts à J. Marouzeau*, Paris 1948, pp. 483–90. Pippidi would suppose that Aristotle saw in Thucydides' History '*non pas la chronique d'une guerre*, quelle que fût son importance, *mais un essai de philosophie politique*, fondé sur la conviction (qui était également sienne) que les mêmes causes engendrent toujours les mêmes effets' (pp. 489–90). [Pippidi's italics.]
41 The fullest discussion is that of Weil, op. cit. (n. 3), especially pp. 97–116.
42 Note the interesting analogy Aristotle draws between different species of animals and different forms of constitutions, in *Pol.* 4.4, 1290$^b$ 25–38.
43 See the beginning of the second paragraph of this essay. Contrast the attitude of Wilamowitz, who said that after the publication of the London papyrus of the *Ath. Pol.* Aristotle 'fortan nicht mehr als Historiker gelten darf', and that he 'kein geschichtlicher Forscher ist. (*Aristoteles und Athen*, Berlin 1893, vol. 1, p. 373); 'in diesem Buche [the *Ath. Pol.*] wirklich geschichtliche Forschung so gut wie gar nicht steckt' (p. 308). These judgements have recently been quoted with approval by J. Day and M. Chambers, *Aristotle's History of Athenian Democracy* (*Univ. of California Publications in Hist.*, vol. 73, Berkeley and Los Angeles 1962), who seem to view Aristotle primarily as a philosopher who would not hesitate to make historical distortions and even inventions dictated by his a priori philosophical theories – a point of view with which I deeply disagree. I cannot resist quoting here the unintentionally comic remark by J. Zürcher, *Aristoteles' Werk und Geist*, Paderborn 1952, p. 258, that Aristotle must have conceived the idea of collecting constitutions at an early stage in his development: 'es passt ja sogar besser in die vorphilosophische Periode eines Mensch'!
44 Tod *GHI* 2.187 = *SIG*$^3$ 275. For the date, see D. M. Lewis, *CR*, N.S, vol. 8, 1958, p. 108. See also Weil, op. cit. (n. 3), pp. 133–7.
45 See Weil, op. cit., pp. 131–3.
46 See Weil, op. cit., pp. 137–9.
47 See Weil, op. cit., pp. 116–21.
48 See Weil, op. cit., pp. 127–30.

[49] See Weil, op. cit., p. 130; and H. Bloch, 'Studies in Historical Literature of the Fourth Century B.C.' in *Athenian Studies Presented to W. S. Ferguson* (*HSC*, Suppl. I. 1940), at pp. 355–76.

[50] Cf. n. 43 above.

[51] Cf. the famous passage in *De Part. An.* 1.5, 644$^{\mathrm{b}}$22–5$^{\mathrm{a}}$36.

G. E. M. de Ste. Croix,
New College,
Oxford.

# 5

# Hellenistic Cities of Judaea and its Vicinity – some New Aspects

It is not the aim of this paper to give a comprehensive account of the Hellenistic towns of Eretz Yisrael in the period between Alexander the Great and the end of the Roman Empire. Our knowledge is still very limited, and real progress can only be made by excavation, of which not a great deal is being done. The intention here is to raise problems, and the method will be discursive.[1]

I shall begin by sketching the topographical siting of some of the Hellenistic towns, because perhaps not enough attention has been paid to this aspect. Here again, the material is far from complete. The Hellenistic cities fall into three main groups; the coastal towns, those in the central mountain massif, and those in Transjordan, including the important cluster north-east and south of Lake Kinneret in Bashan, Hauran and Gilead. Of the latter, we may begin with Raphana, which is Er-Rife (five kilometres south of Sheikh Misqin) an isolated mound about ten kilometres west of the lava field of the Lejja, the ancient Trachonitis; it obviously originated as a military post to watch the area, which was a classic hideout of habitual raiders and plunderers.[2]

*Canatha*,[3] between the Jebel Hauran and el-Lejje, is set between Wadi Kanwat on the north-east and another deep wadi on its south. The city appears to have extended farther east and west at some period, but the known enceinte probably marks the original fortified area, apparently enclosing some 120 hectares. A copious spring exists to the south-west of the town.

Next, *Hippos*,[4] the Semitic Susita, on the east shore of Kinneret. This stands on an elongated elliptical hill, 345 metres above the lake, and is defended by steep slopes on all sides but the south-eastern, where a narrow saddle descending to the gorge (W.e-Jammusiyeh) alone gave access. The area of the Byzantine town is about 25 hectares. *Abila,* surrounded on three sides by valleys, with a wide command south of the River Yarmuq,[5] also occupies an isolated tell. *Capitolias,* Bet Ras, overlooking a tributary of the Yarmuq, stands on a high spur projecting westward from the mountains, being thus inaccessible from the west, south, and north. Officially it became a city only in Trajan's reign, but it may well have been important before that.[6]

Tell el-Ash'ari, probably the ancient *Dium,*[7] is a tell poised 24–30 m. on a promontory above the plain of the Yarmuq; its west side falls abruptly into the river-gorge, and its south side is defined by a deep chasm. Oliphant described it as 'an impregnable position'.

*Gadara* (Um el-Qeiss),[8] on the south edge of the Yarmuq, stands on a west-jutting spur of the plateau 835 metres above sea-level; its north scarp overlooks the river. It also commands a southern slope.

*Pella,*[9] facing Beth Shean–Scythopolis, is built on a terrace of the western plateau scarp, on a tell some 60 hectares in area. This is linked to the plain by a saddle on the east, but all the other sides fall steeply, and the south side is protected by the Wadi Jurm el-Moz.

For *Gerasa,*[10] on the ancient north-south highway along the fringe of the Arabian desert connecting the Gulf of Eilat and the Arabian peninsula with Damascus, a low south-eastern hill-spur between the River Chrysoroas and one of its western tributaries was chosen; the original Hellenistic site was on a projecting eminence in the centre of the spur.

West of Jordan, the nearest urban centre was *Beth Shean–Scythopolis.*[11] The Hellenistic town was sited originally, it would seem, on the very photogenic Tell el-Hosn, which is a steep-sloped eminently defensive and splendidly commanding position in a well-watered plain, with long-range observation on all sides.

In the south of the country we may note Idumaean *Marissa,* represented by Tell es-Sandehanna, not far south of Beth Govrin.[12] Here the area and fortifications of the early Hellenistic site speak more eloquently than the topographical situation: its total area is about 2–2·4 hectares, its walls are 3–4 metres thick. The town's internal buildings remind us of a pocket battleship; the dwellings are crowded together, the streets minimal and narrow, the agora about 30 x 24 m. in area. The original fourth-century fortified area of *Samaria*,[13] with its immensely strong round towers, was not much larger than Marissa — perhaps 2·8 hectares.

As to the coastal towns, their original early plans are practically unknown. Straton's Tower, however, seems to have been only a fraction of the size of Herod's Caesarea Maritima[14] and Ptolemais–'Akko expanded far beyond the original Phoenician settlement which, in a manner typical of Phoenician coastal sites, occupied a peninsula which was turned by the Greek settlers into their acropolis.[15] At Ashdod and Ascalon,[16] the original pre-Hellenistic city-mounds appear to have done duty as the Greek *acropoleis*. At Apollonia (Arsuf) Hellenistic finds are known only over a very restricted area within the Roman-Byzantine settlement.[17]

What is the conclusion to be drawn from the siting of the Transjordan cities and those west of Jordan, but not on the coast? They were, except for Canatha, comparatively small, and those we have scrutinised were essentially defensive positions. Defence was the primary consideration in their selection, whether or not they occupied the sites of older settlements. Water supply was only secondary,[18] nor can proximity to trade-routes always be observed. Plans are economical, and in Marissa and Hippos there are possible traces of a regular Hippodamian street-plan. When we look at Marissa and Samaria, we realise that we are in the presence of a military minority aware that the country is against them.

We have next to no material to tell us what the natives of the country thought of the Greek cities before the period of the Maccabees, from which we learn that the non-Hellenisers among the Jews were less hostile to cities as such (after all, Jerusalem was a city) than to the religious and social implications of Hellenisation. But one interesting passage in the *Letter of Aristeas*[19] suggests that a distinctive attitude did exist among some Jews towards the city as a phenomenon.

In paragraphs 83—116 of the *Letter*, the writer, an Egyptian Jew, describes both Jewish agriculture in Judaea and the city of Jerusalem. Both were idealising accounts written with religious motives; it is doubtful if the author had ever been in the country. He was probably influenced by the well-known Hellenistic school of authors who wrote the 'archaeologies' of various Greek cities.[20] But he was also influenced by the current mentality which sought utopian forms of government and favoured city-planning, such as had begun in the fifth century but found full scope only with Alexander's conquests.[21] He has some strong criticisms to make of the idleness and luxury bred by city life (108–9), citing Alexandria and referring to the Ptolemaic regulation restricting the period which rural elements were allowed to spend in that city, in order that agriculture should not be neglected. And he sums up by saying that the Jews in their homeland were careful to maintain a balance between town and country (113). This reminds us of Hecataeus' attribution to Moses of a policy of compelling the Jews to educate their children in the countryside in order to maintain the population.[22] An echo of the same attitude is perhaps to be traced in the tradition quoted by Josephus in the *Antiquities*, which makes Cain the first builder of cities, which he fortified and in which he forced his kinsmen to settle.[23]

For historians of the nineteenth and most of the twentieth century so far, the Hasmonean attitude to the Greek cities was no problem.[24] The Hasmoneans were destroyers of Greek urban civilisation, and that was that. But today it is evident that the picture is not so simple. For one thing, as able soldiers, the Hasmoneans must early have realised the tactical, strategic, and logistic value of fortified towns. They were quick to occupy Gezer and Jaffa. But the historical situation shows why they saw the Greek towns as targets of attack. Tcherikover wrote that if the struggle with Antiochus Epiphanes was political, the struggle with the Greek towns was economic.[25] Eleazar Galili pointed out[26] that the wars of the Hasmoneans fall into two phases: the struggle with the Seleucid dynasty based on Syria, and that with the Greek cities after they had fallen back on their own resources; this second phase had its economic and mercantile aspect, but was fundamentally a life and death struggle for the country as such. It is generally assumed that the Hasmoneans destroyed cities whose gentile inhabitants they expelled if they refused to Judaise. In effect destruction seems to have overtaken Arethusa, Philoteria, Gadara, Pella, and Gaza. Josephus[27] adds Hippos, Scythopolis, Samaria, Iamnia, and Azotus. On some centres we have no information, but the destruction of Pella has been confirmed by archaeology at least in the excavated areas, where occupation was lacking from the second century B.C. to the time of Pompey. Yet even here the Hellenistic stratum yielded a coin of John Hyrcanus.[28] The complete abandonment of Shechem, on the other hand, was demonstrated by a thick stratum of soil deliberately tipped over the site by the same ruler.[29] The picture is different at some other sites. Gerasa yielded sufficient Hasmonean coins to suggest that occupation continued after Yannai's capture of the place.[30] At Ashdod the burnt stratum reflecting the destruction by John Hyrcanus was found, but a second overlying stratum beginning in the late second century shows that the town was rehabilitated and reoccupied.[31] At Samaria too, the number of coins of the later Hasmoneans (47) gave evidence that life there did not end between the Jewish capture of 107 and the rebuilding by Gabinius.[32] The 1924 excavations at Dor of the temenos in the north-west of the tell recovered from the fill between the temple podium and the temenos wall pottery which ran continuously from the third to the first century B.C.; this makes it improbable that the Jewish occupation caused a cessation in the life of the town.[33] On the site of Straton's Tower in the northern part of the later Herodian Caesarea,[34] while pottery ceased in the first century before the current era, the first Jewish synagogue was built on the early Hellenistic occupation, and pre-Herodian pottery was associated with material that included 'West Slope' wares, so that Jewish occupation may have continued on the site. At Marissa, as at Beth Zur and Gezer, Jewish coins ceased in about 100 B.C. but occupation continued,[35] suggesting that while the Jewish garrison had been removed, friendly elements — at Marissa and Beth Zur perhaps Idumaean proselytes — remained in occupation. Jaffa, of course, was firmly held by the Hasmoneans from the time it was occupied by Simon.[36] At Scythopolis— Beth Shean, on present information, Hellenistic material does not begin before the second century B.C.,[37] and the temple on Tell Hosn is now known to belong to the early Roman period.[38] The bulk of the tombs recently excavated to the north-east of the city do not contain material earlier than the first century B.C.[39] *Megillat Ta'anit*[40] records the evacuation of the place by its gentile population after its capture by Yannai, yet Strabo (16, p. 763) says that Scythopolis was surrounded by forts either by Yannai or by his sons.[41] Gamala in Gaulanitis, though not formally a city, was of some importance as a strong point, as events during the rebellion of 66–73 witness. It was, so far as we know, a non-Jewish settlement when captured by Yannai, but in 66 it was a Jewish centre.[42] Ascalon, as is well known, maintained its independent existence unimpaired by the Hasmoneans and in alliance with them.[43] Ptolemais—

'Akko and Philadelphia were never taken by them, and Philadelphia was (like Scythopolis) surrounded by Hasmonean forts. We thus have a new picture — one of Hasmonean urban colonisation.

How did the Hellenistic cities react to the Hasmonean attack from an internal point of view? One of the phenomena characterising their development in the later second and earlier first centuries B.C. is the emergence of tyrants, at Straton's Tower, at Dor, Philadelphia, Gerasa, and elsewhere. These are presumably not tyrants of the fifth-century classical model;[44] it may be supposed that they were the products of a military situation which produced the breakdown of a very superficial and artificial democracy imposed upon communities too inexperienced to maintain it under strain. The democracy of the Hellenistic cities was in any case externally limited by the monarchs,[45] and even in the coastal cities, where a Phoenician tradition had created comparatively stable mercantile oligarchies used to administration, they rested on a very narrow basis,[46] and these communities must have been extremely heterogeneous in origin. There may have been a conflict between these oligarchies and the strong men emerging to tackle the new military situation in which the cities had to fall back entirely on their own resources. But there might occasionally be a popular opposition to both; and if a Greek city like Ascalon could grasp that a compromise with the Hasmoneans was possible,[47] some popular leaders elsewhere might realise it too.

Something like this appears to have occurred at Ptolemais—'Akko at the beginning of the reign of Yannai (104/3 B.C.), according to Josephus' account in *Antiquities* 13.324 ff. The city, under threat from Yannai, had called upon Ptolemy Lathyros for help, thus bringing down upon itself Cleopatra III, Lathyros' aggressive and hostile mother. At this point there appeared at Ptolemais one Demainetos, a native of the city, described as a demagogue who commanded the confidence of the populace; he attempted to persuade them that it would be better to venture an accord with the Jews than to accept obvious slavery from Lathyros or Cleopatra. As a result, the city closed its gates to Lathyros. The rest of the story has a certain pungency; excavations at 'Akko in 1958 revealed something of the havoc wrought as the result of the capture of the town by Cleopatra; it involved the destruction of a small shrine to Zeus Soter and probably much beside; in the area of excavation nothing of significance superseded the destruction till the time of Caesar. When it came to the matter of behaviour towards Greek cities, the Ptolemies, it seems, were no better than Hyrcanus or Yannai. But there may have been a special factor here, namely the Jewish troops of Cleopatra, commanded by Ananias; probably to them should be ascribed the destruction of the shrine of Zeus Soter and perhaps other buildings in its vicinity. It were also well to recall that the said area appears to have been occupied, at least in part, by a military depot.[48] But as regards Demainetos, let us note his name, which is suggestive of a democratic family tradition,[49] and recall that there were Athenian merchants at Ptolemais even before Alexander the Great overran the country.[50]

We know very little of the details of the social structure of these urban communities; but it should be remembered that there were in Hellenistic Eretz Yisrael not a few communities which were secondary urban centres; they possessed no official city-status, but appear to have acquired some degree of Hellenistic organisation. Examples are Gezer, Camous, Gephrous, Pergamon, and Gamala. These cannot be discussed fully here, but attention should be drawn to two inscriptions connected with Qaddesh Naphtali in north-east Galilee, because they throw considerable light on the question of the social structure of these, and perhaps more important places.

The first document[51] is a Greek curse-tablet of the fifth century B.C., found at Selinus in Sicily, and belonging to a time when there were Carthaginians resident in the city. Some of the names are Greek, but several are Punic or Phoenician, and one is Κάδοσιν τὸν Ματυλαῖο. Now the Metu'alim are today a Shi'ite community who live north of the Jewish colony of Metullah, and Qaddesh Naphtali lies about 12 miles to the south-east. The inscription suggests that the name of the Shi'ite community is over two thousand years older than has been thought,[52] and the father of Kadosis must have been known by this name when he settled in Qaddesh; his son, when he emigrated for some reason to Sicily, bore the name of the town Qaddesh where he was born. Evidently then in the fifth century B.C. a process was taking place of the settlement of tribal elements in urban centres; in the first century of the Christian era, according to Josephus,[53] Quaddesh Naphtali was a strong town with a Tyrian population, in a state of continual war with the Jewish peasantry of Galilee. Another inscription from the place throws further light on the social structure of Qaddesh.[54] It is a dedication set up under Hadrian through the agency of three men with pronouncedly Semitic names, on behalf of the συγγένια of the God of Heaven, presumably Zeus Haddad. Συγγένια is a kinship group (Arabic ḥamullah).[55] We may recall that the erstwhile pastoral communities of Bashan and Hauran in the Roman period transferred their tribal structure unimpaired to the framework of village organisation when they passed to settled life, and so successfully built up, in the course of the third and fourth centuries, an organic village democracy evidenced by numerous inscriptions.[56] Their success was probably due to two factors: first, that no Greek cities existed in their areas to break up their natural social organisms; and second, that such cities as did grow up subsequently in this area were not endowed with wide city-territories which enabled them to dominate and exploit the villagers.[57] This picture is something of a negative commentary on the social rôle of the Hellenistic and doubtless the Graeco-Roman urbanisation of Syria and Eretz Yisrael.

There may, indeed, be signs of over-urbanisation in Judaea and the Decapolis in the later second and third centuries. The Harvard Expedition reported that many of the columns of the Forum of Samaria and its attached basilica had been overthrown before the Severan period.[58] The later British excavation found that the Herodian Stadium had been ruined by floods from the city-area above.[59] The theatre at Beth Shean, built under the Severi, had been reduced in scale in mid-building and was ruinous by the end of the third century. The third-century rabbi Rish Laquish (Tos. *'Erubin,* 4. 11: Jer. *'Erubin,* 5. 10) noted that the stadium of Tiberias was full of ruined houses in his time. The town-extension implied by Hadrian's triumphal arch at Gerasa appears never to have developed to the extent of being walled; the city's funds in the later second century were devoted chiefly to ambitious temple-building. My own observations at Susita (Antiochia ad Hippum) suggest that there was considerable public building there in the Severan period, but that many of the edifices concerned were in ruins by the early fifth century.

The last question which may be briefly discussed is that of the cultural level of the Hellenistic cities. Most of the evidence of cultural creativity that we possess in relation to the Greek cities of Eretz Yisrael and its vicinity belongs to the Roman period. Yet let us consider a statue found in the theatre of Scythopolis—Beth Shean in 1961.[60] The theatre is Severan; the head is earlier than the rest of the figure, which was plainly made for the head much later. Probably the original statue, which was part of a very high relief, fell victim to Jewish iconoclasm in the time of Yannai. The head is of the school of Lysippos, and there is a replica from Ialysos in Rhodes, now in the Metropolitan Museum, New York. Another parallel, not quite so close, comes from Cyrene, where Stucchi identified it as a portrait of Ptolemy III Euergetes. A miniature replica adorned with a diadem (so proving the royal identity of the portrait) exists in the Rockefeller Museum at Jerusalem. Unfortunately its provenance is unknown.[61] Being a copy, the Beth Shean head is difficult to date, but it does suggest that Scythopolis already existed as a Greek city in the second half of the third century B.C.

Other sculptures of interest come from Caesarea, and another from Gadara.[62] A Zeus and a Heracles from Caesarea are of the same school and spirit, although the latter is hardly earlier than the third century of the Christian era. What the two have in common is that they possess a pronouncedly local native quality, of some artistic value. How individual they are can be seen by comparing a Medusa from Caesarea, far more polished and by no means lacking in spirit, but much less original and showing affinities with a similar conventional school found at Ascalon[63] and Lepcis Magna (Tripolitania)[64] in the age of the Severi. Not far removed from it, chronologically, but much less conventional, is the satyr from Gadara,[65] the only example of art I have seen so far from that, the most cultured city of the Transjordanian Decapolis.[66]

The important thing about the Caesarea local school is that it presupposes a longish local development that might take us back into the Hellenistic period. Further discoveries might show, either that the local Hellenistic culture was not uprooted by the Hasmoneans, but maintained a successful continuity,[67] or, alternatively, from what quarter came the new populations of some of the Greek towns rebuilt by Pompey and Gabinius. We may yet have to revise our estimate of the cultural level of some of the Greek urban foundations in Eretz Yisrael before the Roman era.

## Notes

[1] On the Hellenistic cities of Judaea, Philistia, Transjordan, and Phoenicia, see V. Tcherikover, *Die hellenistische Städte-*

*gründungen von Alexander dem Grossen bis auf die Römerzeit,*
Philol. Supplem. vol. 19, Leipzig 1927, pp. 182 ff.; *E. Schürer,*
*Geschichte des jüdischen Volkes in Zeitalter Jesu Christi,* vol. 1,
Leipzig 1907, pp. 94 ff.; A. H. M. Jones, *The Greek City from*
*Alexander to Justinian,* Oxford 1940; *Cities of the Eastern*
*Roman Provinces,* ed. 2, Oxford 1971, Chap. 10; H. Bietenhard,
'The Decapolis from Pompey to Trajan' *ZDPV* vol. 79, 1963,
pp. 24 ff.; U. Rappaport, 'A Biography of works on Jewish
History in the Hellenistic and Roman Periods' *Studies in the*
*History of the Jewish People and of Israel* vol. 2, Haifa 1972,
pp. 247 ff. (Eng. and Heb.); especially pp. 266–267; A. Schalit,
*König Herodes, Der Mann und sein Werk,* Berlin 1969;
R. Martin, *L'Urbanisation dans la Grèce antique,* Paris 1951,
pp. 163 ff.; A. Alt, 'Hellenistic Cities and Domains in Galilee'
*Kleine Schriften,* vol. 2, Munich 1953, pp. 384 ff.

[2] For information on the topographical siting of a number of
the cities discussed here, I am indebted to Professor M. Braver.

[3] R. E. Brünnow, A. von Domaszewski, *Die Provincia Arabia,*
Strasbourg 1909, Plate x, p. 108.

[4] K. Schumacher, *The Jaulan,* London 1888, plan, p. 195;
*Abila of the Decapolis,* London 1889.

[5] *ZDPV* vol. 37, 1914, Taf. 4B (Tell Abil); cf. Bietenhard, art.
cit. (n. 1), p. 24.

[6] L. Oliphant, *The Land of Gilead,* Edinburgh 1880, p. 114;
Trajanic era: *CIL* 6.210; 10.532; 8.18084, line 89.

[7] G. Schumacher, *Across the Jordan,* London 1866, p. 203.

[8] G. Schumacher, *Abila of the Decapolis,* London 1889,
frontispiece.

[9] Schumacher, *Pella,* London 1888; *PEFQS,* 1934, p. 18;
*AASOR* vol. 6, 1924, pp. 13 ff.; vols 25–28, 1945–9,
pp. 254–57.

[10] C. Kraeling, *Gerasa, City of the Decapolis,* New Haven,
Conn., 1938.

[11] Map – N. Tzori, *IEJ* vol. 16, 1966, p. 123. For the
acropolis, *SEG* 20. 456, to Zeus Akraios Soter (Hadrianic).

[12] F. J. Bliss, R. A. S. Macalister, *Excavations in Palestine*
*during the Years 1898–1900,* London 1902.

[13] S. W. Crowfoot, K. Kenyon, E. L. Sukenik, *The Buildings*
*of Samaria,* London 1942, p. 24.

[14] *Encyclopedia of Excavations,* Giva'tayyim-Ramat Gan
1970, vol. 2, s.v. Caesarea, p. 50 (Heb.); *IEJ* vol. 6, 1956,
p. 260.

[15] Harpocration, *Lexicon* (Dindorf), s.v.

[16] Ashdod: *Enc. of Excavs.* (n. 14), vol. 1, s.v., p. 15; Ascalon; *PEFQS* 1922, pp. 112–119; air photograph, *Enc. of Excavs.*, vol. 1, p. 21.

[17] I am indebted to Mrs. Eva Danielus for information on the site of Apollonia and for guidance on the site itself.

[18] Characteristic was the situation of Philadelphia–Amman, taken by Antiochus III only after he had cut off the city's water supply, which came from outside (Pol. 5.71).

[19] There is a growing consensus of scholarly opinion that the letter was composed towards the end of the third century B.C. For bibliography from 1949–1972, Rappaport, op. cit. (n. 1), pp. 287 ff.

[20] Poetry was also written to celebrate given Greek cities in the third and second centuries B.C.; these works were paralleled by the Jew Philo, 'the epic poet', who wrote Greek verse in honour of Jerusalem, probably in the second century B.C. – see Y. Gutman, *Scripta Hierosolymitana*, vol. 1, The Hebrew University, Jerusalem 1954, pp. 36 ff.

[21] Cf. Martin, op. cit. (n. 1), pp. 163ff.; A. von Gerkan, *Griechische Städteanlagen*, Berlin and Leipzig 1924, pp. 62 ff.

[22] Diod. 40.3.7.

[23] *AJ* 1.62.

[24] E.g. E. Meyer, Ursprung und Anfang des Christentums, vol. 2, Stuttgart 1921, p. 280; E. Bevan, *Jerusalem of the High Priests*, London 1904, pp. 98–128.

[25] *Hellenistic Civilisation and the Jews*, Philadelphia and Jerusalem 1959, p. 235.

[26] 'Against whom did the Maccabees fight?' *Molad*, no. 218, 1968, pp. 168 ff. (Heb.).

[27] Jos., *BJ* 1.156.

[28] *Archaeology* vol. 21, 1968, pp. 134 ff.

[29] *Biblical Archaeologist* vol. 26, 1963, p. 25. We also learn (ibid.) that the destruction by Hyrcanus was followed by a brief but extensive re-occupation, tentatively dated 128–100 B.C.

[30] A. Bellinger ap. C. Kraeling, *Gerasa*, p. 500.

[31] M. Dothan, D. N. Freedman, *'Atiqot* (Eng. series) vol. 7, 1967, p. 27.

[32] J. W. Crowfoot et al., *Buildings at Samaria*, p. 31.

[33] Dor – *Bull. Brit. School Arch., Jerus.*, vol. 4, 1924, pp. 35 ff.; vol. 6, 1924, pp. 65 ff.; vol. 7, 1925, pp. 80 ff.

[34] The Caesarea synagogue – *IEJ* vol. 6, 1956, p. 260; vol. 13, 1963, p. 146; *Rabbinowitz Bulletin of Ancient Synagogue Research* vol. 1, 1949, p. 17; vol. 2, 1951, p. 28 ff.

[35] Avi-Yonah in *Encyc. of Excavs.* vol. 2, pp. 400–401, s.v. Marissa.

[36] I *Macc.* 10.75.

[37] Mr N. Tzori has material of the second century B.C. from the northern part of the town.

[38] Information by the kindness of Dr E. Oren, who has re-examined the dating material found by Messrs. Rowe and Fitzgerald.

[40] *Megillat Ta'anit*, for the 15th and 16th of Sivan – ed. Z. Liechtenstein, p. 63, line 10.

[41] Strabo's precise terms are λῃστήρια καὶ γαζοφυλάκια – hardly to be taken literally. Mr Rami 'Arav, of Qibbutz Reshafim, has located a fortress with casemate walls on Mount Gilboa south-west of Beth Shean; the pottery finds, which he was kind enough to show me, are Hellenistic. The fort's plan is characteristically Jewish, and the structure can, I think, be identified with one of the Hasmonean forts round Beth Shean referred to by Strabo.

[42] Yannai's capture, Jos., *AJ* 13.394; Jewish population – *Vita* 47. According to Josephus (*BJ* 1.166), it was rebuilt by Gabinius, but other MSS have Γάβαλα, and the Latin version has Gadara. As Gamala would be the only settlement without city-status to be mentioned in this list, and it was overwhelmingly Jewish in 66, it is clear that 'Gamala' is not the correct reading here. The identification of the town with Tell Aḥdab near Jameleh in southeast Golan cannot be reconciled with Josephus' topographical description (*BJ* 4.1 – opposite Tarichaeae); it has recently been re-identified with es-Salem south-east of Bir Qaruah, Israel Grid 256.4/219.5, which possesses the appropriate situation, remains, and natural features. See S. Guttman, in *The Roman Period in Eretz Yisrael*, Dept. of Local Knowledge of the Qibbutz Movement, Tel Aviv 1973, pp. 199 ff. (Heb.).

[43] I *Macc.* 10.86; 11.60. For the political constellation which secured Ascalon's continued independence, see M. Stern, 'The Political Background of the Wars of Alexander Yannai' *Tarbiz* vol. 33, 1963, pp. 183 ff.; B. Kanael, 'Remarks on Yannai's Conquests of the Coastal Region' ibid., vol. 24, 1955, pp. 15 ff. (Heb.).

[44] Most relevant is the study of C. Mossé, *La tyrannie dans la Grèce antique*, Paris 1969, who points out (p. 204) that while the pre-classical tyranny prepared the way for democracy and the strengthening of the city-constitutions by destroying aristo-

cratic domination, later tyrannies destroyed the free city political system by exploiting the conflict between rich and poor. It is nevertheless a question how far democracy was ever so developed in most of the Hellenistic cities of the orient as to make Mossé's formulation applicable to them.

[45] E. Bickermann in *Mélanges Dussaud*, Paris 1939, p. 99.

[46] F. K. Movers, *Die Phönizier*, Aalen 1849, vol. 2, pp. 479 ff. for Phoenician and Punic constitutions; popular assemblies later became active in some cities (e.g. Tyre, Utica — see Movers, op. cit., pp. 515 ff.).

[47] Jews and Ascalonites would have rubbed shoulders, for instance, at Delos in the second century B.C. W. A. Laidlaw, *Hist. of Delos*, Oxford 1933, p. 210 f., for Ascalonites in the island; the probable synagogue — E. Goodenough, *Jewish Symbols in the Graeco-Roman Period*, New York 1953, vol. 2, pp. 71 ff.

[48] Cleopatra's Jewish force, Jos. *AJ* 13.351–355. The excavations at 'Akko were conducted by the writer on the site of the new post office in Ben 'Ami Street in 1959 (*IEJ* vol. 9, 1959, p. 274). Several sculptural reliefs, so smashed as to be unrecognisable, were also found in the area. The identification of the quarter as a military depot rested on the recovery of a dedication by a chief secretary of the forces (Landau, *IEJ* vol. 11, 1961, pp. 118 ff.; *SEG* 20.413), and of the bone of an elephant.

[49] For the name, Pape-Benseler, *Wörterbuch der griechischen Eigennamen*,[3] Graz 1911, ad voc.; it occurs at Athens but also elsewhere.

[50] Dem. 52.20.

[51] *SEG* 16.573, line 13.

[52] I am indebted to Mr A. H. Hourani for advice on the question of the Metua'lim; he tells me that despite the generally accepted view that their name and sect originated in the eighteenth century, preliminary examination suggests that there is no authority for the origin of the name at this date.

[53] *BJ* 4.105.

[54] *SEG* 8.2.

[55] An organised group of Jewish fishermen at Jaffa in the Roman period is called συγγενική (*CIJ* 2.1145). Our information on the derivation of the non-Greek population of the Greek towns under discussion is not extensive. Philistines and Phoenicians may be assumed to have been among the components of the coastal cities. Gaza is known to have been

recolonised by Alexander the Great with Arabs (Arrian 2.27.7; Nabataeans may be meant); Marissa in the late third century B.C. contained Idumaeans and Sidonians (Peters, Thiersch, *The Painted Tombs of the Necropolis of Marissa*, London 1905); Scythopolis was formerly known as Trikomia (Malalas 5.5.139—140) implying that part of its population was synoecised from Semitic villages of the vicinity. For Avi-Yonah's suggestion of the nucleus of Scythian military settlers here, see *Essays and Studies in the Lore of the Holy Land*, Tel Aviv and Jerusalem 1962, pp. 366 ff. (Heb.). The population of Philadelphia—Amman appears to have included Phoenicians (Tcherikover, *Hell. Civilisation and the Jews*, p. 100).

[56] A. H. M. Jones, *Cities of the Eastern Roman Provinces*, pp. 285 ff.; *JRS* vol. 21, 1931, p. 270; Harper, *YCS* vol. 1, 1928, pp. 143 ff.

[57] For the parasitism of the cities on the countryside, Jones, *The Greek City*, pp. 268; 274.

[58] Reisner, Fisher, Lyon, *Harvard Excs. at Sam.*, Cambridge, Mass., 1924, vol. 3, p. 211; cf. p. 185.

[59] Crowfoot et al., *Buildings*, p. 41.

[60] *Bulletin of the Museum Ha-aretz, Tel Aviv*, 13 June, 1971, pp. 14 ff.

[61] S. Stucchi, *Cirene 1957—1966*, Tripoli 1967, pp. 121—127; figs. 97, 100, 102, 114, 116. I am indebted to Mr L. Y. Raḥmani of the Dept of Antiquities and Museums of Israel, for information concerning the Rockefeller Museum exhibit.

[62] The finds here discussed are exhibited in the Museum of Ancient Art of the Haifa Municipality. They were acquired and first published by the late Mr Rosh, Keeper of the Collection, in a *Handbook of the Collection of Ancient Art; Provincial Sculpture*, Haifa 1950.

[63] *Encyc. of Excavs.*, vol. 1, p. 25 (illus.).

[64] *The Encyclopedia of World Art*, vol. 3, New York 1958 pl. 357.

[65] From the Haifa collection, above n. 62.

[66] Πόλις Ἑλληνίς — Jos. *AJ* 17.320; χρηστομούσια — Clermont-Ganneau, *Recueil d'archéologie orientale*, vol. 2, Paris 1897, p.142.

[67] It may not be without significance that the two cities of the region known to have produced men of intellectual note in the Roman period were Ascalon and Gadara. Ascalon remained independent and unimpaired throughout the Hasmonean and Roman periods; Gadara, though evacuated by its Greek

inhabitants under the pressure of Yannai shortly after 104 B.C. (*AJ* 13.356), and reoccupied only in 64 B.C., was restored by one of its own citizens, Demetrius, who returned with Pompey (*AJ* 14.75). This suggests some measure of cultural continuity.

Shimon Applebaum,
Department of Classical Studies,
Tel Aviv University.

# 6

# Two Cohorts from Camerinum[1]

In any consideration of Marius' influence on the subsequent demise of the Republic his army reforms of 107 B.C. usually occupy a prominent position.[2] There is no need to emphasise the consequences which stemmed from his appeal for volunteers, but it also seems to be a proper judgement of Marius' achievement that he instituted a new form of *clientela*.

The senatorial aristocracy of the period before Marius had always thrived on its clients: *clientela* hitherto had not been a revolutionary weapon (although the Gracchi may have used it as such) nor even a military one, for it was only incidental to its main purpose that it functioned in war when the *plebs* refused their services and *patroni* led out their clients, always in the service of the State, to battle. But with Marius it was not a question of calling clients to serve, rather of making clients those who responded to a call for volunteers. Marius' popularity and his avowed intention of rewarding faithful service made him a new-style *patronus*, the first of those who found themselves able to build their power in the army instead of taking it with them.

The private army recruitment which developed after Marius has an organic connection with the mobilisation of support by *patroni* for political purposes in earlier days.[3] The old system of *clientela* now received its fullest expression by converting what had been an irregular employment of clients into an almost continuous performance of loyalty to new-style *patroni* on the battlefield, and the novelty which the last century B.C. produced was one which killed the *respublica*: those who wished to destroy the prepared positions of the governing clique came, after the example of Marius, to find their support more in the army than outside it and thus built up a new *clientela* that was at once more revolutionary, more powerful than any following of a civil order, and fated to produce an internal war.[4]

It may also be true to say that the significance of the army recruitment which was practised by the new-style *patroni* in the last century B.C. was not primarily economic in character. While it may have been an economic necessity that the poorest of the population should eventually come to fill the legions, economic causes in themselves are not an adequate explanation of what was nothing less than a phenomenon of power politics. The economic background to army recruitment in the last decades of the Republic has been exaggerated.[5]

Complementary to the emergence of the new *patronus—cliens* relationship in local recruitment in Rome is the phenomenon as it appears in Italy before the Social War and in the provinces after it. The Roman oligarchy with Roman dependents gave way to dynasts who knew how to exploit the support of non-Roman adherents. 'The Roman monarchy is a product . . . of obscure people . . whose name is legion.'[6] The pun repays examination.

Provincial commands had always been able to bring the governor special friends and followers. It was equally an honourable tradition that a non-Roman fighting for Rome could be rewarded for a display of valour by an offer of the citizenship and that in the process a relationship of *clientela* could be instituted: the client, winning his deserts for *virtus*, became tied to his patron by a chain which might have for its links money, decorations, and the citizenship.[7] The mechanism for such grants is clear: a general might advise, but it was the people on the Senate's recommendation who would actually make the grant.[8]

In the first four centuries of the Republic such grants of citizenship were fitful, the yield thin. It is a striking break with tradition,[9] both in the manner of conferment and in the numbers involved, when Marius during the Cimbric War enfranchises two whole cohorts of Camertes.[10]

Plutarch's figure of one thousand men may be a maximum for the soldiers directly involved, though the full number of those who benefited directly and indirectly would, of course, be far more. It was a tremendous advance on anything done hitherto in this narrow field of reward for military services rendered, and its impact must have been considerable on the Italians.[11] Furthermore, it was Marius himself who conferred the citizenship; he had no authority to do so, and pleaded 'inter armorum strepitum verba se iuris civilis exaudire non potuisse'.[12] Against his critics Marius had no defence save that of his *auctoritas*. The weakness of his position is revealed by Cicero's frequent *argumenta ad hominem*.[13] The grant, we are told, was made *in ipsa acie*;[14] if this can be taken literally it is surely a possibility[15] that Marius drafted in the Camertes to fill gaps left in the legionary ranks caused by the destruction of two Roman cohorts.[16]

It was one thing to select *boni et locupletes* for rewards, quite another to make a largess at random. Perhaps in the past there had been a frequent correlation between *virtus* displayed on the field of battle by individuals, and that sterling character in family life, social intercourse, and politics which adorned the 'best' type of Roman. Why should this be expected from the cohorts of Camertes? The two might not be coincidental in Optimate eyes even if there were those who could delicately suggest that the one sprang from the other.[17] Balbus could deserve more than a medal for his bravery[18] but not necessarily canonisation for his virtue. His family might not support a searching examination.[19] The best soldiers are not always the 'best' men, and those from Camerinum might fit uneasily into the Roman timocracy.

It could be argued that the consequences which flowed from Marius' illegal grant of citizenship to the Camertes were as disruptive as those which followed on his reforms of 107 B.C. Large scale grants of the *civitas* for *virtus* could make men dependent on their benefactors. So long as the new *patroni* represented themselves as the holders of *imperia* conferred upon them by the State and as the State's agents, the connections that developed could be made to work in the State's favour. But the action of Marius in making the grant of the citizenship an award whose source was to be traced no deeper than to a general in the field, and possibly in correlating that citizenship with military service in the legions, opened up new fields for personal enterprise. At the same time his emphasis on volunteers forged the bond of *clientela* between general and soldier so strongly that it could not be loosened merely by the withdrawal of the latter from military service. In the years before the Bellum Italicum the allies, and after it the provincials, were encouraged to recognise in their rewards for *virtus* an invitation to continue to display their valour not only as servants of their new *patria* but as loyal *clientes* of their general as well.

One of the secrets of the long life of Rome was that, perhaps unconsciously, new sources both for the citizen body and for the army were constantly being tapped which were bound through the criteria governing awards of the citizenship to revive the *res Romana*.[20] What at first sight seems a necessary cause of the fall of the Roman Republic was essentially, *sub specie aeternitatis*, a vital contribution to the birth of the Principate and the continuation of Roman civilisation for years to come. It was the combination of military superiority and political ambition, and indeed the intermixture of the two, that kept Rome alive. It should not be forgotten that in the Bellum Italicum one of the chief claims of the allies to participation in the Roman ἡγεμονία was that their labours in the field had made Rome what she was. It is the prompt recognition of this claim after 90 B.C. which ironically destroys one society and builds another. The development of the old tradition that *virtus* on the battlefield might be rewarded by a grant of the citizenship into a system whereby a commander built himself a following, the innovation of Marius in giving the tradition a twist and in drawing into the citizenship large numbers of *socii*, both combined to prolong the *res Romana*, to undermine the *respublica* and to prepare for centuries of monarchy.

Marius may have enrolled the Camertes into the legions but there were more subtle ways of forming an army. It was easy to pervert the older practice and to offer the citizenship, nominally for valour, to men of influence in the provinces who could be of service as officers,[21] of greater use if they brought over to their benefactor a host of clients whose sons at least might be potential *pedites* in a *legio vernacula*. Against this background it becomes difficult to tell the white sheep from the black.

Before the present century the evidence was tenuous, literary, and undistinguished. An inscription[22] then threw new light. During the Social War Pompeius Strabo awarded the citizenship and other honours to a *turma* of Spanish *equites* under the provisions of the Lex Julia,[23] and conveniently had the award commemorated on a bronze plaque. The connection seems difficult: how can Spaniards have been given the citizenship under a *lex* born out of the crisis of the Bellum Italicum? The law may have been intentionally vague so as to cover all cases. We do not know it in detail. Yet a doubt remains. Those who find legal lopholes are just as adept at citing the evidence as those who abide by the spirit. Pompeius Strabo may have been exploiting a weakness. Ancient judgements on his character and his other activity are suggestive.[24] Gelzer[25] at one time thought his application of the lex Julia to non-Italians might have offended.

During and after the Social War the evidence for grants of the citizenship to provincials *virtutis causa* multiplies.[26] Sulla gave the citizenship to Spaniards and Gauls,[27] yet saw no service in Spain. Almost certainly these are *auxilia* serving during the Bellum Italicum.[28] The young Pompey is quick to take the lesson: his awards to the Ovii, to Cn. Pompeius Basiliscus of Messana and to Uticenses[29] are probably to be dated to his Sicilian and African campaigns of the late eighties. Sertorius seems to have operated on a large scale, using his own methods to cope with a shortage of Roman legionaries and at the same time to bind the provincials to him.[30] During the struggle in Spain Pompey enfranchised Balbus *virtutis causa*,[31] and Metellus competed.[32] Later evidence for Pompey's *clientela* points to heavy but undocumented activity in this period.[33] This activity had to be guaranteed: hence the Lex Gellia Cornelia of 72 B.C. and no doubt others.[34] The law had a reference to *singillatim*: no-one, of course, could count the number of clients a new citizen brought with him.

The case of Balbus, well-documented even if by a prejudiced source, can be a pointer for the period. In 56 B.C. Cicero's *pro Balbo* defended through a particular instance the general policy of the dynasts in the field of the citizenship. Cicero lent his support to the methods by which Marius, Pompeius Strabo and his son, and finally Caesar imposed their several wills on the *respublica*. What was actually involved in the case of 56 B.C., although not explicitly mentioned in the charge itself, was the right of Pompey, Crassus, and Caesar to make citizens as they chose. The trial is an important one. It was natural that Pompey and Crassus, for all their inadequacy as orators,[35] should take their stand. The closing sections of the speech show that Caesar was heavily under fire.

It was straightforward for Cicero to point to the confirming Lex Gellia Cornelia and to take it for granted that all was as it used to be, Rome's representative rewarding for valour in the field and Rome's senate and people gladly confirming. But 'fecisse Pompeium quod ei facere non licuerit': was it a charge that could be refuted simply by putting a man from Gades in his place? Some indeed might have wanted to add what to Cicero was the weaker accusation, 'quod non oportuerit', and to contend that it was a charge no less serious. Cicero's reminder that the grant of citizenship to Balbus had been made 'de consilii sententia'[36] might prove compliance with the law, but it would also bring to mind Pompeius Strabo and Caesar's clique in Gaul. Cicero asks what sort of *amicitia* or *foedus* it is if Rome must not reward those who exposed themselves for her sake in battle[37]: 'dignissimi sunt qui civitate ea donentur pro qua pericula ac tela subierunt'.[38] But what really mattered was how many were going to be admitted, and by whom, and what were to be the terms of their admission. A firm stand in 56 B.C. could have checked the enfranchisement of provincials for private ends, the building of *legiones vernaculae*,[39] and even the later civil wars — or was it too late? Some might have said nearly fifty years too late. But Cicero in the *pro Balbo* is not prepared to admit that the system by which generals could confer the citizenship had got out of hand, and even makes the point that what was agreed for the orator was sour grapes for the soldier.[40] This was an argument he deserved to have thrown in his teeth when Caesar and his provincial hordes invaded Rome. It was one thing to welcome a cultivated civilian to the citizenship for services in the courts, another to greet a soldier when he marched on the capital. *Propugnatores imperii*[41] could easily become *propugnatores imperatoris*, and Caesar was to drive home the lesson that his uncle had demonstrated as far back as the Cimbric War.

In Caesar's time the province of Cisalpine Gaul was hardly a unity as far as the status of its inhabitants was concerned. After Pompeius Strabo's work in 89 B.C.[42] Cispadane Gaul is almost entirely Roman, the Transpadana is conspicuous for the number of native *oppida* which have acquired Latin rights. In the case of the Cispadana the merger with Italy in 42 B.C. was no more than the official recognition of what was already well known in practice, for Transpadane Gaul the grant of citizenship in 49 B.C. was an essential preliminary.[43] The province, with its reserves of free labour, its wealth and prosperity, could hardly fail to commend itself as a recruiting ground for the legions. There was a precedent in the eighties.[44] Cicero knew that it could provide an invaluable force in time of disturbance.[45] The Pompeian hold was strong: a legion was raised there in 55 B.C.[46]

For all the powerful, constitutional reserves of Cispadane

Gaul there were some who preferred to tap resources north of the Po and to summon to legionary service those who did not yet enjoy the full citizenship, members of towns which had been given *ius Latii* by Pompeius Strabo. The Transpadana offered rich prizes to the ambitious, not least because of the discontent felt by its inhabitants over their lack of the citizenship, a discontent which mounted as the years passed and which found its chief expression in the towns that had acquired *Latium*.[47] It was a region which could be exploited not only in political fashion[48] but in ways more provocative and more deadly.

Although it is not always possible to be certain from Caesar's own remarks whether he recruited north or south of the Po during his Gallic campaigns,[49] the whole development of legionary recruitment in the late Republic suggests the former. Formation of *clientela* by inclusion in the legions is unlikely to have escaped Caesar's notice in this area if it had commended itself to Pompey and others elsewhere. Constitutional problems that would arise over the status of the Transpadane legionaries might have been neglected by Caesar at the time — even if the *pro Balbo* suggests that there were others who were prepared to challenge what was being done.[50] Hardy[51] started from the premiss that Latins were not eligible for the legions and had to conclude that arrangements for recruiting in the Transpadana until 49 B.C. were vague, often at the whim of the proconsul. The conclusion can be reached independently of the premiss which may be true but which certainly admits exceptions.[52] This is not a period of rigid observance of tradition even if the Pompeius Strabo inscription and the Lex Gellia Cornelia suggest it. Laws can bolster, they are rarely the mattress now. It seems better to emphasise the evidence we do have that Transpadanes were taken into the legions.[53] Hardy's reminder that the magistrates of the Transpadani would in the forty years after the Bellum Italicum be producing Roman citizens is not enough to explain the phenomenon. And it was one which did not come and go in a moment. If it did not take long in the new fashion to make a man a citizen, the later armies of the civil wars were not built in a day. Caesar was preparing for years.[54]

It was clear, when the final struggle came, that whereas the rest of Cisalpine Gaul might be persuaded, Caesar's ties with the Transpadanes were such that the situation there was hopeless.[55] Even Pompey's extensive control of clients could not shake the allegiance shown to Caesar north of the Po. Not least important is the fact that contemporary comment strongly suggests that Caesar in the main recruited in Transpadane Gaul. Cicero for example points to the work of agitators,[56] Antony's connection with Caesar later tempted him to rely on Transpadane support.[57] Caesar's hold on the Transpadana was firm because it had ties, and ties of a military kind, with him. Opitergium contributed auxiliaries.[58] Regular use of Transpadanes in the *auxilia*, no doubt with promises of later enfranchisement, was an important feature.[59] In 49 B.C. the whole of Cisalpine Gaul received its reward but the *civitas* which came to it by the Lex Roscia was particularly welcomed in the Transpadana, there to bring the region up to the status of the returning veterans so that resettlement might be made easier.[60]

The nature of the northern sector of the Transpadana raises an important point. Here the phenomenon of *attributio* is securely attested and it is possible to trace the introduction to legionary service of those who were only recently made full members of the Roman world. *Attributio*, an attachment to a town of a commune or communes which were unfitted by themselves for urban organisation,[61] is attested in Pompeius Strabo's settlement;[62] Caesar had first-hand experience of an analogous situation in Gaul.[63] Its importance for the development of a town, and therefore for widening the sources of legionary recruitment, is attested by Tacitus' description of Cremona's rise.[64] When a province came to receive the citizenship as Cisalpine Gaul did, the *attributi* could play an important part as legionaries; until that time their participation in the town was a useful preparation. As for the *incolae*, the 'residents',[65] men with ties with two states (that in which their *domicilia* lay and that of their *origines*), they were liable for such *munera* as military service in the *colonia* in which they were residing as well as in the town where they were born.[66] A passage in the Lex Ursonensis attests their liability in Caesar's time.[67]

The grant of *Latium* to Transpadane Gaul in 89 B.C. brought with it the incorporation of tribes hitherto independent and unattached. The Bergalei are found attributed to Comum,[68] the Anauni, Sinduni, and Tulliasses to Tridentum.[69] There need be little doubt that Eporedia was a useful centre.[70] It seems unlikely that *attributi* would have been enrolled in the legions, even by Caesar, before they had attained Latin status, and indeed the large resources of Transpadane Gaul in Latins, together with the fact that there was discontent among the Latin colonies themselves which he might care to foster, suggest that up to 49 B.C. the Alpine tribes would have served exclusively in the *auxilia*. After that date, however, with the grant of citizenship to Cisalpine Gaul and the corresponding rise in status of the *attributi*, it is possible that the legions began to receive them on a large scale. It had been the settlement of Pompeius Strabo in 89 B.C. which had prepared the way for their eventual participation.

Caesar suceeded in the struggle for Rome because he relied on an army drawing its main strength from the Cisalpina. On his arrival in his province in 58 B.C. he found three veteran legions[71] at Aquileia and one in Narbonensis.[72] To these he added two more in 58 B.C.[73] and a further two in the following year.[74] It should be quite clear that these additional legions were unauthorised,[75] that pay for them was not forthcoming until 56 B.C.,[76] and that they were levied in Cisalpine Gaul, probably in the Transpadana.[77] Three new legions were added in 54/3 B.C. thanks to Pompey's generosity and Caesar's own recruitment — and all three had come from the Cisalpina.[78] By 53 B.C., allowing for additions and deductions,[79] Caesar had ten legions. There follow *supplementa*[80] but it is not until 51 B.C. that any increase in the number of the legions is directly attested.[81] In this year a legion is sent to Cisalpine Gaul on garrison duty, yet there are still ten available elsewhere for active service.[82] One has clearly been added, almost certainly recruited in the Cisalpina. Then there is the Legio Alaudae which never, alone of all Caesar's legions, carries a number until its members receive the citizenship and which was almost certainly in existence by 50 B.C., despite the fact that Hirtius never mentions it, probably for the very good reason that its members were Gauls.[83]

In the Civil Wars the pattern continues. Caesar raises a legion *ex tumultuaribus militibus* in Pontus[84] and gives the citizenship at Gades in return for, in all probability, legionary service.[85] *Legiones vernaculae* appear, legions of non-citizens born in the provinces.[86] Caesar used them although he never says that he formed one: the only legion on the Caesarian side which is given its proper title of *legio vernacula* is that of Q. Cassius.[87] This needs no explanation. The claims of propaganda had to be heard and it was a winner to dub the other side non-Romans and, whenever possible, Orientals.[88] Pompey and his followers knew the value of *legiones vernaculae*, even before the Civil War broke out.[89]

Long-term commands in the provinces, together with the tendency to make use of provincial manpower even to the extent of enrolling it in the legions, combined to produce men who were soldiers first and citizens second, and then soldiers of a particular general. While citizenship was so closely associated with legionary service which was often the prelude to it, army claims and army aspirations were prior to political ones. Provincial *clientes* were likely to be as sturdy in their loyalty and as complete in their *virtus* as any Italian, more so if they owed their presence in the Roman scheme of things to a Pompey or a Caesar. It is no accident that the ambitious turn the services of the underprivileged to their own advantage, nor that in using such material they presented themselves as threats to the *respublica*. Powerful support was theirs in return for promises of advancement, and the support was powerful just because it was concentrated into one field, that of war, and not allowed to dissipate itself in a maze of political institutions. Throughout the first century B.C. the realisation grows that there were others besides Roman *proletarii* who could promote *ambitio*. The *legiones vernaculae*, offspring of the Marian cohorts of Camertes, were men united by the hope of enfranchisement, and they devoted their strength to attaining this end.

Here the *Bellum Hispaniense* has some lessons to offer.[90] The work indicates both in its outlook and in its treatment of important incidents how deep and how extensive was the attachment of a soldier in this period to his general. This, of course, was as true of the Italian as it was of the provincial , but whereas the former had before his service savoured something of the delights of power in the Roman world, even if this meant no more than the observation of elections at Rome or in his home town, the latter, often enjoying his first contact with *res Romana* other than its judiciary, serving a general who boasted that he would soon have the whole world at his mercy and who promised rich rewards for loyalty and devotion, might be excused for seeing in his military service the full life of a Roman and for pledging himself utterly to his commander's cause. His meagre acquaintance with the higher reaches of Roman power and ambition would not prevent him from identifying his benefactor with the majesty of Rome itself. So the remarks of

Tullius the legate[9][1] could lie as easily in the mouth of Cato the Lusitanian who accompanies him; for him it is not important to consider whether Caesar has any justification for the invasion of Spain or whether the struggle there is to free the world of Rome's enemies or to relieve Caesar of encumbrances. The sole question is whether he should be the soldier of Pompey or of Caesar, and the alternative of service to Rome does not arise.[9][2] A Spaniard would have added that in the late Republic the last was becoming more difficult to understand if separated from the service to those dynasts who appeared in Spain from time to time. Men served in a *legio vernacula* not from love of Rome but to ingratiate themselves with a *dux* who was nominally Rome's representative, and to further the cause of one who promised them some advancement.

If Marius discovered that the most useful reward for valour was direct enrolment in the legions, it was left to later generals to drive the lesson home. What had originated as *singillatim* grants of the citizenship for particular acts of bravery were extended by Marius to cohorts and by his successors to whole legions. By the end of the Republic it was a regular occurrence that the foreigner should serve in the legion first and be rewarded later with the citizenship. What started the rot was the unchecked recognition of skill in battle, and from it developed the armies of clients who were the eager followers to their generals.

## Notes

[1] I am very much in Professor Badian's debt for help with this paper.

[2] On these see R. E. Smith, *Service in the Post-Marian Army*, Manchester 1958, with an important addendum by P. A. Brunt, *JRS* vol. 52, 1962, p. 69f. The work of E. Gabba in this field (*Ath.* N.S., vol. 29, 1949, p. 175f.; vol. 31, 1951, p. 171f. = *Esercito e Società*, Florence 1973, p. 1f.; p. 47f.) is fundamental. On Marius see Carney, *A Biography of Marius*, *PACA*, Suppl. 1, 1962.

[3] Well emphasised , but not in a wholly acceptable way, by A. von Premerstein, *Vom Werden und Wesen des Prinzipats, Abh. der bay. Akad. der Wiss. (Phil. – hist. Abt.)* N. F. Heft 15, 1937, p. 22f., and not completely exploited by E. Badian, *Foreign Clientelae*, Oxford 1958.

[4] It is along lines such as these that an answer has to be found to A. Momigliano's question in *JRS* vol. 30, 1940, p. 78: 'The clientships of the old days had been the strength of the senatorial aristocracy. The clientships of the last century B.C. destroyed the senatorial government. Why?'

[5] I hope to explore this in a later paper.

[6] Momigliano, loc. cit.

[7] See Badian, op. cit., pp. 252f. and 302f. (details of grants). I have not been able to consult Krawczuk, *Virtutis erga* . . ., Krakow 1963.

[8] Pol. 6. 14. 4; Cic., *pro Balbo*; 10. 25; 24. 55. See Th. Mommsen, *St.* vol. 2. $2^3$, p. 890f.; 3. 1. p. 134f. id. *Herm.* vol. 19, 1884, p. 11f. (= *Ges Schr.* vol. 6, p. 30f.).

[9] Well emphasised by Badian, op. cit., p. 252f.

[10] Cic., *pro Balbo* 20. 46; cf. Val. Max. 5. 2. 8; Plut., *Vit. Mar.* 28: idem, *Reg. et Imp. Apophth., Mar.* 5. Brunt, *JRS* vol. 55, 1965, p. 106, makes two mistakes when he calls them 'a troop of horse'. Nothing is known of M. Annius Appius of Iguvium whom Cicero conjoins with the Camertes.

[11] Not recognised by Brunt, op. cit. (n. 10), nor by any modern commentator on the causes of the Social War. Taken in conjunction with the move in 100 B.C. to settle *allied* veterans (Appian, *BC* 1. 29. 132) it would be an important factor in any Italian decision to fight for recognition.

[12] Val. Max., loc. cit.

[13] *Pro Balbo* 21. 49. On the question of the precise nature of Marius' illegality see Badian, op. cit., p. 261, n.1. Professor Badian, although not agreeing with my reconstruction at this point, has been kind enough to remind me that Cicero nowhere says that Marius acted *de consilii sententia,* though this would have been a strong point for him.

[14] Val. Max., loc. cit.

[15] I owe this suggestion to C. E. Stevens. There is no actual evidence for Badian's 'after the battle' (op. cit., p. 261).

[16] On the origin of the Roman cohort, which was certainly established by this date, see M. J. V. Bell, *Hist.* vol. 14, 1965, p. 404f.

[17] Caes., *BG* 1. 47. 4: 'C. Valerium Procillum . . . summa virtute et humanitate adulescentem, cuius pater a C. Valerio Flacco civitate donatus erat'; cf. ibid. 1. 19. 3; 53. 5–6. R. Syme, *JRS* vol. 27, 1937, p. 131, calls him 'a civilised provincial' (cf. idem, *CQ* vol. 32, 1938, p. 41: 'a cultivated and

admirable young man') and thereby swallows Caesar's propaganda. We do not need to be told that his father received the citizenship for military services.

[18] See p. 79ff.

[19] See Syme, *RR*, p. 80, n. 2.

[20] See some penetrating observations of H. Last in *JRS* vol. 37, 1947, p. 152.

[21] E.g. the uncle of Pompeius Trogus was in charge of *auxilia* in the war against Mithridates (Justin 43.5.11). It is outside the scope of this paper to deal with the type of new citizen, his background, later progress, etc.

[22] *CIL* 1².709 = 6.37045 = 16, p. 145, no. 9 = *ILS* 8888 = *ILLRP* 515 (best text). The most useful discussion is still C.Cichorius, *Röm. Studien*, Leipzig, etc., 1922, p. 130f.

[23] Provisions anticipated by the Lex Calpurnia (Sisenna, fr. 120P).

[24] See the observations of Badian, op. cit., p. 203 et al.

[25] *Die Nobilität der röm. Republik*, Berlin 1912, p. 78 — withdrawn, however, as Badian, op. cit., p. 261, n.4, observes in *Röm. Studien,* vol. 2, Leipzig 1943, p. 72 ( = *Kl. Schr.*, vol. 2, p. 118).

[26] Down to 70 B.C. Badian, op. cit., p. 252f., is fundamental. I have tried to include some items on which, to my mind, he has not laid sufficient emphasis.

[27] Cic., *pro Archia* 10. 25: cf. *pro Balbo* 22. 50 (text corrupt, but he rewarded the Gaditani) and Exsuperantius 5.

[28] On the activity of Q. Metellus Pius and M. Licinius Crassus in the eighties see Badian, op. cit., p. 266f.

[29] Cic., *pro Balbo* 22. 51; *in Verr.* 2. 4. 11. 25. See Tenney Frank, *AJP* vol. 56, 1935, p. 63f.

[30] Plut., *Sert.* 12. 2: δισχιλίοις γὰρ ἑξακοσίοις οὓς ὠνόμαξε 'Ρωμαίους (cf. Exsuperantius 8). Surely for military purposes. Note the legacy in Caesar, *BG* 3. 23. 5.

[31] Cic., *pro Balbo* 3. 6; cf. Pliny, *NH* 5. 5. 36; *SHA* 21. 7. 3. On his name see Badian, op. cit., p. 303.

[32] Cf. Cic., *pro Archia* 10. 26. On the foundation of Metellinum see *RE*, vol. 15, s.v. *Metellinum*, col. 1371.

[33] Besides the evidence in Badian, op. cit., p. 302f. and that to be gathered from a study of *nomina* (ibid., p. 253f.), n.b. Caes., *BC* 1. 29. 3; 61. 3; 2. 18. 7; App., *BC* 5. 556; 596; Dio 43. 30. 1 (cf. 42. 56. 4; 45. 10. 1; App., *BC* 4. 349). For a Gaul who probably received the citizenship from Pompey see Caes.,

*BC* 5. 36. 1. On Pompeius Paullinus, one of whose ancestors was also probably given the same honour, see Syme, *CQ* vol. 22, 1938, p. 41, n.7.

[34] See Badian, op. cit., p. 260.

[35] Cic., *Brutus* 68. 239 (Pompey); 66. 233 (Crassus).

[36] *Pro Balbo* 8. 19.

[37] Ibid., 9. 23f.

[38] Ibid., 22. 51.

[39] See p. 83ff.

[40] *Pro Balbo* 23. 54.

[41] Ibid., 22. 51.

[42] See U. Ewins, *PBSR* vol. 23, 1955, p. 73f.

[43] On this see p. 82ff.

[44] App., *BC* 1. 303; 393 (Badian, op. cit., p. 268, n.4).

[45] *Ad Q. F.* 2. 3. 4.

[46] Caes., *BG* 6. 1. 1–2.

[47] Cf. Cic., *de Off.* 3. 22. 88; Suet., *Div. Iul.* 8; Dio 37. 9. 3f. Among them would probably be Verona (*Panegyr.* 9. 8; Ewins, op. cit., p. 75 and n. 11).

[48] Caesar's activity in this field (e.g. at Comum) is a subject in itself.

[49] BG 1. 10. 3; 24. 2; 2. 2. 1; 6. 1; 7. 1. 1. Explicit mention of *trans Padum* in 5. 24. 4.

[50] 27. 61 ('idem' — the Senate — 'in angustiis aerarii victorem exercitum stipendo adfecit') suggests that Caesar's new legions were not paid by the Aerarium until 56 B.C.

[51] *Some Problems in Roman History*, Oxford 1924, p. 53.

[52] F. Vittinghoff, *Röm. Kolonisation und Bürgerrechts-politik unter Caes. und Aug., Akad. der Wiss. und der Lit. (Abhandl. der Geisten- und Socialwiss. Klasse XIV)*, Wiesbaden 1951, pp. 1262 (46); 1278 (62), has drawn attention to the fact that men are found serving in the legions whose known places of origin enjoyed a status no higher than Latin, and that we have no grounds for supposing that they are immigrants.

[53] Caes., *BC* 3. 87. 4: 'hae copiae quas videtis ex dilectibus horum annorum in citeriore Gallia sunt refectae, et plerique ex coloniis Transpadanis'. Labienus is not necessarily exaggerating, *pace* G. E. F. Chilver, *Cisalpine Gaul*, Oxford 1940, p. 112, n.5 (cf. n.49 above).

[54] E.g. Tac., *Ann.* 3. 40. 1 (Julius Florus and Julius Sacrovir): 'nobilitas ambobus et maiorum *bona facta, eoque* Romana civitas olim data, cum id rarum nec nisi *virtuti* pretium esset.' Once again (see n.17 above) we have the 'slide' from 'valour' to

'virtue'. For the hypothesis that an ancestor of Julius Africanus (Tac., *Ann*. 6. 7. 4) was taken into service in Gaul by Caesar see *RE*, vol. 10, s. v. *Julius* no. 45, col. 114f. Scandal in Tacitus, *Hist*. 4. 55. 2.

⁵⁵ Cic., *ad Fam*. 16. 12. 4. The flogging of the Novocomensis (Cic., *ad Att*. 5. 11. 2, etc.) was a particularly stupid act at this juncture.

⁵⁶ *Ad Att*. 5. 2. 3; *ad Fam*. 8. 1. 2.

⁵⁷ Cic., *Phil*. 10. 5. 10; 12. 4. 10 (more likely the result of Caesar's grant of the citizenship to the area, though indirectly Caesar's recruitment there earlier is suggested).

⁵⁸ Livy, *Per*. 90; Florus 2. 13. 33; Schol. Bern. apud Lucan, *Phars*. 4. 462: Mommsen, *CIL* 5, p. 186.

⁵⁹ See T. Yoshimura, *Hist*. vol. 10, 1961, p. 473f. for the evidence.

⁶⁰ See M. I. Henderson, *JRS* vol. 43, 1953, p. 140; cf. Ewins, op. cit., pp. 91–94.

⁶¹ See *RE* Suppl. 7, s.v. *attributio*, col. 65f.; U. Laffi, *Adtributio e Contributio*, Pisa 1966.

⁶² Pliny, *NH* 3. 138.

⁶³ *BG* 7. 9.6; 76. 1; Hirtius, *BG* 8. 6. 2 (see Laffi, op. cit., p. 46f.).

⁶⁴ *Hist*. 3. 34: 'igitur numero colonorum, opportunitate fluminum, ubere agri, adnexu conubiisque gentium adolevit floruitque' where 'adnexu' is clearly Tacitus' word for *attributio*, whatever the description of the actual phenomenon should be (Laffi, op. cit., pp. 54–55).

⁶⁵ This is the meaning of the word, not 'natives' as Vittinghoff takes them to be: cf. *inter alia Cod. Just.* 10. 39 (38). 1; 40 (39). 4; *Dig*., 50. 1. 29, and the inscriptions listed in *RE*, vol. 9, s.v. *incola*, col. 1250. The language of Asconius, p.3C, is not to be taken too seriously.

⁶⁶ *Dig*., loc. cit.

⁶⁷ CIII. On this difficult passage, and the emendations which have been suggested, see Laffi, op. cit., p. 129f. There is no need to believe that *attributi* are referred to here.

⁶⁸ Cf. *CIL* 5. 5050 = *ILS* 206.

⁶⁹ See Mommsen, *Herm*., loc. cit. ( = *Ges. Schr.*, vol. 4, p. 304) for the suggestion that the *attributio* dates to the Republic; *contra*, A. N. Sherwin-White, *The Roman Citizenship*, Oxford 1939, p. 175; Chilver, op. cit., p. 23f.

⁷⁰ See P. Fraccaro, *Annali dei Lavori Pubblici* vol. 79, 1941, p. 719f. ( = *Opuscula*, vol. 3, p. 93f.).

[71] Caes., *BG* 1. 10. 3. That they were veteran is shown by Hirtius, *BG* 8. 8. 2. However, not all the legionaries in leg. VII were hardened campaigners: see *ILS* 2225 for Q. Canuleius who died in Gaul at the age of eighteen.

[72] Caes., *BG* 1.7.2.

[73] Ibid., 1. 10. 3.

[74] Ibid., 2. 2. 1.

[75] T. Rice Holmes, *Caesar's Conquest of Gaul²*, Oxford 1911, p. 557. It is not likely that a governor had power to levy troops in his province unless authorised in advance or unless there was a *tumultus*.

[76] I take this to be the full implication of Cic., *pro Balbo* 27. 61 (quoted in n.50 above).

[77] See above p. 81ff.

[78] Caes., *BG* 6. 1.

[79] N.B. loss of Titurius Sabinus' legion (*BG* 5. 32f.).

[80] Ibid., 7. 1. 1; 7. 5.

[81] Ten legions only in 53 B.C. (Caes., *BG* 6. 32. 5–33. 3) and 52 B.C. (7. 34. 2). There is no hint that there was one garrisoning Cisalpine Gaul at this stage, and Hirtius, *BG* 8, 24, 3, seems to rule it out.

[82] Leg. VI is attested for the first time in 51 B.C. (Hirtius, *BG* 8. 4. 3). Rice Holmes, *Roman Republic*, vol. 3, Oxford 1923, p. 356f., refuted Groebe's theory that leg. VI was originally Pompey's leg. I and that when this was returned in 50 B.C. a new leg. VI was raised. Leg. VI is called *veterana* in 47 B.C. (*Bell. Alex.* 69. 1), a fair enough description given the events of the last three years.

[83] On the *legio Alaudae* (Suet., *Div. Iul.* 24. 2) see Mommsen, *Herm.* vol. 19, 1884, p. 13 ( = *Ges. Schr.*, vol. 6 p. 32f.); Marquardt, *Röm. Staatsverw.* vol. 2², p. 433, n.1; V. Ehrenberg, *Klio* vol. 19, 1925, p. 198 and n. 4; Rice Holmes, *Roman Republic*, vol. 3, p. 355, n. 3 etc.

[84] *Bell. Alex.* 34. 5.

[85] Dio 41. 24. 1.

[86] *Bell. Alex.* 53. 5 is the *locus classicus* (Mommsen, *Herm.* vol. 19, 1884, p. 13, n. 2 ( = *Ges. Schr.*, vol. 6, p. 31, n. 3)). See also *Bell. Hisp.* 7. 4 (distinction between *legio vernacula* and *legio facta ex coloniis*); 12. 1; 20. 5 (slaves serving in legio V). I do not accept Gabba's interpretation of *Bell. Alex.*

[87] *Bell. Alex.*, 53. 5.

[88] For propaganda points see for example Caes., *BC* 3. 4. 2f.; 3. 102. 2.

[89] Yoshimura has shown that Pompey anticipated Caesar in the formation of a *legio vernacula* between 55 and 52 B.C. *(using Bell. Alex.* 61. 1 and referring the 'multa proelia' there to the wars mentioned in *Caes., BC* 1. 44. 2; see Gabba, *Esercito e Società*, p. 480. Cf. Caes., *BC* 2. 20. 4; *Bell. Hisp.* 7.4; 10. 3; 12. 1; 20. 2. For Spain cf. Caes., *BC*. 1. 85. 6 (N.B. 'VI legiones ... septimamque ibi conscriptam'; but Cic., *ad Fam.* 16. 12. 4, recognises only six); 86. 3; 87. 4–5. There is no mention of Spanish troops in the catalogue of Caes., *BC* 3. 4, but some of the cohorts which Caesar allowed to return to their homes in Spain after the capitulation of Afranius probably served at Pharsalus (see Rice Holmes, *Roman Republic*, vol. 3, p. 469, on Caes., *BC*. 3. 88. 2). Pompey's son could raise some nine legions in Spain (*Bell. Hisp.* 7. 4–5). Mommsen, *Herm.* vol. 19, 1884, p. 12 ( = *Ges. Schr.*, vol. 6, p. 31) took 'Gallos Germanosque' in Caes., *BC* 3. 4. 4, to be legionaries, but they are listed among *auxilia*.

[90] See H. Drexler, *Herm.* vol. 70, 1935, p. 208f.; Gabba, *Ath.* N.S., vol. 29, 1951, p. 186f. ( = *Esercito e Società*, p. 65f.).

[91] *Bell. Hisp.* 17.

[92] Cf. the protest of Cic., *Phil.* 10. 5. 12, and the centurion's remarks in *Bell. Ar.* 45. 2f.

P. J. Cuff,
Pembroke College,
Oxford.

# 7

## Priscae Gallorum Memoriae: some Comments on Sources for a History of Gaul

Among the published letters of Q. Aurelius Symmachus is one which he wrote to his Gaulish friend Protadius in the year A.D. 396, advising on sources for a history of Gaul.[1] The previous year had seen Protadius at Milan, where his brother Minervius had held a position, perhaps that of *magister epistularum,* in the secretariat of Honorius, while his second brother, Florentinus, had been *quaestor sacri palatii* before departing for Rome in the summer of 395 to take up office as *praefectus urbi.* Protadius had hoped for some prize through the patronage of his brothers.[2] His turn was to come, but meanwhile he returned in temporary disappointment to estates in Gaul.[3] He had not abandoned the literary pursuits which he had in common with Symmachus, and had expressed a desire to compose a history of Gaul, to which end he wished to borrow from his friend's library. 'Asperserat nos ille iamdudum facundiae suae floribus, et sibi Galliarum prisca monumenta iuvando otio exscribenda mandaverat', is how Symmachus described Protadius' ambition in a letter he wrote to Minervius in Milan,[4] and under cover of which he sent the aforementioned one to the would-be historian, with the following response:

> 'priscas Gallorum memorias deferri in manus tuas postulas. revolve Patavini scriptoris extrema, quibus res Gai Caesaris explicantur, aut si inpar est desiderio tuo Livius, sume ephemeridem C. Caesaris decerptam bibliotheculae meae, ut tibi muneri mitteretur. haec te origines situs pugnas, et quidquid fuit in moribus aut legibus Galliarum, docebit. enitar, si fors votum iuvet, etiam Plinii Secundi Germanica bella conquirere. tantisper esto contentus. . . .'

The letter tantalises by what it does not make explicit. Exactly where was Protadius? Most probably in his estates in the Five Provinces, to judge by the tales of relaxation, since Protadius' other recorded abode, Trier, was associated with duty.[5] Also not completely clear is whether Protadius had his own copy of Livy, or whether that, too, was sent along with the manuscript of Caesar: the former is perhaps the more natural reading. The passage does, however, shed light not only on the procedures which Protadius was expected to adopt, but also on the availability of the sources. Livy presented no problem, and the way the reference is phrased suggests that it was a full text, not an epitome, the end of which Protadius was to unroll: this would indeed be natural among members of a circle which was so deeply concerned with the manuscript tradition of that author.[6] Pliny's German Wars are another matter: after being utilised as source material by Tacitus, who did not however have a high opinion of their author,[7] they seem to have virtually disappeared from view, and even the bibliophile Symmachus was uncertain whether he could lay his hands on a copy. Between the two comes Caesar, possessed by Symmachus himself but apparently considered valuable, or at least unusual.

Here, however, the use of the word *ephemeris* causes a further uncertainty when we seek to know just exactly what it was that Symmachus sent to his friend. And in order to answer the question of whether it was or was not the work that we usually think of as the Commentaries on the Gallic War, a further, double question must be posed and answered: what was the original title of that work, and was there extant another published work, to which the name *ephemeris* might be given?

The second half of the question is best considered first. It is a suggestion made by various people at various times, though it has been less in vogue since firmly dismissed with magisterial sarcasm by Nipperdey in the introduction to his 1847 edition of the Gallic Wars.[8]

To start with, it is relevant to consider episodes in Caesar's campaigns mentioned by other writers, the source for which is not Caesar as we have him, and to consider what clues there may be to alternative sources. Frontinus in his *Strategemata* lists a few such incidents. One, the story of how Caesar, stumbling after disembarkation, turned a bad omen into a good by claiming to embrace Mother Earth, occurs with slight variations in Suetonius and Dio:[9] such a tale could have found wide circulation in oral tradition, or it may be considered by some to be a literary commonplace. A reference to Gaulish scythed chariots likewise requires explanation, since Caesar says nothing of Gaulish war-chariots, and archaeology is ignorant of the scythes.[10] Here, someone seems to have attributed to the Gauls the scythed chariots of Pharnaces mentioned in the *Bellum Alexandrinum*: the idea took firm root, since we find in Pomponius Mela and Statius references to scythes with the Celtic name *covinnus* adding apparently circumstantial detail.[11]

The most interesting and precise stories in Frontinus are one from the Gallic and one from the Civil Wars, the absence of which from the Commentaries is not too hard to explain, since they show Caesar and his men in a poor light. The first is the flight of Commius the Atrebate when, by spreading the sails on ships still beached by low tide, he caused Caesar to drop pursuit.[12] Though there is a difficulty in locating the incident, Frontinus' story has won general acceptance.[13] The other, where a Pompeian slipped through Caesar's sentries at Ategua by employing a ruse to learn the password, is recounted also by Dio, but not by the author of the Spanish War.[14] It is Dio, too, who tells us that Caesar's most embittered enemy, Vercingetorix, had once been his friend.[15]

Sources for such stories are however not hard to suggest. Whether from oral tradition or via the letters of Caesar and his subordinates, they could easily have found their way into the writings on Caesar by Cornelius Balbus and Oppius, the histories of Asinius Pollio, Tanusius Geminus, and Aelius Tubero, and thence to Livy.

Slightly more complicated are the questions raised by the Greek writer on stratagems, Polyaenus. He has details of the sieges of Gergovia and Alesia which partly correspond with Caesar, and an intriguing tale of his camouflaging part of his army in a wood.[16] Now it is normally held against Polyaenus that he was careless, and that convenient character, the muddling intermediary or compiler, can also be supposed to have confused accounts which might in any case have come from Timagenes, Nicolaus of Damascus or the Greek Asinius Pollio of Tralles rather than directly from Caesar.[17] When it comes to Caesar taking advantage of a morning mist while crossing the Alps, Polyaenus (or his source) is accused of having lifted a passage on Hannibal from Livy,[18] though there are many ways in which the account could have found its way into the tradition. Of Polyaenus' stories, the most remarkable (and notorious) is undoubtedly that of the armoured elephant in

Britain, which is said to have helped Caesar cross a big river in his advance against Cassivellaunus by terrifying the natives, who had never before seen such a portentous beast. In Caesar's account, his legionaries, though supported only by the more normal quadrupeds of the cavalry, nevertheless advanced with such impetus that the Britons could not withstand the onslaught.[19] Has there been a gross muddle between Caesar and Claudius, who according to Dio included elephants (in the plural) among his preparations for Britain, though we are not told that he actually employed them in the battle for the Thames crossing?[20] Yet Polyaenus at least had the name of Caesar's enemy approximately right. Or, as has been suggested by others, has one of Hannibal's elephants been light-heartedly detached to Caesar, so that the tale is merely 'impudenter fictum'?[21] In fact, there are reasons to support its credibility. It can be argued that it helps make sense of the battle, while for the motif of the elephant in connection with Caesar's campaigns in Gaul there is the corroborating evidence of the coinage (though this may fall a little later than previously thought).[22] Moreover, the suggested explanation that Caesar intended parading round Britain on an elephant in order to spite and ridicule Domitius Ahenobarbus, whose grandfather had thus circumperambulated Narbonensis, is so attractively appropriate that it is tempting here to fly in the face of methodology (which cannot of itself guarantee a truthful reconstruction) and use the hypothesis as supporting evidence.[23] Since Caesar's British campaigns did not bring the total success hoped for, the absence of any such story from the Commentaries is not hard to explain, and it may be doubted whether it would figure in official dispatches.[24] At the very least, if Polyaenus is to be dismissed the case must be more fully argued.

In any case, we have to turn to authorities other than Caesar if we are to grasp the excitement caused at Rome by Caesar's visits to Britain, and the reasons for some of it. The twenty days' thanksgiving accorded to him is better understood when we read in Plutarch that many authorities of Caesar's day did not believe in the existence of Britain, so that merely to have gone there testified to remarkable audacity.[25] A much later passage, in the anonymous panegyric to Constantius when newly returned from Britain, echoes Plutarch, but expressly ascribes to Caesar himself what is not to be found in the Commentaries:[26]

'(sc. Britannia) quam Caesar ille auctor vestri nominis cum Romanorum primus intrasset, alium se orbem terrarum scripsit reperisse, tantae magnitudinis arbitratus ut non circumfusa Oceano sed complexa ipsum Oceanum videretur ... prope ut hoc uno Caesar gloriari in illa expeditione debuerit quod navigasset Oceanum'.

Although similar, this is not a direct copy of the Plutarch passage, and indeed, unless the panegyrist had got his imperial references wrong, his source should be something that Caesar himself wrote, and which might also lie behind Plutarch. Here, Caesar's dispatches to the senate, which we know to have been extant at least till Suetonius' day, and information from which could have found its way into Livy, are a likely source.[27]

Finally, we come to two direct references to an *ephemeris*, the first in Symmachus' letter, the other in Servius' commentary on Virgil's *Aeneid* 11. 743.[28] Servius, who wrote around A.D. 500, tells us that once Caesar, in the thick of a battle, was being carried off by a Gaul on horseback when another Gaul, recognising him, called out his name in derision: but since the word Caesar, or some approximation to it, denoted 'release' in Gaulish, Caesar was able to escape his uncomfortable predicament. Certainly not in the Commentaries, though Servius claims to have found it 'in ephemeride sua ... ubi propriam commemorat felicitatem'. Here Nipperdey was moved to take up his knife again in exasperation: 'tota res a nugatore conficta est, qui, ut fidem ineptiis adderet, impudenter haec in ephemeride Caesaris legi affirmavit, hoc est, in commentariis'.[29] Certainly the tale is a strange one, and although Nipperdey did not endeavour to explain why the trifler should have made it up, that he could have done so with impunity is not out of the question, given the apparent scarcity of manuscripts of Caesar. Or had he read it somewhere else, and made a slip in attributing it to Caesar? Yet another possibility may present itself — that there was indeed extant an *ephemeris C. Caesaris*, but that it was not necessarily genuine.[30]

There is however a single, simple solution to a number of the problems: it is that an *ephemeris* by Caesar, distinct from the Commentaries, did exist. Its existence is not a necessary hypothesis, since all the passages mentioned can be explained away, though with varying degrees of conviction. Those who have a predilection for wielding Occam's razor will therefore be disposed to dismiss it. Those whose curiosity remains unsatisfied will wish to examine further the question of whether such a work is likely to have existed. And this leads us to a consideration of just how the Commentaries were composed, as well as to the question of their original title, temporarily abandoned a little while back.

As to the latter the early Latin *testimonia* are unanimous in referring to the works as *commentarii,* and without too much difficulty the common denominator *C. Iulii Caesaris commentarii rerum gestarum* (or *rerum suarum*) can be extracted, a title which avoids any embarrassing references to a Gallic, or, worse, a Civil, War. Whether Caesar himself gave them this (or any) precise title is less certain: at any rate, the manuscript tradition was subsequently to show a variation at odds with the clarity of the early references.[31]

The pedigree of the genre *commentarii* turns out to be largely Roman, though by Caesar's time crossed with a strain of Greek.[32] *Commentarii* to the Romans were originally the private records of a public man, such as were kept by *pontifices* and magistrates, but without the intention of publication. The dispatches which proconsuls or propraetors were expected to send to the senate were not *commentarii* but *litterae.*[33] By the last century B.C. the Roman *commentarii* had come close to overlapping with the Greek *hypomnemata,* which had a very extensive range of meanings, and the identification was firmly made by Cicero, who uses both words of the accounts he wrote of his consulship in Latin and Greek. From this time on, the words are used interchangeably, and sometimes denote a sketch or unfinished work, one of the meanings of *hypomnemata.* This may explain the comments of Cicero and Hirtius, who understood Caesar to be providing raw material for the historian (unless they simply meant that Caesar's writing did not fall into the regular genre of history).[34] Perhaps Caesar himself saw them as a finished, published version of true Roman *commentarii,* while others interpreted them through the mists of the Greek *hypomnemata.* Certainly, as we might expect, *hypomnemata* is the word which Strabo uses as the Greek equivalent of *commentarii.*[35]

It is not necessary here to discuss the vexed question of exactly when the *commentarii* on Gaul were written, for the point at issue is rather just what Caesar had in front of him to use as sources for the final version. That copies of his dispatches to the senate, together with the dispatches which his lieutenants delivered to him when reporting on their various activities, played an important part, is undisputed. But the stringing together of dispatches, with a little ethnographical padding, would scarcely have sufficed to produce the Commentaries as we have them, and the question arises whether Caesar kept by dictation something closer to a day-by-day account: such would be in the tradition of the Roman *commentarii,* but in Greek would very likely be called *ephemeris* or *ephemerides,* the word commonly used for court diaries and implying a day-by-day record.[36] The idea was again scornfully dismissed by Nipperdey:[37]

> '... ut, qui eum his (sc. epistolis) adiutum componere commentarios post quamvis longum tempus potuisse negabit, is sibi Claudio aliquo obliviosorem Caesarem fingat necesse sit'.

Possibly, though it may be noted that Cicero, despite dispatches and letters, was apparently unable to keep in mind what part of Gaul the Nervii inhabited.[38] But against Nipperdey it may be argued that the keeping of a more continuous record was customary. Moreover, though Caesar himself may have been able to recollect everything, can the same be said for Hirtius and the less able compiler of the African and Spanish Wars? The fact that these additions to Caesar keep closer to a day-by-day account suggests strongly that quite detailed dated records survived to be used, and indeed this is the opinion of many modern scholars.[39]

That some such detailed but relatively shapeless account did exist, and that it might be called *ephemerides* in Greek, is then likely enough, but this is a very different matter from showing that it was published separately. That Caesar could have found time and interest to supervise such a publication is highly doubtful, and there is strong negative evidence to hand in the silence of Suetonius, who mentions the publication of Caesar's dispatches and correspondence, as well as his non-military works.[40] That the material could have been employed by Balbus and Oppius as well as Hirtius is however more likely than not, so that they could have transmitted genuine material which Caesar preferred to omit. Might the word *ephemerides,* alternatively, have been used of the published dispatches? This would represent quite a departure from the original connotations, and in fact, when we meet the word used of Caesar's writings by Plutarch (references in Appian are less clear), the most natural interpretation is to take it as meaning the *commentarii.*[41] Originally existing distinctions between *commentarii, hypomnemata*, and *ephemerides* seem to have grown slighter with time, and the pairing of Caesar with Alexander may have helped the identification between first and last.[42]

What then of Symmachus' use of the word? Here, too, the most natural interpretation is that he means the Commentaries (become rare because not included in the normal school-room curriculum). And although a man who addressed a friend by saying 'hilarasti mihi diem litteris tuis'[43] might simply as a trick of style prefer a Greek word to a simple Latin one, there could be an additional reason for his choice. For in some of the manuscripts the title is given as *C. Caesaris Ephemeris* (or *Ephimeris*), and it may be that Symmachus' own manuscript was thus entitled even before it came into his hands.[44] That the manuscript tradition of Caesar's works was already divided and muddled over the titles and attribution is very likely. For Orosius, when he summarised the Gallic Wars for his history, was under the impression that he was consulting Suetonius, and indeed there is a numerous class of manuscripts in which Caesar's work is ascribed to that author, apparently from the belief that the same man had written Commentaries and Life, perhaps too because Caesar's use of the third person to refer to himself had proved misleading. And this leads to one last puzzling reference, which may yet have clues to give. Sidonius Apollinaris, writing to a friend Burgundio who was preparing to deliver a *Laus Caesaris* as a rhetorical exercise, comments on the difficulties:

> 'nam si omittantur quae de titulis dictatoris invicti scripta Patavinis sunt voluminibus, quis opera Suetonii, quis Iuventii Martialis historiam quisve ad extremum Balbi ephemeridem fando adaequaverit?'[45]

Now 'opera Suetonii' should mean Commentaries and Life, and suggests that Sidonius had seen a manuscript with the same type of title as had Orosius. But what of the last two items? Once again, Occam's razor can be wielded. Sidonius, it has been claimed, is quoting Symmachus, but from memory, with the result that Pliny has been replaced by an imaginary author Martialis (*fictus* again, whether *pudenter* or *impudenter*), while 'ephemeris Balbi' is a muddled reference to the 8th book of the Gallic Wars, where the preface is addressed to Balbus, though the work is always correctly ascribed to Hirtius in the manuscript tradition.[46] But there is a difficulty over this last point, for even granted that Sidonius did not have a copy of Caesar to hand, it is hard to see how he could attribute the main body of the work to Suetonius and an addition to Balbus.[47] Others have therefore seen a genuine reference to a Life of Caesar by Balbus, which could have survived, perhaps because its style was in keeping with the taste of subsequent ages: certainly the account of portents before Caesar's death, borrowed by Suetonius , shows that Balbus had a taste for the remarkable.[48] What then of Martialis? Dismissed as fiction by some, ascribed to the second century by others,[49] he might equally well be explained as the supposed author of some late fourth-century compilation in the tradition of the Scriptores Historiae Augustae.

To sum up, it *can* be argued that nothing by Caesar and nothing specifically on Caesar survived beyond the second century except the Commentaries and the Life by Suetonius, with Plutarch for those who could still read Greek (the passage from the panegyrist would on this view be a quotation from memory of Plutarch, with a wrong ascription to Caesar). Hardest to explain on this hypothesis, the main virtue of which is sweeping simplicity, is the passage in Servius, who does indeed then require to be dismissed as a 'nugator'. The simple explanation at the other end of the spectrum, the survival of a true *ephemeris* by Caesar, is on the whole unlikely. A middle way, admitting the survival of at least one work on Caesar, or even claiming to be by him, is perhaps the most satisfactory. One likely candidate is the account by Balbus, however entitled, while another is a later compilation perhaps belonging to the fourth century: Juventius Martialis could be identical with the latter, or something else again. The work by Balbus, incorporating material from Caesar's dispatches and unpublished reports, could explain Polyaenus as well as the panegyrist, while on any of these hypotheses the serious-minded Servius was guilty only of a minor misattribution.

The argument has carried us on a circuitous voyage, leaving Protadius and his self-appointed task for a time out of view. We are now free to return to him, equipped with his Livy and, most probably, Caesar's Commentaries (probably not Pliny, since we hear no more of him), and to speculate on what sort of history he had in mind. Whether he finished it is unknown: the following year saw him back at court in Milan, with less leisure for the task.

Now Protadius was one of a large group of Gauls who, in the late years of the fourth century, enjoyed distinguished public careers but nevertheless remained faithful to their Gaulish origin.[50] Protadius' own interest in Gaul is further illustrated by the nature of his proposed undertaking. He was, moreover, excellently situated to consult source material long unavailable to us, notably in the form of the provincial archives. Is there any chance that he might have done this, so breaking out of the traditional mould and attempting to bridge the gap between the beginnings of Roman Gaul and his own day? Could the stirrings of Gaulish feeling which we glimpse, intermittently, in Ausonius, when he writes of the cities, countryside, and rivers of his homeland, or describes the defeat of Treveran forces near Bingen as a Gallic Cannae,[51] have led to some significant new departure in Protadius? Not many years later, a new outlook was to manifest itself, though not exactly in these directions. It occurs in the *Histories* of Orosius when, after recounting Caesar's campaigns, he conjures up a vision of a personified Gaul, pale, worn and distraught from the long fever of fighting, and into her mouth puts words which end with the great accusation, 'ita me Romani inclinaverunt ut nec ad Gothos surgam'.[52] Although inspired by a desire to show the darker side of the old pagan heroes rather than by any deep sympathy for the lot of Roman provincials, and following distantly in the tradition of Tacitus' famous 'ubi sollitudinem faciunt, pacem appellant', the speech and epigram have yet been specifically moulded to fit a new situation.

There is, however, little to suggest that Protadius would have moved in any of these directions. We note the absence of Tacitus from the list, and wonder whether he thought of consulting that other Gaul who wrote on Gaul, Pompeius Trogus: if a full text was not readily available, the epitome by Justin should have been.[53] More likely, Protadius merely planned a literary exercise, a compilation or epitome (doubtless tricked out with a little Gaulish rhetoric) from restricted sources only, perhaps dealing only with the conquest, and not so far in spirit from the rhetorical *thema* of Sidonius' friend Burgundio. Just as Ausonius or Sidonius, when writing of their villas, omit much of the information we would nowadays like to have,[54] so it probably never crossed Protadius' mind that much of the history of Gaul was to be found written not in ink but in much harder materials such as the stones and mortar of the buildings around him, or in such fleeting and undignified affairs as the daily life of his own slaves and estate workers. If it has been often, and rightly, said that we must treat Late Antiquity as a period worthy of respect in its own right, the terms on which we have to accept many of its leading figures include their own ardent desire to identify themselves with a bygone age.[55] Alas, Protadius might well have fallen into the trap which Cicero considered sane men would avoid when he wrote of Caesar's *commentarii:*

> 'sed dum voluit alios habere parata, unde sumerent, qui vellent scribere historiam, ineptis gratum fortasse fecit, qui volent illa calamistris inurere: sanos quidem homines a scribendo deterruit'.[56]

It has been suggested that the invasions of 406–7, the Visigothic settlement ten years later, and the intervening taking of Rome by Alaric might have changed Protadius' view of past history, and of the relationship between his two homelands, Gaul and Rome.[57] But certainly, we look in vain for any such major re-adjustment in Rutilius Namatianus, who met Protadius in 417, and who, while lamenting the fate of Gaulish cities and countryside, nevertheless continued to idealise eternal Rome;[58] nor, despite the harshness of the times, do we really find it in Paulinus of Pella, Sidonius, or even Salvian. The total and persistent acceptance of Rome as the *communis patria* is indeed a remarkable phenomenon, while the insistence on continuity to the point of identification with the past obscured a true appreciation of either past or present. If any contrary inclinations were felt, they were considered either incapable or unworthy of expression.

Attitudes of the modern historian to the past and to his sources have been moulded in manifold ways by the intervening ages, by such phenomena as the emergence of the European nation-state and most recently by our own contemporary age with its emphasis on anti-heroes and de-colonialisation. In addition, the last century or so has seen the blossoming of many separate yet interconnected scholarly disciplines — archaeology both classical and prehistoric, numismatics and epigraphy, as well as more traditional studies — all of them giving the would-be historian of Gaul a chance to reconstruct events which would once have been considered unknowable, and perhaps best left so. Moreover, whether consciously or not, the modern student tends to follow the precepts of R. G. Collingwood, reconstructing the past by seeking in the evidence answers to specific questions, frequently questions such as a previous generation would not have thought to ask. We therefore contemplate Protadius across a deep gulf, yet, even as we seek to bridge it, not without some sympathy, let it be hoped, arising from common interests and goals.

## Notes

[1] (Symm.,) *Ep.* 4. 18, ed. O. Seeck (Berlin 1883, = *MGH* Auct. Antiq. 6. 1). I follow Seeck's dating.

[2] On the family, *Ep.* ed. O. Seeck, intro. pp. cxli—cxliii; see also under Minervius, Florentinus, Protadius in K. F. Stroheker, *Der senatorische Adel im spätantiken Gallien,* Tübingen 1948, and A. H. M. Jones, J. R. Martindale, J. Morris, *The Prosopography of the Later Roman Empire,* vol. 1, Cambridge 1971.

[3] *Ep.* 4. 18, 4. 32 and cf. 4. 50.

[4] *Ep.* 4. 36.

[5] *Ep.* 4. 30. there is a problem over the dating, which Seeck gives variously as 495 (intro. pp. lxiv, cxliv) and 496. For the suggestion that *civica religio* means attendance at the court, J. F. Matthews, 'Gallic Supporters of Theodosius', *Lat.* vol. 30, 1971, p. 1096. Regardless of the actual date of the transference of the prefecture from Trier to Arles — after 400 according to E. Stein, *Hist. du Bas-Emp.* vol. 1, 1959, p. 248, about 395 J.-R. Palanque, 'La date du transfert de la préfecture des Gaules de Trèves à Arles' *REA* vol. 36, 1934, pp. 359—364 — *Ep.* 4. 28 may be taken as reinforcing Seeck's idea of a Treveran origin, since Protadius is still in the north after the court has left.

[6] H. Bloch in *Paganism and Christianity in the Fourth Century,* ed. A. Momigliano, Oxford 1963, pp. 215—216.

[7] Tac., *Ann.* 15. 53; *Hist.* 3. 28.

[8] *C. Iulii Caesaris Commentarii,* ed. C. Nipperdey, Leipzig 1847, praef. 5—8.

[9] Frontin. *Strat.* 1. 12. 2, Suet., *Div. Iul.* 59, Dio 41. 24. 2.

[10] Frontin., *Strat.* 2. 3. 18. Archaeology knows most of funerary vehicles: recently P. Harbison, 'The Chariot of Celtic Funerary Tradition', in *Marburger Beiträge zur Archäologie der Kelten, Festschrift W. Dehn,* ed. O.-H. Frey, Bonn 1969, pp. 34—58.

[11] Mela 6. 52, Statius *Silv.* 17. 417.

[12] Frontin. *Strat.* 2. 13. 11.

[13] Hirtius, *BG* 8. 48. 8–9: see for instance S. S. Frere, *Britannia,* London 1967, p. 40.

[14] Frontin. *Strat.* 3. 14. 1, Dio 43. 33–34, *Bell. Hisp.* 18–19. Admittedly, these incidents belong to the period covered by the supplements.

[15] Dio 40. 41. 1.

[16] Polyaen. 8. 23. 10, (Caes.) *BG* 7. 45; Polyaen. 8. 23. 11, *BG* 7. 80–82, 87–88; Polyaen, 8. 23. 7, *BG* 5. 49–51.

[17] See W. W. Tarn in *OCD* and F. Lammert (a more positive view) in *RE* vol. 21, 1951, cols 1432–1436.

[18] *C. Iulii Caesaris commentarii rerum gestarum* vol. 1, *Bellum Gallicum,* ed. O. Seel, Leipzig 1968, p. 321.

[19] Polyaen. 8. 23. 5, *BG* 5. 18.

[20] Dio 50. 21. 2.

[21] *BG* ed. Seel, p. 333, following Klotz.

[22] See Lammert, *RE* vol. 21, col. 1434; E. A. Sydenham, *The Coinage of the Roman Republic,* London 1952, p. 167, and, for a later dating, M. H. Crawford, *Roman Republican Coin Hoards,* London 1969, table 14.

[23] Suet., *Nero* 2; C. E. Stevens, 'Julius Caesar's Elephant' *History Today* vol. 9, 1959, pp. 626–627.

[24] Stevens (loc. cit.) supposed it might.

[25] *BG* 4. 38. 5; Plut., *Caes.* 23. 2, *Cato Min.* 51. 1.

[26] *Paneg.* 8 (5) 11 (OCT) = 4 (8) 11 (Budé).

[27] As suggested by C. E. Stevens, '55 B.C. and 54 B.C.' *Antiquity* vol. 21, 1947, p. 5 n. 6, listing other passages emphasising Ocean, including *ILS* 216.

[28] *Servii in Vergilii carmina commentarii 2,* ed. G. Thilo, Leipzig and Berlin 1923, p. 561, where the passage is attributed to the original Servius.

[29] See above, n. 8, and note the editorial commonplace 'impudenter'.

[30] R. Syme, *Ammianus and the Historia Augusta,* Oxford 1968 and *Emperors and Biography,* Oxford 1971.

[31] *Testimonia* and MS titles conveniently collected in *BG* ed. Seel, intro. pp. cxiv–cxxii.

[32] Major contributions are U. Knoche, 'Caesar's Commentarii, ihr Gegenstand und ihre Absicht' *Gymnasium* vol. 58, 1951, pp. 139–160 and F. Bömer, 'Der Commentarius' *Herm.* vol. 81, 1953, pp. 210–250. Oppermann's less convincing views are now briefly re-stated in *Caesar,* ed. D. Rasmussen, Darmstadt 1967 (= *Wege der Forschung* 63), pp. 499ff.

[33] For *litterae* = dispatches, *BG* 2. 55. 4; 4. 38. 5, and cf. 7. 90; Cic. *in Pis*. 16. 38, *ad Fam*. 15. 1. 1 and 2; 15. 3. 2.

[34] For Cicero's accounts of his consulship, Cic., *ad Att*. 1. 19. 10; 1. 20. 6; 2. 1. 1. For *commentarii* = sketch, Cic., *Brut*. 164, cf. Bömer, *Hermes* vol. 81, 1953, p. 216 ff. For comments on Caesar, Cic., *Brut*. 262, Hirtius, *BG* 8, *praef*. 4–7.

[35] Strabo 4. p. 177.

[36] On the use of dispatches, besides Knoche and Bömer (above n. 32), E. Norden, *Die germanische Urgeschichte in Tacitus' Germania*, repr. Darmstadt 1971, p. 87 ff.; M. Gelzer, *Kleine Schriften* vol. 2, Wiesbaden 1963, p. 312ff.; M. Rambaud, *L'Art de la déformation historique dans les commentaires de César*[2], Paris 1966, pp. 7–96. On *ephemerides*, Kaerst, *RE* vol. 5, cols 2749–2753. For Caesar's energy, Fronto, *de bell. Parth*. 9.

[37] See above n. 8.

[38] Cic., *ad Q. fr*. 3. 8. 2.

[39] Thus Knoche speaks of 'Amtsbuch', Bömer of 'Kriegstagebuch' or more generally 'Unterlage', Rambaud of 'dossier' or 'journaux de marche', though there may be a danger here of being misled by modern parallels: *contra*, Schanz-Hosius vol. 1[4], 1927, p. 337.

[40] Suet., *Div. Jul*. 56, cf. Gell. 17. 9. 1.

[41] App., *BC*. 1. 90, Plut., *Caes*. 22. 2. For the suggestion that *ephemerides* could mean dispatches, S. Reinach, 'Les communiqués de César' *Rev. Phil*. vol. 39, 1915, pp. 29–49, cf. C. E. Stevens, *Lat*. vol. 11, 1952, p. 4.

[42] *Ephemerides* frequently but not invariably seem to mean something rather more trivial, cf. the *Ephemeris id est totius diei negotium* of Ausonius, but also *ILS* 1575 (*proc. ab ephemeride*).

[43] *Ep*. 4. 20.

[44] See above n. 31. also F. W. Kelsey, 'The Title of Caesar's Work' *TAPA* vol. 36, 1905, pp. 211–238. Symmachus himself did not borrow from Caesar; J. A. McGeachy, *Q. Aurelius Symmachus and the Senatorial Aristocracy of the West*, diss. Chicago 1942, p. 167.

[45] Oros. 6. 7, Sid., *Ep*. 9. 4. One further reference which should be added is Arator, *Ep. ad Parthenium* 38–40 (Migne *PL* vol. 68, p. 250; H. J. Arntz in *PL* took this as meaning a private diary by Caesar.

[46] *BG* ed. Seel., intro. p. cxii; Schanz-Hosius vol. 1[4], 1927, p. 350, Teuffel vol. 1[6], 1965, p. 448.

[47] Though muddles of mistaken identity certainly could occur; cf. Orosius' belief that Sallust wrote on Domitian, Oros. 7. 10.

[48] Suet., *Div. Iul.* 81; Münzer, *RE* vol. 4, col. 1268, arguing that it would be the elder Balbus rather than the younger.

[49] Schanz-Hosius vol. 3,[3] 1922, p. 77, Teuffel vol. 3[6], 1965, pp. 61—62.

[50] Stroheker (above, n.2) and Matthews, *Lat.* vol. 30, 1971, pp. 1097—1098.

[51] Auson., *Mosella* 3.

[52] Oros. 6. 12.

[53] For the use of Justin, see A. Klotz, *RE* vol. 21, cols 2311—2312.

[54] Auson., *de Herediolo* (3. 1 ed. Peiper), Sid. *Ep.* 2. 2, and elsewhere.

[55] *Inter alios* by Gelzer, *Kleine Schriften* vol. 2, pp. 387—400, and, with special reference to Symmachus' circle, McGeachy, op. cit. (n. 44), pp. 153—191. A good example in miniature of Symmachus' attitudes is his lifting of Scipio's letter to Jugurtha from Sallust to apply it verbatim to Florentinus; *Ep.* 4. 24.

[56] Cic., *Brut.* 261.

[57] Matthews, *Lat.* vol. 30, 1971, p. 1097.

[58] Rutil. Nam., *de Reditu Suo*, especially 47 ff., and, on Protadius, 543—558. Acceptance of Rome had had a long history in Gaul; on lack of bitterness in Trogus' family, O. Seel, *Eine römische Weltgeschichte,* Nuremberg, 1972, p. 88 ff.

E. M. Wightman,
History Department,
McMaster University,
Hamilton,
Ontario,

# 8

# Octavian and Eclogue 1

Horace has told us in *Sat.* 1.5 how he was introduced to
Maecenas by Virgil, probably in the spring of 38 B.C. But he
does not tell us how he came to know Virgil, nor allude to the
circumstances and date of that even more momentous event,
the first meetings of Virgil himself with Maecenas, and with
Octavian. The writer of the *Culex* seems to address the future
Augustus as 'Octavius' and as 'puer', as if before his adoption by
Julius Caesar's will, in 45 B.C. or earlier. But the ancient *Lives*
and commentaries have it that Virgil was recommended to
Octavian, at the time of the confiscations of land for the
veterans in 41 B.C., by Pollio or Cornelius Gallus, and so had his
estate exempted or at least was compensated for its loss.
*E[clogue]* 1 was taken as an expression of thanks for this
restoration to the unnamed 'young man' who figures in the very
centre of the poem, though Servius was aware that the poem
was also an attack on Octavian[1]. This identification has become
accepted almost universally in modern times also. Yet, if Virgil
celebrated Octavian in 41–40 B.C., it was not until 38 that he
seems to have become known to Maecenas, shortly before he
introduced Horace, presumably when the *Eclogues* were published under his name, and Horace was introduced because
he had written poems that had influenced the *Eclogues*.
Vollmer[2] in 1909 argued from *G[eorgics]* 2. 198–9 that Virgil
lost his estate once and for all. The lines are often quoted as
proof only of Mantua's general loss, while Virgil himself was
exempted or restored or compensated. But the reference to
swans looks back to *E*9. 27–9, where Virgil himself (or more
strictly speaking Menalcas) is the swan of Mantua. Virgil

therefore includes himself among the victims at Mantua, and *G*3. 10ff. confirm this: he may return eventually to Mantua but only when he is celebrated as an epic poet. I doubt if he could have otherwise written *G*1. 507 either. *Catalepton* 8 shows that Siro's villa near Naples was Virgil's home, and there is every reason to believe that he lived there until his death, and prepared his tomb there, not at Mantua. If then he so casually informs us of his loss, it must be because he did not want it to be thought that he had been 'converted' to Octavian, and was promising him the future epic, by the restoration of the estate, but in spite of its loss. Horace, *Ep.* 2.1.247, mentions gifts made by Augustus to Virgil, but no restoration or compensation at Mantua. Perhaps already in 30 B.C. the young man of *E*1 was being identified with Octavian (and *G*1. 500 encouraged this) because the precise historical setting was by then obscured. Virgil's position (or his father's) is expressed, and with much more feeling, by Meliboeus; yet a little later in *E*6 Virgil makes Apollo address him as Tityrus, as though he were the old slave who saw Rome for the first time in 41 B.C. In what sense then are they, Meliboeus and Tityrus, with Menalcas, Moeris, and Lycidas in *E*9 masks for Virgil himself?

Our only hope is to date the *Eclogues* as precisely as possible and reconstruct their immediate setting with the help of the historical evidence, which is ample and detailed enough, rejecting completely as suspect what the ancient commentaries assert. The authors of the ancient *Lives* and commentaries did not trouble to read the *Histories* of Pollio, but it seems that we can perhaps in the form that our fullest source, Appian, *Bellum Civile,* has transmitted them to us,[3] and it is only through Pollio that we can get at Virgil's probable attitude in those years, since he regarded himself as under Pollio's patronage until the end of 39 B.C. It should not now be necessary to argue that there was no board of 'triumviri agris dividundis',[4] and that Pollio and Gallus had nothing to do with the plantation of veterans.[5]

Very different views have been held of the date of the first contact of Pollio and Virgil, and of Pollio's suggestion that Virgil should try Theocritean pastoral. But it seems likely that they met before Virgil abandoned all thought of a political career and retired from Rome to sit at the feet of the Epicurean philosopher Siro near Naples, according to *Catalepton* 5, and that must have been before the outbreak of the civil war in 49 B.C. anyhow precluded such a career.[6] Pollio may well in these years before 49 have kept Catullus' circle of poets together and recruited promising younger men, but the civil war broke up such circles, and Pollio was absent from Italy until 45. *Catalepton* 8, genuine like 5, shows Virgil in 41 still at Naples, having now inherited Siro's villa and made it his home. His health was not robust, and once he discovered the charms and climate of South Italy, he is unlikely to have returned except briefly in spring or autumn to the icy damp of the Po valley in winter or its humid heat in summer. Pollio was governor of Gallia Cisalpina for Antony in 42–40, but those hazardous and agitated years can hardly have been opportune for literary studies. If then *E*8. 11–12 'accipe iussis / carmina coepta tuis' refer to Pollio's suggestion of pastoral to Virgil, the only plausible date is the year of his praetorship in 45 B.C. after his campaigns in Spain and before his return there as pro-praetor. He could then have assembled what remained of the new poets' and elicited one of Virgil's rare visits to Rome, to reprove him for his poetic silence, if the Muses had not revisited him even 'pudenter et raro'. To suggest 45 B.C. is to reject the scholiasts' period of three years for the *Eclogues,* beginning when Virgil was twenty-eight (in 42 B.C.). But the three years may well be only an inference from the three datable poems, 9, 4, and 8, 41–39 B.C. But if 2, 3, and 5 (and 1 and 7) are earlier than *E*9 they must be compressed into the previous or the same year, and such a burst of production seems unlikely. The reference to the 'frigora Rheni' in *E*10. 47 suggests the winter of 39–8 or of 38–7, when Agrippa crossed the Rhine, Dio 48. 49. 3 before or after his defeat of the Aquitanians, App. *BC* 5. 386. The *Eclogues* can be spaced out over eight years, with a gradual acceleration that leads on to the *Georgics* at a rate of about one line a day, and the *Aeneid* much faster.

The chronological order of the *Eclogues* has been much discussed.[7] I adopt the order 27359146810. The dates then become 2 and 7 in 45; 3 in 43, and sent to Pollio in Spain (44 after 15 March was a bad year, see *G*1. 466ff.); 5 in 42, the year of the formal deification of Julius Caesar, of which 5 is a criticism, putting up a rival candidate; 9 in 41 when Virgil's father was evicted and took refuge with him in Siro's villa, *Catalepton* 8, before the outbreak of the Perusine war; 1 in mid 40, replying to Horace, *Epode* 16, which, as we shall see, alludes to the Parthian advance into Asia Minor and Syria in the spring of 40, or even earlier; 4 in October 40 when Pollio was able to assume his promised consulship after the peace of Brundisium; 6 in early 39 in reaction to the ecstatic hope in *E*4. 53–9 of some day becoming a great epic poet, but itself more than a pastoral and suggesting a Callimachean didactic poem, an 'aition', 'origo', to be written by Virgil's exact contemporary, Gallus; 8 in October 39 when Pollio was expected in Rome for his triumph on 25 October 39 (if we reject, as we shall, Bowersock's and Clausen's reference of the lines 6–13 to Octavian in 35 B.C.); 10 in 38 or 37, when Gallus failed to write a poem on his desertion by Lycoris (and presumably began the military career under Octavian which ended in the governorship of Egypt and suicide); Virgil stepped in with a poem for him, transposing elegy into pastoral in order to bid a second farewell to pastoral, though carrying with him as inescapable their common theme, tragic love, which *E*8 had not exhausted. But the first nine *Eclogues* had been published, in late 39 or early 38, under his name, with *E*8 as the last. Before he could see his way to adopt for himself what he had suggested for Gallus, as the *Georgics*, there was a considerable pause (as in the later transition from the *Georgics* to the *Aeneid*, 30/29 to 26 B.C.), in which Virgil was won over by Maecenas.

But if Maecenas, and Octavian, got hold of Virgil, and through him of Horace only on the publication of the nine *Eclogues,* the poems separately and anonymously must have been in circulation and perhaps widely popular and at once performed as mimes on the stage. The anecdote in Servius on *E*6. 11 that Cicero was present at a performance by Lycoris and expressed his astonished admiration in the words 'magnae spes altera Romae', later used by Virgil in *A*[*eneid*] 12. 168, is a malicious invention (by Pollio perhaps?), but the *Eclogues* were so performed, and it was they, not the *Georgics* or *Aeneid,* which won the acclaim of which Tacitus speaks in the *Dialogus.* Their authorship was of course known to a circle of friends to whom Virgil or Pollio (his 'lector', *E*3. 85) read them, but they would get out to a wider public, especially when topical. Horace's *Epodes* were not 'published' until 30 B.C. or so, but, some of them were known to Maecenas before he invited Virgil to produce the unknown author. The *Eclogues* can be dated largely because of Virgil's habit of quoting his own earlier poems, in order to claim them and yet remain anonymous. There was indeed no need to conceal the authorship of timeless, purely pastoral, poems such as *E*2 and 7. If in *E*3 Virgil attacks Bavius and Maevius, it was as well to indicate that he had the support of Pollio; and in *E*5, if it makes Daphnis, not Julius Caesar, a god, he claims *E*3 and so implicitly the support of

Pollio. But *E*9 and 1 are overtly political and if, as I shall argue, attacks on Octavian, dangerous. Pollio refrained from writing against the man who could proscribe; Virgil himself refers to *E*1 in the last line of *G*4 as produced by him 'audax iuventa', and Horace too speaks of his boldness in his earliest poems, 'paupertas impulit *audax* / ut versus facerem', *Ep.* 2.2. 51—2. He can have meant only *Epodes* 7 and 16, which are undoubtedly attacks on the Triumvirs. The boldness is, I suggest, political rather than literary in Virgil also.

The game of echoing earlier poems takes a new turn when another poet joins in and caps his predecessor's verse by either heightening or contradicting it. This raises the great question whether *E*4 precedes *Epode* 16 or the other way round.[8] But if *E*1 is earlier than *E*4, the whole controversy can be circumvented, since Virgil's lines *E*1. 70—1 beginning with the words 'impius' and 'barbarus' are a more complex idea, a heightening and therefore echo of *Epode* 16. 9 and 11, successive hexameters, beginning 'impia' and 'barbarus'. In Horace the barbarian horseman is generally accepted as meaning the Parthians, whereas Virgil's barbarian is the Roman soldiery,[9] the veterans who are displacing the real Roman citizens. It has also been argued that the 'contagia' are better placed in Horace, 61 than in *E*1. 50.[10] Sallust, *Hist.* 1, has been put forward as Horace's source for the 'beata arva, divitesque insulas', 41—2,[11] and dated 37—6 or even 35 B.C. But Horace could have used Sallust's source, and anyhow Sertorius, Spartacus, 5, and the Allobroges, 6, were surely notorious.

But the historical arguments for an early date, Spring 40, of *Epode* 16 are more important.[12] The Parthians, referred to as such in *Epode* 7. 9, are to be recognised in the 'eques' of *Epode* 16. 12. The danger that they constituted for the Roman East was known long before and after, but in 40 B.C., or even in late 41, under Pacorus, the King's son, and Quintus Labienus, who had been sent by Brutus and Cassius to the Parthian court as ambassador, they conquered Syria and swept across Asia Minor as far as Cilicia and Ionia, Lydia and Asia.[13] Horace's tone of urgency, even desperation, fits 40, and would have been out of place after 39, and the boldness of his outburst would have sunk by 38 to very little. Moreover he attributes his boldness to his poverty. His acquisition of a post in the quaestors' office, as 'scriba', cannot be dated precisely, but Fraenkel says 'probably in 41 B.C.',[14] suggesting that to begin with the post must have kept Horace too busy to write *Epode* 16, and that only later could he treat it as a sinecure, as when he went on the journey to Brundisium. But before he obtained the post Horace was poor and otherwise unoccupied, and anyhow how could he have bought ('comparavit') the post, as Suetonius says? When the poem came into Virgil's hands, he surely sought out its author, and Virgil's friends, e.g. Alfenus Varus, were in a position to help, when Virgil himself could not. Varus, as ex-praetor, was a senator and so exempt from confiscation, Dio 48. 8. 5. Under the influence of *Epode* 16 Virgil, when it seemed that the Perusine war would lead to war with Marcus Antonius, looked back on the evictions and sharpened the point of *E*9, but soon the Peace of Brundisium enabled him to reply with new confidence in *E*4 to the *Epode* and to Catullus' Song of the Fates. *E*4 is addressed to Pollio, when at last he could assume his promised consulship, ten months late, and surely celebrates the marriage of Antonius to Octavia, and for Virgil as for Pollio Antonius, a second Achilles, is greater and more important than Octavian.

But was he still an adherent of Pollio, sharing his view of events in late 39 B.C.? It has been generally accepted that the lines 6–13 of *E*8 refer to Pollio and his triumph over the Parthini in Macedonia to be celebrated on 25 October. But the lines have recently come under attack, as to their authenticity by Peter Levi,[15] and as to their reference to Pollio by Bowersock (followed by Clausen),[16] who argues for Octavian (as assumed by Servius) and a date in 35 B.C., when he campaigned in Illyria. Octavian was hailed as god and saviour in Italy only after the defeat of Sextus Pompeius in 36 B.C.

As they stand now, the lines are incomplete and out of place, but they can be defended as the remains of the first edition of the *Eclogues,* without *E*10. There must, however, have been one or two lines at the beginning, naming the recipient, and the whole passage must have stood at the head of the poem. Did Virgil himself truncate them and slip them in to interrupt the poem or did Pollio preserve them for a later editor or scholiast to insert them? The formula, regularly reserved for a god or a sovereign, was put to a new use by Virgil. He does not mean to put Pollio's name first and last in this *Eclogue,* but refers to his first and last *Eclogues,* as is clear from the explanation 'accipe iussis / carmina coepta tuis'.

Levi alludes to the difficulty of Pollio's 'unverifiable' journey along the coast of Illyria past the mouth of the Timavus, on which Bowersock has seized. His scepticism about the ancient

*Lives* and scholiasts allows him (and me) a new dating, not restricted to three years and Virgil's twenty-eighth year. The Parthini, over whom Pollio triumphed, lived in Macedonia, a province of Antony's, of which, it is usually assumed, Pollio was pro-consular governor for 39 B.C. He sailed from Brundisium, App. *BC* 5. 272–6; Dio 48.41.7; one would expect him to return there. So what was he doing over 400 miles away from the Parthini in Octavian's province? Returning to Italy for Virgil in Mantua? But what if Virgil were in Naples? Pollio may have been given a special commission by both triumvirs to operate against rebels whether in Macedonia or Illyria. He resigned the consulship before the end of the year and was back in Rome by the following October; this does not look like the annual tenure of a province. Octavian may have stipulated that Pollio's legions were to return to Gallia Cisalpina, not to central Italy, in the general rearrangement of legions between him and Antonius. There may have been trouble in Istria also.[17] After the fall of Perusia Pollio had retreated to Ravenna, App., *BC* 5. 50, and beyond to Altinum, Velleius 2.76.2, and held Venetia for Antonius. It is easier to suppose that Virgil knew of Pollio's movements than that he inserted an apostrophe much later than the rest of the *Eclogues,* when he was engaged on the *Georgics,* and that an apostrophe to Octavian was beheaded and displaced. The *Eclogues* were surely begun (whether in 45 or 42 B.C.) before Virgil had come into contact with Octavian, at Pollio's suggestion. The apostrophe then must be accepted as of Pollio and of October 39.

But Clausen, accepting Bowersock's conclusions about *E*8, dates *E*1 also to the year 35 because, if it is dated to the year 40, 'there is no way of accounting for the style and tone of the references to Octavian'. Certainly in spring 40 a reference in *E*1 to Octavian is very unexpected, but why should he not be named explicitly in 35? Clausen's explanation that his name in the most Roman of all the *Eclogues* would have offended Roman sensibility, whereas the entirely Greek context of *G*1, 24–31 excuses the one Roman feature, the name Caesar, is unconvincing. The name of Caesar occurs in *E*9. It seems easier to deny the identification of the 'iuvenis' in *E*1 with Octavian than to disrupt the whole chronology of the *Eclogues* and of Virgil's development.

'Pollio was no friend of Octavian' at this time, indeed they were virtually at war, their armies confronting each other, precisely in the period to which *E*9 and 1 are assigned. Octavian wrote obscene epigrams against Pollio, who disdained to reply in kind, Macrobius 2.4.21. Could Virgil praise Octavian as a god and preserver of his poetical vocation in *E*1 and then write *E*4 and *E*8 for Pollio? Some scholars have spoken of Pollio writing a letter to recommend Virgil to Octavian, or of Pollio as a member of Maecenas' circle. Pollio of course was a Caesarian of a kind. In 49 B.C. he took Julius Caesar's side as a personal friend, assuredly not approving all of his behaviour and policies. *E*5 has been taken as the first evidence of Virgil's adherence to the Caesars. The official deification of Julius Caesar is, I would concede, alluded to, but by proposing a better candidate, the archetypal poet who can enchant even inanimate nature. This figure is, more often even in the *Eclogues*, celebrated by Virgil as Orpheus and the importance of the idea for Virgil as a poet is clear. Pollio at least is unlikely to have approved of the unrepublican deification of Julius. Antonius had checked Octavian's appeal to the populace in demanding special honours for Julius, App., *BC* 3. 28 — a passage remarkable for its failure to mention the famous comet that appeared during the games that Octavian offered in July 44 in honour of Julius.

But, it will be said, surely in *E*9. 46—50 there is unequivocal evidence of Virgil's adherence to Octavian? For, if Julius' apotheosis is meant in the first place, Octavian as 'divi filius' cannot be excluded. In themselves the verses express an unambiguous and emphatic confidence. But their setting in the poem shows that this confidence was unfounded and that the hopes have been belied; 'quod nunquam veriti sumus', 3, has occurred. We do know from the great passage in *G*1. 463—514 what he thought of the consequences of Julius' murder, and there, 488, he mentions comets as portents of woe. Virgil can scarcely have thought of Julius' deification as altering his picture of Italy. If so, by Caesar in *E*9 he meant Octavian, and he may well have been aware of Octavian's private interpretation of the comet. Servius says that Octavian insisted on the comet as the soul of his father and put a star on Julius' statues; 'but some believed it to belong to the glorification of the young Caesar', and concludes that 'the lines are written in honour of Augustus', mentioning Augustus' memoirs of his life. But Pliny, *NH* 2.93—4, too seldom quoted by the commentators, gives us an invaluable quotation from the *Memoirs*: the populace, *vulgus*, believed it to be Julius' soul taken to heaven. But Pliny adds, 'haec ille (Octavian) in publicum: interiore gaudio sibi illum natum seque in eo nasci interpretatus est, et si verum fatemur, salutare id terris fuit': the comet signifies the descent of divinity into Octavian. Cicero seems to have known what was in Octavian's mind at the time, *ad Att.* 16.15.3, after 11 November 44, when he reports on Octavian's speech to the people (App., *BC* 3.41; Dio 45.12.4). If Virgil suspected Octavian's designs, as Pollio probably did (if he is Appian's source, he disdained to mention the comet, contrast Dio 45.7.1), the irony in the context of *E*9. 46–51 is all the sharper, and in his next poem Virgil put this irony explicitly into the very words of Menalcas which he quoted: 'Insere, Daphni, piros' becomes 'Insere nunc, Meliboee, piros'. If there is any confidence in *E*9, it is not due to the comet, but to the unexplained belief in Menalcas' return, 55, 67. Virgil felt that as poet he had handled and overcome the evictions.

But in *E*1 under the influence of Horace's *Epode* 16, he sharpens the attack. The displaced landowner-poet is not absent, but brought on the scene in Meliboeus, so much more like Virgil in economic status and sensibility than Tityrus.

The status of Moeris in *E*9 and of Tityrus in *E*1 has been much discussed. A seldom quoted passage from a historian, Dio 48.6.3–7.2, can help: Octavian confiscated estates complete with their slaves and equipment. Moeris is a slave who has gone with the estate; he represents the whole 'familia' and so his master is called 'vester', 10. Likewise Tityrus is in danger of being included with the estate, and is addressed in the plural, 'pueri', 45, probably as 'vilicus' or manager of the estate and 'familia'. But his position is peculiar in that he does not wait for his master's visit (usually at harvest time), but goes up to Rome (40, 'neque servitio alibi exire licebat') and is absent for many days.[18] If so, he must be working on some kind of 'ager publicus', perhaps confiscated in the proscriptions, which is under a Roman magistrate, not a master, absentee or resident. We do not know to whom he would be responsible, neither does he, as he speaks of several 'praesentis . . . divos', 41, and this gives a natural meaning to 'primus', 44. Tityrus, we may suppose, goes first to the finance office of the quaestors, and when they decline to act against the Triumvir, he tries the legal officer, 'praetor urbanus', with the same result. And next? we are asked to believe that the Triumvir sabotaged his own decree for an old slave, at least on the literal level, on which alone an allegory can be founded. But the consul, Lucius Antonius, could have done such a thing; he alone received suppliants, App., *BC* 5. 74, and, after the arbitration forced on him and

Octavian by the soldiers at Teanum in summer 41, App., *BC* 5. 79, he was to exercise his regular powers without hindrance by the Triumvirs, or he could have acted independently at an earlier stage, for instance when Octavian was absent from Rome on one of his numerous expeditions to plant veterans himself. Virgil has taken an actual event, perhaps a notorious provocation of Octavian by Lucius, as the basis of his poem; he alludes to it just enough for immediate contemporaries to understand. Likewise the 'responsum' of the 'iuvenis' has been found difficult, because there is no mention of emancipation. But it is taken for granted as implied in the concession of the slaves' 'peculium', not in the gift of the whole estate that is confiscated, since what Meliboeus describes in 46–50 is poor little 'rura' or 'ager relictus et extra clusus', cf. *G* 4. 127–9, too small to be liable to confiscation, Dio 48.8.5, being less than a veteran's allotment, too poor to be included by the surveyors in the sort of land that Meliboeus is forced to leave. If the 'iuvenis' were Octavian, how could Meliboeus fail to exclaim 'so your god is my devil!'. But he knew who championed the evicted land-owners and so accepts Tityrus' description without comment.

To a constitutionalist and traditionalist, even if, like Pollio, he well understood that after Philippi the restoration of the Republic was a vain hope, App., *BC* 4.138, who could better represent Rome, twice mentioned in *E* 1.19 and 26, than the consul? *E* 4 alludes in mythological terms to the Triumvir Antonius, but twice speaks of the consul, 5 and 11. Public opinion, not only the dispossessed, was on the side of Lucius Antonius, App., *BC* 5. 106. Appian speaks of the Italians' support of him, and Syme goes so far as to say, *RR* p. 208, that under his banner Italy rose against Rome for the last time, but later, p. 453, after Actium, he can say that Italy perhaps more than Rome prevailed: 'the Principate itself may, in a certain sense, be regarded as a triumph of Italy over Rome'. The Caesarian party, so largely recruited from Roman knights of the towns of Italy, defeated the 'nobiles'. Here we have one clue to Virgil's undoubted later conversion to Octavian as restorer of Italy, but it could scarcely have been operative in 38 B.C., when Virgil first appears in the circle of Maecenas.

In 41–40 Virgil is likely to have shared the feelings of his class, as landowner and Italian. In the histories of Appian Lucius Antonius is idealised as the champion of liberty, and 'Libertas' is emphasised in *E* 1. 27, as the cause of Tityrus' journey to Rome. Under its literal sense some have scented an allegory. Lucius called on the Triumvirs to lay down their despotic powers. The case for Pollio as Appian's ultimate source is a strong one, and, even if he is not, the source was a contemporary historian, deeply interested in agrarian Italy, a supporter of Marcus Antonius, and an opponent of Octavian, but disdaining vulgar propaganda (the 'arae Perusinae'!) with a strong sympathy for Lucius Antonius, holding a balance between the dispossessed and the soldiers. But Pollio, as general of seven legions, understood Octavian's problem very well. Should we not expect this attitude in Virgil too, if we did not know of the proems of *G* 1 and *G* 3, and the 'iuvenis' of *G* 1. 500 (and of the *Aeneid*), and read the *Georgics* without them? Virgil, as we have seen, speaks of the boldness of *E* 1. Was he bold because he praised Octavian at a time when he was extremely unpopular and in great danger within Italy and without from both Marcus Antonius and Sextus Pompeius? Or because he praised Lucius Antonius, probably after the fall of Perusia, perhaps after Lucius' death, in spring or summer 40, looking back at an event of a year ago and finding in it a symbol of his own position? He had been reduced from the owner of (or heir to) a large estate to a smallholder. But his smallholding in the field of poetry, the pastoral, had enabled him to absorb into it a contemporary Roman theme, and to influence opinion in Rome, if those *Eclogues* were at once put on the stage as mimes. This is enough to explain the place of *E* 1 at the head of the collection. If he had attacked Octavian, he had in retrospect been bold indeed; no wonder, after the great climax of Orpheus in *G* 4, that he recalls his bitter 'adynaton' of *E* 8. 55 'sit Tityrus Orpheus'.

How then are we to imagine Maecenas winning Virgil over? As soon as the *Eclogues* appeared under Virgil's name, Maecenas must have sought him out, recognising his genius in spite of its use to pillory the evictions, in spite of the absence of all 'Augustan' elements in the *Eclogues.* In spite of the loss of his estate Virgil was flattered and encouraged by such recognition. The tact of Maecenas and Octavian was different from the curt and sharp criticisms of Pollio. This 'in spite of' on both sides is more creditable to both than the usual reconstruction. How Pollio took his loss of Virgil we have no hint, but he vanishes from Virgil's life, so far as we know, but only after *E* 8, not after *E* 1. The epic, the great estate in the realm of poetry, conceived first for the son of Antonius and Octavia, then transferred with impatience and diffidence ('en erit unquam / ille dies?') to Pollio, was in the *Georgics* grandly anticipated for the young Caesar. But when he in his turn was displaced by Aeneas he was in a way promoted, the culmination of a process of which Virgil treated the origins. This was much more satisfactory than to be the protagonist of a *Bellum Siculum* or *Bellum Actiacum*. The subject of epic for Virgil is the City that grows up out of a united land, 'Roma caput Italiae' (*G*2. 532–5), so that at Actium Caesar leads the Italians, not the Roman army, *A*8. 678, cf. *A*12, 827. This Italian note is found in Virgil, not in Horace or Propertius, and in Appian, not in our other historical sources.[19]

## Notes

[1] Servius on *E*1. 12: cf. on 27 and 70. On 42 he says simply 'Caesarem dicit Octavianum Augustum'.

[2] F. Vollmer, *Sitzungsb. der Münch. Akad.*, 1909, no. 9.2, pp. 5–11, against W. Kroll, *RM* vol. 64, 1909, pp. 50–5.

[3] See the arguments of E. Gabba, *Appiano e la Storia delle Guerre Civili*, Florence 1956, and his edition of Appian, *BC* 5, Florence 1970, with introduction and commentary; and of *BC* 1, Florence 1958 and 1967; also several supporting articles: *Riv. Stor. Ital.* vol. 67, 1955, p. 325ff.; *Ath.* N.S., vol. 27, 1949, p. 198ff.; 29, 1951, p. 183ff.; in *Studi Fanfani*, 1962, vol. 1, pp. 41–50; *Miscellanea Ferrero*, Turin 1971 p. 185ff.; *Parola del Passato* vol. 8, 1953, p. 106ff.; 'The Perusine War and Triumviral Italy' *HSCP* vol. 75, 1971, pp. 139–60. But the reviewers have not on the whole been convinced. Syme, *RR* p. 6: 'The great work of Pollio has perished, save for inconsiderable fragments or supposed borrowings in subsequent historians'; p. 484 (from 60 B.C. only as far as Philippi, not as Actium, hence Pollio as source of Appian, *BC* 5, excluded).

[4] Mr Stevens long ago pointed out to me the source of the error. The words 'triumvirorum iussu' of course meant the 'IIIviri reipublicae constituendae', but as Lepidus was enfeebled and Antony absent, the scholiasts thought only of Octavian and looked round for 'triumviri agris dividundis' in the *Eclogues* and of course found them.

[5] G. Jachmann, *Neue Jahrb. f. das Klass. Altert.* vol. 49, 1922, pp. 101–20, p. 117 n.1.

[6] R. E. H. Westendorp Boerma, *Catalepton* vol. 1, Assen 1949, collects the evidence for Siro and Virgil pp. 99–100, and

discusses the date of *Catalepton* 5, pp. 101–2, inclining to 45 B.C. amid the range of 50 to 43.

[7] E. de Saint-Denis, *Virgile Bucoliques,* ed. 2, Paris 1967, pp. 6–7, has a convenient conspectus.

[8] The latest discussion, to my knowledge, is that of D. Ableitinger-Grünberger, *Der junge Horaz und die Politik,* Heidelberg 1971, with p. 66 for bibliography of the controversy.

[9] Already in January 49 Cicero, *ad Att.* 7. 13. 3, calls Caesar's soldiers 'barbari', where Shackleton Bailey quotes 7. 7. 6; and 8. 11. 4; 9. 13. 4; Lucan 1. 481; Diod. 41. 8.

[10] J. Kroll, *Herm.* vol. 49, 1914, pp. 629–32. But C. Becker, *Herm.* vol. 83, 1955, p. 343ff. reverses the relation.

[11] R. Syme, *Sallust,* Berkeley and Los Angeles 1964, pp. 284–5.

[12] H. Janne, 'L'Épode XVI et l'histoire du second triumvirat', in *Études Horatiennes,* 1937, pp. 119–37. D. Ableitinger-Grünberger's criticisms, op. cit., p. 61, do not convince. The outbreak of the Perusine War seems much more likely, and the 'scelus' of *Epode* 7. 17, Romulus' fratricide, shows that in *E*4. 13 'nostrum scelus' is not to be confused with 31, 'priscae vestigia fraudis', which affect the whole human race and make the 'altera bella' of 35 necessary before the world is pacified under Rome, 17. G. Jachmann, 'Die vierte Ekloge Vergils' *Annali Pisa* vol. 21, 1952, pp. 13–62, complains of the confusion in *E*1.

[13] App. *BC* 5. 276; Plut. *Ant.* 28 'as far as Lydia and Ionia'; Dio 48, 24–7; 39–41; Strabo 12. p. 574, 14. p. 660; Josephus, *AJ* 14. 330, 434. Syme, *RR* p. 223 'The damage and the disgrace were immense' in 40 B.C.

[14] *Horace,* p. 53, and D. Ableitinger-Grünberger, op. cit., p. 65.

[15] P. Levi, 'The dedication to Pollio in Virgil's Eighth Eclogue' *Herm.* vol. 94, 1966, pp. 73–9; also vol. 99, 1971, p. 126.

[16] G. W. Bowersock, 'A date in the Eighth Eclogue', *HSCP* vol. 75, 1971, pp. 73–83; Wendell Clausen, 'On the date of the First Eclogue' *HSCP* vol. 76, 1972, pp. 201–5.

[17] Velleius 2.78.2: Octavian's 'crebrae in Illyrico Delmatiaque expeditiones', using Pollio's former legions? Cf. App., *BC* 5. 338.

[18] Cf. Varro, *RR* 1. 16. 5; 17. 5–7; 19.3, discussing the *peculium,* not in the sense of money saved to buy freedom, but an allotment of land, 'peculiare aliquid in fundo pascere'.

[19] My views on the endlessly debated problems of the *Eclogues* are to be found also in *Virgil Society Lecture Summary,* No. 42, 1957 on *E*4; No. 50, 1960 on *E*6; *Proceedings of the Virgil Society,* 6, 1966—67, on *E*10; *Jackson Knight Memorial Lecture* No. 3, Abingdon 1971, on the *Georgics; OCD*[2], Cols. 1123—8.

C. G. Hardie,
Magdalen College,
Oxford.

# 9

## Mercy and Moderation on the Coinage of Tiberius

The word Moderatio, or connected words, was often in Tiberius' mouth, and Clementia he also found attractive. These virtues he claimed above Pietas, Iustitia, and even Providentia.[1] His claims were known to Tacitus, who guys or denies them; certainly Suetonius regards Tiberius' Moderatio as a sham.[2]

Contemporaries ascribed the virtues to Tiberius without irony. Moderatio and Clementia are each given a section by Valerius Maximus, with an ancestor, C. Nero, cos. 207, offering an example of the former. Another admirer, Velleius, singles out Tiberius' Moderatio, though in a trivial connection.[3]

The senate, too, knew what would please. In A.D. 28 it dedicated an altar to the Clementia of Tiberius; five years later votive offerings commemorated it.[4] But the utterances of an individual are of greater value. In A.D. 21 M. Aemilius Lepidus made a speech recorded by Tacitus.[5] Lepidus was pleading for Clutorius Priscus who, having written successful verses on the death of Germanicus and having been paid for them, thought to repeat his success and more than double his money with a second set on the death of Drusus. But Drusus was not yet dead: he was presiding over the senatorial court that was trying Priscus. 'Sin flagitia et facinorum sine modo sunt, suppliciis ac remediis *principis moderatio* maiorumque et vestra exempla temperant', pleaded Lepidus. 'Saepe audivi principem nostrum conquerentem, si quis sumpta morte *misericordiam eius* praevenisset.' That appeal could be construed as a clever device to force the Princeps to display the qualities he claimed. But Tiberius was absent; Lepidus was bringing the familiar professions to bear on the senate — a procedure equally likely

123

to anger Tiberius if they had not been sincere. Lepidus found only one consular to support him; Priscus was executed without delay. A veiled rebuke from Campania was followed by a *senatus consultum* that delayed by ten days the registration of decrees — including judicial sentences — in the Aerarium. M. Lepidus was a man of sense, and close to Tiberius.[6] The Princeps believed in his own Clementia and Moderatio; that should cause no surprise even in a man notorious for vindictiveness, and with a streak of violence in him.[7]

Tangible evidence of his preoccupation: the *dupondii* which bear on their reverses a shield containing a bust, with legend CLEMENTIAE S.C. or MODERATIONI(S) S.C.[8] That is not to say that Tiberius personally ordered their issue or that he intended to convince the public that he practised those virtues.[9] Certainly the austerity and conservatism of Tiberius' coinage[10] reflects his distaste for adulation and the intrusion of a personality cult into Roman politics. But that does not show that the choice of types was not the work of an official of discretion, aware of his values.

The significance and date of the *dupondii* remain a matter of controversy. It is profitable to return to the views put forward by C. H. V. Sutherland in 1938. To his mind the shields on the *dupondii* recalled the shield presented to Augustus by the senate, the Clipeus Virtutis.[11] Reviving an idea of R. Mowat,[12] Dr Sutherland suggested that Tiberius was offered an honour in the same form; it came in 21, a year which saw only one conviction for treason, and which was precisely the year in which Tiberius rebuked the senate for the hasty execution of Priscus. By contrast, Dr Sutherland saw the year 28 as a time when the misgivings of the senate prompted them to remind Tiberius of his Clementia: the downfall of the elder Agrippina was imminent.

This has not been accepted without demur. On stylistic grounds, M. Grant prefers a later date for the coins, connecting them with Tiberius' *vicennium*,[13] while R. S. Rogers holds that Tiberian Clementia had a wider reference, including foreign as well as domestic foes. Rogers also did good service in collecting instances of Moderatio and Clementia and in distinguishing more sharply than Dr Sutherland had done between the two.[14] Though related, they do not enjoy equal status. A man practising Clementia is thereby displaying Moderatio; the reverse is not the case. Suetonius devotes a chapter of his biography of Julius Caesar to 'moderationem clementiamque cum in administra-

124

tione tum in victoria belli civilis admirabilem', the bulk to acts of mercy.[15] But Rogers' interpretation is too wide. The Clementia that Tiberius showed towards defeated foreign enemies was indeed the quality that taught the Romans to develop the concept. But as a technique for dealing with foreign powers it was not likely to appeal to the public. Nor was it peculiar to Tiberius; all Romans might display Clementia Romana. Finally, Rogers' examples were not all well chosen; credit must go to men in the field, Germanicus for example, who had independent *imperium*.[16] Tiberian Clementia, like that of the other Principes, was a domestic quality.[17]

Most recently, H. Gesche has followed Grant in advocating a late date for the *dupondii*, on stylistic and typological grounds, because there are no other *dupondii* for the period 34—37, and because of their relative scarcity, which fits the numbers of coins struck in that period rather than those of 22—23.[18] She connects them with the offering made to Jupiter in 33 in recognition of Tiberius' Clementia towards Agrippina and with the amnesty granted her followers and those of Seianus; the busts are those of Germanicus and Drusus Caesars, whom Tiberius had destined his successors (the second dying ten years before the issue of these coins) and in whose honour Tiberius had allowed *imagines clipeatae* to be set up in the Palatine Library. The busts also draw attention to two new heirs: Germanicus' son Gaius (Caligula) and Drusus' Ti. Gemellus.[19]

Dr Gesche's thesis is attractive. It is neat, and it does not preclude us from thinking in terms of clemency exercised at home. (There is no need to look for a date for the exercise of Moderatio, which was something that could be practised every day and in trivial matters, as Suetonius expressly says.[20]) Her view that the busts in the shields are those of the dead *principes* is grateful to those who maintain that Tiberius in his last years proposed to continue the policy of dual succession.[21] And Dr Gesche has put forward strong arguments at least for assigning the *dupondii* a date other than 22—23. Yet her interpretation does not give complete satisfaction. It is a problem to which we shall have to return. Why are Clementia and Moderatio the cardinal virtues of Tiberius Caesar? The answer brings into sharper relief two salient features of the Tiberian principate.

There was no reason why Tiberius should not have settled on Moderatio. Its reputable history could be traced back to worthies of the early Republic. As consul, P. Valerius Poplicola voluntarily shared the *fasces* with a colleague; M. Furius

Camillus hesitated to take up his command before completing the formalities of investiture with the Dictatorship; C. Marcius Rutilus Censorinus and L. Quinctius Cincinnatus declined to be continued in their magistracies; and so on.[22]

Clementia is different. The virtue of an autocrat, of a Caesar – the most important of his virtues –, it was already distasteful to Romans.[23] All the more surprising that it should be taken up by a Princeps of 'Republican' inclinations. True, when M. Lepidus wished to refer to Tiberius' Clementia he chose (if we are to trust the wording of Tacitus' report) another word, Misericordia; yet official language and other speakers were straightforward enough.[24] The motives that induced Tiberius to lay claim to Clementia must have been strong indeed.

Yet the two virtues are related. The specimens of republican Moderatio cited above show men in positions of power (*imperium* or *auctoritas*, it is all one) which they deliberately refrained from using. Nor are all specimens republican. Dionysius of Halicarnassus ascribes Moderatio to Romulus, and for Caesar's sake; Suetonius likewise credits Caesar with this virtue; neither of these writers had to fear the sensibilities of Tiberius.[25] But Tiberius' position was essentially the same as that of his illustrious predecessors, Caesar and all: 'Dixi et nunc et saepe alias, p.c., bonum et salutarem principem, quem vos tanta et tam libera potestate instruxistis, senatui servire debere et universis civibus saepe et plerumque etiam singulis.'[26] This is a key passage to the understanding of Tiberius' principate, and it was C. E. Stevens who first drew my attention to that fact, twenty years ago: like so many of his observations, it has proved its value by its continued fruitfulness. Not many would dispute its relevance to Moderatio, the practice of which continued until well into his principate.[27] But Tiberius' remarks in the senate on the occasion of his accession in A.D. 14, as recorded by Tacitus,[28] are equally striking. What Tiberius was trying to do on that occasion – his 'hesitating to accept the Principate ' – has long been a matter of dispute; the simplest explanation is that he was merely redefining the principate in Tiberian terms: 'solam divi Augusti mentem tantae molis capacem: se . . . didicisse quam arduum, quam subiectum fortunae regendi cuncta onus. proinde in civitate tot inlustribus viris subnixa non ad unum omnia deferrent: plures facilius munia reipublicae sociatis laboribus exsecuturos.' So might Poplicola have said, and Censorinus, and Cincinnatus. In A.D. 14 Tiberius (in spite of the precedent of Camillus) was not 'hesitating to' do anything; he was voluntarily circumscribing the limits of his power, proclaiming Moderatio his watchword.

That Tiberius should adopt Clementia as his other cardinal virtue reveals another preoccupation: desire to end the feuds that had marred his rise to power. The trouble had begun in 9 B.C., when Tiberius' brother Drusus died.[29] That event led directly to a second consulship for Tiberius and a grant of tribunician power in 6 B.C., with *imperium maius* in the eastern provinces. The death of Augustus at that point would have left Tiberius in sole power and in a position that would have been hard to dispute. It was disputed before the situation arose. C. Caesar, the fourteen year old son of Tiberius' wife Julia, was irregularly elected to the consulship of 5 B.C., which Augustus merely postponed for five years. Pride forced Tiberius into retirement. Four years later Julia was exiled for adultery, but her paramours were all men of political importance: Iullus Antonius, the son of M. Antonius the Triumvir, 'singulare exemplum clementiae Caesaris', who was allowed to choose the manner of his death; a Sempronius Gracchus; and others.[30] Julia was accompanied into exile by her mother Scribonia, a severe woman who, by going with her daughter, showed that in her eyes she was innocent. The alleged adulterers were supporting the offspring, descendants, and kinsmen of Augustus' first betrothed and first wife, Claudia and Scribonia, against the upstart who had entered the dynasty only through the chance fact that his mother Livia had married Octavian. When the scandal broke, Tiberius was on Rhodes, and near the end of his *imperium* and tribunician power. Perhaps for this reason Tiberius did not of his own accord divorce his wife (that was done for him by Augustus); repeatedly he begged his step-father for mercy on her behalf.[31]

It was as a result of the deaths of Gaius and Lucius Caesar that Tiberius came to power again in A.D. 4, his position strengthened this time by adoption into the *gens Iulia*.[32] The four years that followed were troubled by rebellion in the Balkans, discontent in the army, famine, fire, and flood in Italy. The same period saw strenuous but unsuccessful efforts being made to improve the position of Agrippa Postumus, the brother of Gaius and Lucius, who had been adopted alongside Tiberius. So we may interpret the beginning of Postumus' misbehaviour in the autumn of 5, his abdication and relegation to Surrentum in 6, the seditious poster campaign investigated in the same year by the senate, his removal to Planasia in 7, the death of his brother-in-law L. Aemilius Paullus, the final exile of his sister Julia the Younger in 8, along with that of Ovid, and the departure of her lover D. Silanus. The connections between the supporters of Agrippa Postumus and the group that surrounded Julia the Elder are based on the close ties of relationship, not only between Julia the Elder and her children Julia and Postumus, but also between Scribonia and Paullus, and on those, less close, that subsisted between Silani, Aemilii, Claudii Pulchri, Sempronii, and Quinctii. The agitation of A.D. 4–8 was a continuation of the agitation of 6–2 B.C., conducted by a related group for a similar purpose: the advancement of their candidates for power against Tiberius and his children Drusus and (from A.D. 4 onwards) Germanicus.

For all Ovid's complaints, the agitators of A.D. 4–8, especially D. Silanus, were treated with leniency. Only Paullus died. Relegation to an island or an obligatory sojourn abroad was the penalty for offenders of rank, a fine for a lesser man.[33] For that leniency more than one reason may be proposed: conciliation of supporters of Agrippa Postumus who still sat in the senate and of his massive following among the people; and Augustus was dealing for the most part with his own relatives. Nor do we know what part, if any, Livia and Tiberius played in Augustus' dealings with Julia and Agrippa. However, in A.D. 8, the year of their final downfall, Augustus, who was now too decrepit to attend senate or courts, travelled all the way to Ariminum in order, as Dio puts it, to advise Tiberius on the conduct of the war in the Balkans.[34] As Tiberius had been conducting the war successfully since A.D. 6 it is legitimate to seek a more plausible explanation for Augustus' remarkable journey, and to ask if it was not Tiberius who was to give the advice, on the dynastic crisis which broke precisely in that year.

If Clementia was exercised in 8 it did not meet with a favourable response from survivors of the clique and their supporters. Disturbances at Rome were expected when Augustus died.[35] What materialised was an abortive attempt to snatch Agrippa Postumus from his island and take him to the troops. It failed and all that the rescuer Clemens came away with was his master's ashes.[36] It was also at the opening of Tiberius' principate that two persons exiled in 2 B.C. perished. Sempronius Gracchus was executed on Cercina; Julia starved herself to death at Rhegium.[37] Perhaps they had engineered the attempt to save Agrippa Postumus.

According to Suetonius it was as early as this that

M. Scribonius Libo Drusus began his plot; whatever the truth of that, nothing came to light until two years had passed. In A.D. 16 Libo Drusus was brought to trial before the senate for *maiestas:* 'nefaria consilia . . . de salute Ti. Caes. liberorumque eius et aliorum principum civitatis deque r.p.'[38] The evidence for a murder plot, as reported by Tacitus, is not strong: consultation of astrologers and of a sorcerer, an annotated list of names of prominent men. The trial continued after Libo commited suicide, but it is unlikely that further evidence was forthcoming.[39] Tacitus considered Libo a harmless if extravagant fool, Seneca a fool who was guilty of cherishing ambitions beyond his capacity.[40]

The same year saw Clemens emerge again,[41] this time disguised as his dead master. Gathering support as he went, he reached Ostia and proceeded to Rome with a large band of followers. There he was quietly arrested, brought to the Palatium, and executed. R. S. Rogers suggested long ago that there was a connexion between the plot of Libo Drusus and the imposture of Clemens. With Tiberius and the *liberi* out of the way, a man of Libo's pedigree might hope for power, especially if he were allied with one who could attract some of the popular support that Agrippa Postumus had enjoyed. Once the *coup* had succeeded (presumably by marching on the Curia and forcing the *patres* to declare for Libo and 'Agrippa' after the assassination of the 'principes civitatis'), the pretender could be dropped.

If Libo did intend to exploit Agrippa's popularity that would be suggestive. So would be the fact that the magician who betrayed him was a Iunius, presumably *e plebe* like the Iunius Novatus who wrote an 'asperrimam epistulam' about Augustus and published it under the name of Agrippa.[42] Libo was a descendant of Pompey the Great; that was the main basis of his claim, but not the only one. When Libo toured the houses of his peers, vainly appealing for help, his only supporters were noblewomen, presumably of his house; and when he decided on suicide one of those noble ladies was by his side, counselling him not to do the work of his enemy — and hers. She is named: his great-aunt Scribonia.[43]

The death of Libo Drusus was nonetheless deplored by Tiberius; he swore that he would have asked for Libo's life.[44] This doubtless was one occasion in Lepidus' mind when he said that he had often heard the Princeps complaining when a suicide forestalled his Misericordia. In 16 Tiberius was successful in exercising Moderatio, if not Clementia: many members of the imperial household, *equites*, and senators, were said to have supplied Clemens with help, material and moral. No enquiry was made.[45]

The next seven years saw the deaths, first of Germanicus, then of Drusus Caesar. Their wives were left in jealous uncertainty over the destinies of their children.[46] But the intentions of Tiberius were clear enough. In A.D. 20, three years before his own son died, he had brought Germanicus' eldest son, Nero Caesar, before the senate and asked for him the remission of a *quinquennium* in the *cursus honorum,* that was the privilege of destined *principes*; three years later, the second son, Drusus Caesar, was accorded the same privilege.[47] Their mother Agrippina had no cause for alarm. But her rival Livilla, Drusus' widow, found a champion in the prefect of the guard, Seianus. Agrippina, who was pushing her sons harder than Tiberius thought decorous, quite soon came to distrust her father-in-law and (doubtless) to remember what had happened to her mother and siblings.[48] Once again Tiberius was called upon to exercise Clementia; and when Agrippina committed suicide he claimed to have done so: 'absumptam criminosissime insectatus, cum diem quoque natalem eius inter nefastos referendum suasisset, imputavit etiam, quod non laqueo strangulatam in Gemonias abiecerit: proque tali clementia interponi decretum passus est, quo sibi gratiae ageretur et Capitolino Iovi donum ex auro sacraretur'.[49] All that can be said is that Tiberius had suffered from Agrippina's kinsmen for more than forty years.

If the two cardinal virtues of Tiberius mark his two peoccupations as Princeps — Moderatio his restraint in his use of his overwhelming powers, Clementia his forbearance to the political group that had consistently and ruthlessly opposed his elevation, the two virtues equally, and tragically, mark Tiberius' most conspicuous failures. Though it is alluded to as late as 25, the senate refused to trust Tiberius' Moderatio; the debates on serious subjects that are prominent in the first four books of the *Annals* are heard little of after the Princeps' departure for Campania and Capri in 26; the formalities were observed, but dynastic intrigues in the absence of the Princeps were taking their attention from regular business by 28: hence the Ara Clementiae.[50] The fall of Agrippina and her eldest sons was followed by that of Seianus himself in 31 and by its attendant atrocities. Henceforward the charge of association with Seianus, true or false, was a weapon usually deadly and the more readily used for that. The last years of the principate saw a frenzy of accusations; all the more relevant, then, and celebrated in its slightest manifestation became the Princeps' Clementia — and all the worse the repute of the Princeps who might have put an end to the trials, if he had cared to interfere with the due process of law to interrupt cases that were, after all, the direct descendants of those fought out by factions in the *quaestiones* of the late republic, or to take out of the hands of the senate the courts for which they had fought for a century.

Dr Gesche has shown how appropriate the issue of the Clementia-Moderatio *dupondii* was to the years 34—37. Yet her numismatic arguments do less than she claims for them. She assumes, like most other writers, that there are only two possibilities: 22—3 and 34—37, the only years after A.D. 15—16 attested for Tiberian issues.[51] Having argued against 22—3, she triumphantly deposits them in 34—37. But these small issues are *sui generis*: is it a well-founded enterprise to try to fit them into a known series? Nor is the absence of *dupondii* from the 34—37 issues a compelling reason for ascribing the Clementia-Moderatio coins to those years; coins are struck because they are needed, not to create a complete and systematic series. As for the arguments from style, Dr Sutherland still holds that the technique and conception of the obverse portrait of the *dupondii*, as well as the age of the sitter (elderly, but still well-fleshed), make it impossible to place them later than 23.[52] Other difficulties arise. The coins are dedicated to Clementia and Moderatio; so too, one might have thought, the shields. On Dr Gesche's view, the shields are those dedicated to the memory of Germanicus and Drusus. And are shields set up in their memory *as distinguished orators* suitable for commemoration on coins that pointed at one of the most serious of the acts of a Princeps: his provision for the succession? What in any case have Germanicus and Drusus or their posterity to do with Clementia and Moderatio? Dr Gesche has an explanation: Tiberius in 34—7 is drawing attention to his forbearance in allowing the child of a woman who had intrigued against him and who had perished for it to succeed him; he had punished only those who were guilty. The explanation is not a happy one. As we survey the history of Clementia and Moderatio during the principate of Tiberius we find that moneyers of earlier years than 34—37 might have felt that they already had sufficient reason to glorify those virtues. Indeed, Moderatio is made more of at the beginning of the principate than it is at the end. And it is near the beginning of the principate that I would place the *dupondii*.

The obverses of these coins, with their legend TI. CAESAR

DIVI AVG F AVGVST IMP VIII, are similar except in respect of the laurel wreath worn by Tiberius to obverses of A.D. 15–16 (IMP VII) and A.D. 22–23, and, Dr Gesche points out, in respect of the laurel also to those of 34–37. But all these types continue the obverse legend on the reverse, providing the Princeps with a complete titulature; it is as if the moneyers of the *dupondii* were unexpectedly making use of an obverse type with which they were already familiar; or as if they wanted to draw attention to the new imperatorial dating of the obverse.

If we take this salutation date seriously we are brought to the late summer or autumn of A.D. 16, which saw Tiberius reach his eighth salutation and provided him with another occasion to wear that laurel wreath which, as one would expect from a stickler for propriety, appears at Rome only on coins that record a salutation.[53] The *dupondii* would then follow the *asses* of A.D. 15–16.

The autumn of 16 has more to offer: the exposure of the conspiracy of Libo Drusus on 13 September, an occasion on which Tiberius drew attention to the Clementia he intended; in the same year, before or after the death of Libo, Tiberius was exercising Moderatio in not pursuing the distinguished adherents of Clemens. Offerings, of what sort we are not told, were made *ex SC* on Libo's downfall to Jupiter, Mars, and Concordia.[54] Shields (there seem to have been two of them, for on most of the dies the design of shields and central roundels differs according to the quality being honoured: the bust on the Clementia types is invariably surrounded by a laurel wreath, and the outer rim of the shield decorated with a formal floral pattern; Moderatio usually, not always, has the laurel wreath outside the roundel on the border of the shield) might be set up in a temple as well as in the Curia or Palatine Library. The temples of Bellona and Capitoline Jove were early receptacles, and the Capitol continued to be their destination in the next principate.[55] That is not suprising if R. Winkes is right in supposing that *imagines clipeatae* were normally carried in triumphal processions, and in connecting them with the two kinds of artistic milieu as well as two kinds of *pompa, triumphalis* and *funebris*. For the recent salutation gave special propriety to the dedication of shields, even if the Virtus they commemorated was not of the battlefield.[56] Whose then are the busts they contain? They are of persons youthful and well endowed with hair, unlike the Princeps. At this date Germanicus and Drusus would be the obvious answer; or the elder sons of Germanicus, Nero and Drusus. Do the shields then become *imagines clipeatae*, set up in their honour? Perhaps we may best explain these tiny busts (for tiny they are compared, say, with the *imago clipeata* of Augustus represented on a coin of Mescinius Rufus) by appealing to Pliny, who describes the shields such as those set up by Ap. Claudius, cos. 79 B.C., as 'decora res, utique si liberum turba parvulis imaginibus ceu nidum aliquem subolis pariter ostendat, quales clupeos nemo non gaudens favensque aspicit'.[57] Tiberius' kinsman seems not only to have commemorated his ancestry but also to have reminded men of the future of his dynasty; so the senate celebrated the virtues of Tiberius on shields that would have been aniconic but for the harmless and charming representation of his grandchildren ('liberi') thereon.[58] It had, after all, been the future of the whole dynasty ('salus Ti. Caes. liberorumque eius') that had been threatened by the conspiracy of Libo.

The value of studying imperial virtues to the historian of imperial politics has not passed unchallenged.[59] And with Tiberius we are dealing with a consummate hypocrite. Yet if at worst 'virtues' are no more than the dishonest professions of an autocrat, at best they may reveal genuinely held ideals. The historian we honour has ever been ready (it is a tribute to him) to recognise that there can be more to a politician than wakeful self-interest; precisely with Tiberius. That prompts a final thought on the relation between Tiberian *dissimulatio* and Tiberian 'virtues'. When a man supremely unpopular betakes himself in reaction to the cultivation of his own *virtutes* it is only an invitation to his detractors to add yet another to the list of vices, public and private: 'nullam aeque .. ex virtutibus suis ... quam dissimulationem diligebat'.[60] The real tragedy was the failure of principle to stand up to half a century's wear and tear.

## Notes

[1] Cardinal virtues: see H. Gesche, 'Datierung und Deutung der CLEMENTIAE-MODERATIONI-Dupondien des Tiberius' *Jahrb. f. Num. u. Geldgesch.* vol. 21, 1971, p. 62 n. 81.

[2] Claims to Moderatio: (Tac.,) *Ann.* 1.14.3 (A.D. 14); 2.36.2 (16); Clementia: 2.31.4 (16); (Suet.,) *Tib.* 53.2, cf. *Ann.* 6.25.2 (33); conscious of the reputation it gives: 4.31.1. Denied: *Ann.* 1.8.6; *Tib.* 57.

[3] Val. Max. 4.1; 5.1; Vell. Pat. 2.122.1.

[4] *Ann.* 4.74.3; 6.25.4 f., cf. *Tib.* 53.2.

[5] *Ann.* 3.49 ff.

[6] See R. Syme, 'Marcus Lepidus, *Capax Imperii'* *JRS* vol. 45 1955, p. 22 ff.

[7] *Ann.* 3.48.3 suggests not vindictiveness but a long memory for good or ill. Suet., *Div. Aug.* 51.3, brought against Tiberius, shows youthful anger on *Augustus'* behalf.

[8] *CREBM* vol. 1, p. 132, nos. 85–90; *RIC* vol. 1, pp. 107–108, nos. 30–31.

[9] Contrast A. H. M. Jones, *Studies Presented to Harold Mattingly*, Oxford 1951, p. 13 ff., and C. H. V. Sutherland, *JRS* vol. 49, 1959, p. 46 ff.

[10] See C. H. V. Sutherland, *Coinage in Roman Imperial Policy*, London 1951, p. 84 ff.

[11] C. H. V. Sutherland, 'Two "Virtues" of Tiberius: a numismatic Contribution to the History of his Reign' *JRS* vol. 28, 1938, p. 129 ff. Clipeus Virtutis: *Res Gestae Divi Augusti* 34.2.

[12] R. Mowat, 'Bronzes remarquables de Tibère', etc, *RN* Ser. 4, vol. 11, 1911, pp. 335 ff., 423 ff. Cf. S. Weinstock, *Divus Julius*, Oxford 1971, p. 241, harmonising the chronologically unharmonisable Dio 59.16.10 and Suet., *Cal.* 16.4, to produce an un-Tiberian ceremony. See H. Gesche, art. cit. (n.1), p. 53.

[13] M. Grant, *From Imperium to Auctoritas*, Cambridge 1946, p. 447, n. 10 f.; *Roman Anniversary Issues*, Cambridge 1950, p. 47 ff.; rejected by C. H. V. Sutherland, op. cit. (n. 10), p. 193 ff.

[14] R. S. Rogers, *Studies in the reign of Tiberius*, Baltimore 1943, pp. 42–3, 74 ff. Note *Tib.* 20 (Fides rather than Clementia), and *Ann.* 2.63.

[15] See S. Weinstock, op. cit. (n. 12), p. 234, with definitions in n. 1, especially Sen., *de Clem.* 2.3.1. The author of the *Rhet. ad Her.* uses Modestia for clemency: 3.3; see S. Weinstock, op. cit., p. 239; Suet. on Moderatio and Clementia: *Div. Iul.* 75, cf. Cic., *ad Att.* 7.7.7.

[16] Powerful criticisms: H. Gesche, art. cit., p. 49. Development of Clementia concept: Weinstock, op. cit., pp. 234–5. Clementia Romana: *Ann.* 4.50.2. Tiberius' aides: 1.58.8; 2.10.1; 22.3; 3.73.4 f.

[17] Tac., *Ann.* 14.12.5 f.; *Hist.* 1.75; *CREBM*, vol. 1, p. 384, no 78 ff

[18] H. Gesche, art. cit. (bibliography).

[19] Offering: above, n. 2. Amnesty: *Ann.* 6.30.1; Dio 58.16.6; 19.1; 21.5. *Imagines: Ann.* 2.83.4; *EJ*[2] 94 A (Germanicus); *Ann.* 4.9.2 (Drusus); see H. Gesche, art. cit., pp. 55 f. and 65 ff. (Caligula and Ti. Gemellus).

[20] *Tib.* 32.2.

[21] See B. Levick, *Lat.* vol. 25, 1966, p. 241.

[22] Val. Max. 4.1.1 ff.; 11; 15.

[23] See M. P. Charlesworth, *PBA* vol. 23, 1937, p. 112 f.; M. Grant, *Roman Anniversary Issues*, Cambridge 1951, p. 48f.; R. Syme, *Tacitus*, Oxford 1958, vol. 2, p. 703; S. Weinstock, op. cit. (n. 12), p. 233 ff.

[24] Cf. S. Weinstock, op. cit., p. 235 f.: 'Clementia never became an exclusive term'. Tiberius' referred to: *Ann.* 3.68.2 (not a verbatim report).

[25] Dion. Hal. 2.18.1 f., with S. Weinstock, op. cit., p. 229; Suet., *Div. Iul.* 75.1. Connection between Moderatio and Clementia : Gesche, art. cit., p.75.

[26] *Tib.* 29.

[27] See *Ann.* 1.7.6; 3.12.1; 69.8; 4.6 (implied reference); 4.38.4 (A.D. 25). See also *Tib.* 30 ff., especially 32.2, and Dio 57.8 ff. (death of Germanicus as the terminal date).

[28] *Ann.* 1.11 ff. Vell. Pat. 2.124 and Dio 57.2 do no damage to this interpretation.

[29] For this decade, see B. Levick, 'Tiberius' Retirement to Rhodes in 6 B.C.' *Lat.* vol. 31, 1972, p. 779 ff.

[30] Vell. Pat. 2.100.4 ('singulare exemplum' differently interpreted by F. W. Shipley in the Loeb translation).

[31] *Tib.* 11.4 (from the *commentarii*?).

[32] For the events of this decade see B. Levick, 'The Fall of Julia the Younger', a paper offered to *Latomus*.

[33] For leniency to D. Silanus, see E. Meise, *Untersuchungen zur Geschichte der Julisch-Claudischen Dynastie,* München 1969, pp. 39 and 46. Meise regards Silanus as innocent of conspiracy. See also Suet., *Div. Aug.* 51.1: 'Iunium Novatum . . . pecunia . . . punire satis habuit'.

[34] Dio 55.34.3.

[35] The appointment of L. Piso as Praefectus Urbi in 13: *PIR*[2] C 289. Trouble expected by Augustus: Suet., *Div. Aug.* 99.1. The funeral route lined with soldiers: *Ann.* 1.8.7. Appointment of a second Praefectus Praetorio: 1.24.3.

[36] *Ann.* 1.6.1 ff.; 2.39.1 ff. (Clemens); *Tib.* 22; Dio 57.3.5 f. J. Mogenet, 'La Conjuration de Clemens' *L'Ant. Class.* vol. 23, 1954, p. 321 ff., regards Tacitus' account as taken over

from the earlier attempts of Audasius and Epicadus (Suet., *Div. Aug.* 19.1).

[37] *Ann.* 1.53.

[38] *Tib.* 25.1. For sources and discussion, see R. S. Rogers, *Criminal Trials and Criminal Legislation under Tiberius*, Middletown 1935, p. 12 ff.; E. Koestermann, *Hist.* vol. 4, 1955, p. 87 ff.,.is less favourable to Tiberius. The official version: *Fasti Amiternini, EJ²*, p. 52.

[39] So F. B. Marsh, *The Reign of Tiberius*, Oxford 1931, p. 291 ff.; but cf. Koestermann, art. cit., p. 89, n. 41.

[40] *Ann.* 2.27.2, cf. 30.2; Sen. *Ep.* 70.10.

[41] *Ann.* 2.39 f.; *Tib.* 25; Dio 57.16.3 f.

[42] *Ann.* 2.28.3; Suet., *Div. Aug.* 51.

[43] 'Primoribus feminis': *Ann.* 2.29.1; Scribonia: 27.2; Sen., *Ep.* 70. 10.

[44] *Ann.* 2.31.4.

[45] *Ann.* 2.40.6.

[46] Rivalry: *Ann.* 2.43.7. (A.D. 17), cf. 4.17.4 (24); 39.6 and 40.3 (25).

[47] *Ann.* 3.29.1; 4.4.1 (with a comment on Drusus' 'benevolentia').

[48] *Ann.* 4.17.

[49] *Tib.* 53.2; cf. *Ann.* 6.25.4 f.

[50] *Ann.* 4.74.3.

[51] But cf. *RIC*, vol. 1, p. 107: 'Circa A.D. 23–32'.

[52] I am greatly indebted to the generosity of Dr Sutherland, who has devoted time and attention to my questions. He will not necessarily share the view I put forward here.

[53] For the eighth salutation, see *Ann.* 2.18.2, with H. Gesche, *Chiron* vol. 2, 1972, p. 339 ff.

[54] *Ann.* 2.32.4.

[55] Pliny, *NH* 35.12 ff. For Gaius see Suet., *Cal.* 16.4. W. H. Gross, 'Clipeata Imago und εἰκὼν ἔνοπλος'' *Convivium, Festgabe für K. Ziegler*, Stuttgart 1954, p. 72, thinks that this *clipeus* bore an *imago*.

[56] R. Winkes, *Clipeata Imago*, Bonn 1969, pp. 41 ff., 97, 101. Cf. Pliny, loc. cit.: 'origo plena virtutis', 'Martio exemplo'. The *imago clipeata* of Augustus appears on the obverse of a coin of which the reverse is devoted to a statue of Mars (*CREBM*, vol. 1, p. 17, no. 90).

[57] Mescinius Rufus, see preceding n. Pliny, loc. cit., misdates Ap. Claudius: see J. Bolten, *Die Imago Clipeata*, Paderborn 1937, p. 10; Gross, art. cit., p. 68 ff.; Winkes, op. cit., p. 35. He

is not thinking of the Erotes, etc., that sometimes supported *clipei* (Boltcn, op. cit., p.12); see Winkes, op. cit., p. 96. 'Pariter' = 'at the same time'; 'liberi' must be children in connection with their parents.

[58] I do not underestimate the differences between the *dupondii* and what Pliny seems to be describing. Pliny apparently thinks of a ring of children's busts round a central (and ancestral) bust. For aniconic gilded shields, with *tituli*, set up in honour of Tiberius, see Philo, *Leg.* 299 ff.

[59] F. W. Walbank, *G and R* vol. 13, 1944, p. 31; R. Syme, *Tacitus*, vol. 2, p. 754.

[60] *Ann.* 4.71.4; cf. 1.75.4; Vell. Pat. 2.126.4; *Tib.* 59.2; W. Süss, *Ethos*, Leipzig and Berlin 1910, p. 251 ff.

B. M. Levick,
St. Hilda's College,
Oxford.

# *10*

# Agricola, the Flavian Dynasty, and Tacitus

Although the opening stages of Agricola's *cursus honorum* were conventional enough, his rise in the 70's was meteoric and has not been adequately explained. He was unique in serving as tribune, legionary legate, and governor in one province.[1] A rapid survey of known careers can produce about fifty senators who held all three posts; but none held them all in the same province and only a handful served even twice with one army.[2] Agricola was unusually young to become consul at 36 or 37 and unusually young to govern the great military province of Britain.[3] Finally, his term of seven years in Britain was quite exceptional for a consular governor.[4] After the unusual circumstances under Tiberius[5] such lengthy tenures are scarcely ever found again.

Agricola's conduct in 69 does not seem to have received sufficient attention. In March or early April the Othonian fleet ravaged the Ligurian coast and Agricola's mother was killed.[6] He set out to fulfil the 'sollemnia pietatis', and was overtaken by the news of Vespasian's bid for empire; he at once joined the Flavian side (*Agr.* 7.2). Disturbed conditions may have delayed his departure, yet he must have been one of the very first to join the Flavians.[7] After all, Vespasian was not proclaimed at Alexandria until 1 July.[8] Agricola may well have been approached by one of those active in the Flavian interest in summer 69, such as Antonius Primus or Cornelius Fuscus (perhaps a fellow-townsman), although to judge from the *Histories* they did not begin active canvassing until late July.[9] A likely ally of Vespasian in summer 69 is the procurator of Narbonensis, Valerius Paulinus, a native of Forum Iulii and hence certainly known to Agricola. This man seized the colony at latest in October, after inducing several communities to swear allegiance to Vespasian. Paulinus had been 'Vespasiano ante fortunam amicus';[10] soon after, he effected the capture of Valens, which brought about a general swing to the Flavians.

Tacitus describes how Agricola was given an appointment by Mucianus: 'is missum ad dilectus agendos Agricolam integre strenueque versatum vicesimae legioni ... praeposuit' (*Agr.* 7.3). He was made legate of XX *after* successful service levying troops: surely this was in 69.[11] Strong elements of the British legions had served in the Vitellian forces.[12] Perhaps he had to provide replacements and take them to Britain, where he was to replace the turbulent Roscius Coelius.[13]

Agricola's speedy adhesion to the *partes*, and assistance from Valerius Paulinus, may have been enough to secure these appointments. And his advancement in the 70's may have followed naturally from this, and from meritorious conduct in the posts with which he was entrusted. But he may have had his own links with the Flavian family. As tribune in Britain[14] he probably had Titus as a colleague. Titus, almost his exact coeval, was tribune in Germany and Britain.[15] No details are recorded, but after the rising of Boudicca the British army, in particular IX Hispana, had to be reinforced by a draft from Germany.[16] A *tribunus laticlavius* would have been the appropriate officer to command this force[17], and one may postulate that Titus was the man.[18] Thereafter, Agricola and Titus had ample opportunity to meet after their return from Britain. Both married, both held the quaestorship.[19] Agricola, who presumably gained a year through the birth of a son,[20] went to Asia to serve under Salvius Titianus, evidently from 63–64.[21] Titus' quaestorship is not specified by Suetonius; he doubtless held it ca. 64. But surprisingly Titus unlike Agricola did not become tribune of the plebs – Agricola was tribune in 66.[22] Two factors may have been relevant. Titus' first wife Arrecina Tertulla had died, leaving him a daughter, Julia;[23] he had remarried, to Marcia Furnilla, daughter of Barea Sura.[24] In 66 Marcia's uncle Barea Soranus succumbed to a charge of high treason. Servilia, Soranus' daughter, also died.[25] Servilia's husband Annius Pollio had already been in trouble,[26] and Pollio's brother mounted a conspiracy later in 66.[27] The family to which Titus had allied himself – very probably on account of Vespasian's friendship with some of these people[28] – was now dangerously suspect. Titus divorced Marcia.[29] On 25 September 66 Nero left for

Achaia.[30] Vespasian was in his train,[31] and presumably Titus also went, soon – still quaestorian in status – to receive a legionary command.[32]

Evidently Agricola's service as legionary legate did not extend into the governorship of Frontinus;[33] hence he was back at Rome in 73, to be made a patrician and appointed legate of Aquitania.[34] There he stayed 'less than three years';[35] thus he presumably relinquished the post before the end of 76. Then came the consulship, the appointment to Britain, the marriage of his daughter to Tacitus, and the pontificate.[36]

Whether the governorship began in 77 or 78 has long been disputed. Discussion must be reserved for another place, but it is here assumed that the year was 77. Vespasian was still emperor, but the power of Titus was immense, unequalled since Tiberius' at the end of Augustus' life – and Titus was prefect of the guard as well.[37] Suetonius is emphatic.[38] But his power did not make him popular. Suetonius dwells on the hatred with which Titus was regarded before his accession. Dio's account is too truncated to be of much use, but the implication of the opening remarks in Xiphilinus' summary of the reign is clear.[39] The contrast in Tacitus' *Histories* is striking. Titus is first mentioned briefly with his father (1.10); but before Vespasian is given a full introduction, Titus is accorded astonishing prominence at the opening of book 2. Men thought Galba had summoned him to be adopted,[40] Tacitus says, describing Titus' journey in 68. Even his dalliance with Berenice is glossed over, and there is only a hint of what Suetonius spells out in such detail. Titus' rôle as conciliator between Vespasian and Mucianus is emphasised also, as it is again in 2.74. In 4.52 he is portrayed begging his father to look more kindly on his errant brother Domitian. Finally, at the opening of book 5 there is another eulogy.

The nature of Tacitus' treatment has not gone unnoticed; and in a recent study R. Urban has analysed it in detail and offered explanations.[41] He notes that at the time of writing it was politic (for Trajan) to hark back to Titus as a model. Further, there may have been 'a personal relationship between the Caesar and Princeps and Tacitus, who was at that time beginning his political career under the protection of Agricola.' Finally, he suggests, Tacitus, who was influenced by the parallel between Tiberius and Domitian, may have likewise modelled his portrayal of Titus on Germanicus.[42]

The picture painted of Domitian in the *Histories* is highly

unflattering: in the *Agricola* the hostility may be understandable; in the later work one might have expected more
restraint, at least in the surviving books, where Domitian's rôle
is minor. But, for whatever reason, this is not the case.[43]

During the reign of Vespasian a major political question was
the succession. The main opposition came from Helvidius
Priscus. Helvidius' views and activities are enigmatic and the
scanty evidence has been interpreted in various ways.[44] Dio
reports a crucial episode, evidently in 70:

> Helvidius, who was then praetor, instead of doing anything
> to honour the emperor, would not stop insulting him. On
> one occasion he was arrested by the tribunes of the plebs
> for this ... Vespasian was overcome with emotion and
> walked out of the Senate in tears, saying: "Either my son
> shall succeed me, or no one".[45]

Suetonius does not link Vespasian's remark with Helvidius but
puts it in an astrological context, although he refers to frequent
conspiracies; and he has 'sons' rather than 'son'.[46] Earlier,
Suetonius had referred to the downfall of Helvidius in a context
reminiscent of Dio's account (*Vesp.* 15). Dio records further
details in a passage preserved only in the *Excerpta Valesiana*
(273): hence it is not clear what relation it has with the previous
passage, nor which year Helvidius died:

> 'It became strikingly clear that Vespasian hated Helvidius
> Priscus, who was denouncing "kingship" and praising
> "democracy", and got together people to insult the rulers,
> stir up the mobs, overthrow the existing order and bring
> about a revolution.'

Dio contrasts Helvidius' behaviour unfavourably with that of
Thrasea under Nero, claims that he had some personal
animosity against Vespasian, and that he would not desist from
attacking him in public and in private, for which he was
eventually to pay the penalty.[47]

According to Rostovtzeff, Helvidius had advocated in the
Senate 'the Stoical or Cynical point of view', that Vespasian
'should adopt the best man of the senatorial class', and that
Vespasian's answer meant: ' "Better the re-establishment of the
Republic than the method adopted by Helvidius".'[48]
Charlesworth was rash enough to claim certainty: 'one thing
seems clear, that [Helvidius] was utterly opposed to *any* form
of Principate, whether hereditary or elective.'[49] Wirszubski was

more judicious, pointing out that Dio's βασιλεία and δημοκρατία are the equivalents of *regnum* and *respublica*. 'All that can be said with certainty about Helvidius', he concludes, 'is that he tried to bring to book the prosecutors of his father-in-law, that he spoke his mind freely, and that he wished to enhance the prestige of the Senate. Anything else is speculation.'[50] This is too restrictive. Vespasian's emotional statement leaves no doubt that Helvidius had spoken strongly in the Senate, opposing the designation of Titus as Vespasian's successor. The occasion might have been — and this *is* speculation — a meeting of the Senate of which there was a motion to confer powers on Titus.[51] How long after 70 Helvidius continued his open hostility is not clear. At first Vespasian evidently tried to silence him by persuasion;[52] then came banishment; and finally death. The process may not have taken very long ,— but it is probable that Titus was actively involved in the final stages.[53] Why the Stoics had opposed him is not difficult to explain in the light of the defects outlined by Suetonius; and apart from this there could have been special loathing — long before Titus' return in 71 — for the man who had divorced Marcia. Titus returned to Rome in summer 71: after that year the legend *libertas* disappeared from the imperial coinage for a quarter of a century.[54]

Tacitus' own attitude to Helvidius, and indeed to the Stoics in general, is enigmatic. The sketch with which he introduces the man is sympathetic enough, but in the comment that to some Helvidius 'adpetentior famae videretur, quando etiam sapientibus cupido gloriae novissima exuitur' (4.6.1), one may detect the same point of view, albeit less passionate, as was earlier expressed towards the end of the *Agricola* (42.3–4).

On the assumption that Agricola's first season in Britain was 77, a fresh examination of his governorship and its aftermath may now be undertaken. In his short first season he completed the conquest of N. Wales and Anglesey, an area he must have known well.[55] In the second season, 78, he consolidated Roman control over Brigantian territory, a task initiated by Cerialis, which must have been continued by Frontinus: 'quibus rebus multae civitates, quae in illum diem ex aequo egerant, datis obsidibus iram posuere, et praesidiis castellisque circumdatae' (20.3). This indicates that he passed beyond the Brigantian *civitas*, into Scotland, meeting little opposition from peoples who had previously fought fiercely ('iram') and on equal terms ('ex aequo') — against Cerialis or Frontinus, or both.[56] In the third season, 79, he pressed on northwards. In mid-season, on 24 June, Vespasian died and Titus assumed power.[57] Agricola carried on, up to the Tay. Titus recognised his great success by taking his fifteenth imperatorial acclamation, as Dio specifically records. Agricola 'novas gentes aperuit'; and he had more success than his predecessors against those who had previously fought with Rome.[58] In 80, his fourth season, when he may have expected recall, work of consolidation was undertaken: 'omnis propior sinus', south of Clyde and Forth, was secured.[59] In 81 he began a further drive forwards, crossing the Clyde — that is unambiguous — and pacifying 'ignotas ad id tempus gentes crebris simul ac properis proeliis' (24.1) Since in his fourth season 'omnis propior sinus tenebatur', the 'unknown peoples' must have lived beyond the Clyde.[60] Hence it is conceivable that Agricola drew up his forces on the tip of Kintyre for his celebrated gaze at Ireland. It is possible that during 80 Agricola corresponded with Titus about initiating the conquest of Hibernia. He certainly received authority for pushing further forward in Britain.

Soon after the end of the fifth season he must have had the news of Titus' death, which occurred on 13 September 81.[61] The implications for himself were no doubt obvious. He had had two and a half years from Vespasian and two and a half from Titus. His career had advanced spectacularly with their blessing — and both of them had served in Britain and presumably took an interest in the province. The accession of Domitian made a change inevitable:

> '[Domitian] quite outdid himself in visiting disgrace and ruin on the friends of his father and brother ... he regarded as his enemy anyone who had enjoyed his father's or his brother's affection beyond the ordinary, or who had been particularly influential.'[62]

Within a year, or eighteen months at the most, 'many of the leading men' were removed, by banishment or death.[63] It is difficult to exclude Agricola from the category of those who had 'enjoyed the imperial affection beyond the ordinary'. But unlike the men whom Domitian crushed in 82 and 83, Agricola had an army of four legions and a large force of auxiliaries. Besides this, his campaign had been followed with some interest at Rome,[64] and he must have been able to convince the new emperor that the 'terminus Britanniae' was within his grasp.[65]

Any prospect of invading Hibernia, had it been mooted, must have been firmly dropped.

During 82 Domitian began making preparations for the campaign which was to give him the military renown which he had craved, and of which he had felt cheated — despite efforts by propagandists to boost his rôle in the events of 69–70.[66] The 'dux magnus' summoned the *proceres* to the 'arx Albana'.[67] They discussed Britain,[68] but the Chatti and the 'torvi Sycambri' proved to be the principal theme.[69] The advisers included one Pompeius, now convincingly identified with M. Pompeius Silvanus, evidently designated to a third consulship for 83.[70] Silvanus must have died before the end of 82, and the man who actually held the *fasces* as Domitian's colleague was Q. Petillius Rufus, perhaps none other than Q. Petillius Cerialis Caesius Rufus, Agricola's former commander-in-chief, a close kinsman of Domitian and formerly his close associate in the year 70.[71] Another adviser of Domitian for the German war was Agricola's immediate predecessor Frontinus.[72] Cerialis and Frontinus may both have felt that Agricola was due for recall: by 82 he had had twice as long in Britain as each of them.

During 82, his sixth season, Agricola had perhaps already furnished troops to reinforce the Rhine armies for their coming offensive.[73] This was the war that Domitian had hoped to wage in 70. Now, after standing so long in the shadow of his brother, his chance had come. Agricola was given one more season, and then recalled. He had certainly achieved a great deal. Tacitus may underrate somewhat the achievements of Agricola's predecessors, and depreciate their capacities by innuendo.[74] But Agricola had been very successful. To be sure, he was due for recall. But he might have felt that at the time of Titus' death he needed only one more season *at full strength* to complete the conquest. Had not the enemy eluded him, 'debellatum illa victoria foret' (26.2), Tacitus comments on the major battle of the sixth season; and he had already mentioned that the ninth legion was 'maxime invalida' — by implication the others were also below full strength. Nonetheless, Mons Graupius ensured that Britain was indeed *perdomita* (10.1).

Agricola returned to Rome in 84, to spend the remaining nine and a half years of his life in frustrated inactivity. All that he was given was the *ornamenta triumphalia* — perhaps merely a confirmation of what Titus had already conferred.[75] His three predecessors had all received something more: Bolanus the proconsulship of Asia; Cerialis a second consulship, perhaps a third; Frontinus the proconsulship of Asia.[76] Tacitus himself was away from Rome during the last four years of Agricola's life, 90–93.[77] During the years 85–89 they must have had numerous discussions, about Britain, about Agricola's career, and about the contemporary political scene.[78] It is during those years that Agricola must have been accustomed to tell how 'se prima in iuventa studium philosophiae acrius, ultra quam concessum Romano ac senatori, hausisse, ni prudentia matris incensum ac flagrantem animum coercuisset' (*Agr.* 4.3). Those words acquire additional point if, at the end of this period before Tacitus' departure, the devotees of philosophy, those who *had* drunk it in 'ultra quam concessum Romano ac senatori', were being persecuted.[79] What is more, several of them were making clear their refusal to play a part in public life.[80] To a man desperately anxious for further employment,[81] but who was not offered any, this attitude may well have been maddening. The withdrawal of one of the four British legions, very soon after Agricola's departure from Britain, and the abandonment of much of the territory which he had overrun, will no doubt have made him even more indignant.[82]

On the murder of Domitian there was a drastic change in the political situation. The surviving Stoics crawled out from under their stones and basked in the sunshine of popular approval.[83] But 'considerable turmoil was created by the fact that everyone was accusing everyone else', Dio reports, and 'Nerva ordered that this state of affairs should cease for the future'[84] – but it did not, or not completely. 'Occiso Domitiano statui mecum ac deliberavi, esse magnam pulchramque materiam insectandi nocentes, miseros vindicandi, se proferendi', Pliny records: he assailed Publicius Certus, whose victim the younger Helvidius had been in 93. The attack was dropped in the end.[85]

At this juncture Tacitus may have reflected that when all eyes were on the Stoic martyrs and their heirs, he ought to speak up for men of a different kind. At the opening of the *Agricola* he refers to the laudatory biographies of Thrasea and the elder Helvidius.[86] At the end of his work he reverts to the theme of *laus*:

'sciant quibus moris est illicita mirari, posse etiam sub malis principibus magnos viros esse, obsequiumque ac modestiam, si industria ac vigor adsint, eo laudis excedere,

146

quo plerique per abrupta, sed in nullum rei publicae usum, ambitiosa morte inclaruerunt' (42.3–4).[87]

The elder Helvidius had sprung to the defence of his dead father-in-law when the tyrant Nero was dead, as Tacitus was to relate in the *Histories*.[88] Now he himself could do the same on the fall of the tyrant Domitian, reminding his contemporaries that the Stoics deserved less praise than men like Agricola.

He emphasises that Domitian hated Agricola.[89] One need not call this special pleading, hiding an untruth.[90] As has been argued above, Agricola was doomed to rejection by Domitian, as a friend and *protégé* of Titus. Nor need one doubt that Agricola's feelings about Domitian were less than cordial. The abandonment of his British conquests must have rankled not least: the point is made emphatically in the *Histories* (1.2.1) – 'perdomita Britannia', echoing *Agr.* 10.1, 'et statim missa', a phrase which recent archaeological research has at last restored to its true and obvious meaning, that the conquests of Agricola in North Britain had all been given up by the death of Domitian (if not, indeed, by the time of Agricola's own death).[91] Tacitus, and one must assume Agricola also, were imperialists:[92] they surely could not admire the apparently pusillanimous foreign and frontier policy of Domitian. Tacitus was to turn to a closely relevant theme immediately afterwards: the *Germania* is designed not least to show that Domitian's German conquest had been a fake.[93] As for the Stoics, they shared Domitian's displeasure: but Tacitus (and Agricola) may have felt that they deserved it. To be sure, Tacitus displays some admiration for them in his later writings: their fortitude must have compelled it. But in both *Histories* and *Annals* there are reservations which show that his admiration was strictly limited, and that Tacitus, like Agricola, thought that 'studium philosophiae' could be overdone. Caution was required when confronted with the 'pulchritudinem ac speciem magnae excelsaeque gloriae'. Agricola, after all, 'retinuit, quod est difficillimum, ex sapientia modum'.[94] Thoughts of Britain and the Stoics must have been closely intertwined at the time when he wrote those words: in 97 or 98 one of the Stoics, a friend of Thrasea, T. Avidius Quietus, was made governor of the province.[95]

I am happy to offer this paper as a tribute to C. E. Stevens: I hope he will believe some of it.

## Notes

[1] The point has been duly noted: see e.g. A. R. Burn, *Agricola and Roman Britain,* London 1953, p. 92.

[2] Apart from Agricola, I can only find the following cases of men governing provinces where they had served as legionary legates: Q. Petillius Cerialis ((Tac.), *Ann.* 14.32; *Agr.* 8.17); Q. Pomponius Rufus (*AE* 1948.3); L. Burbuleius Optatus (*ILS* 1066); Q. Pompeius Falco (*ILS* 1035–6); Cn Julius Verus (*ILS* 1057); M. Nonius Macrinus (*ILS* 8820); C. Vettius Sabinianus (*AE* 1920.45); P. Septimius Geta (*AE* 1946.131); Q. Venidius Rufus (*CIL* 13.7994, 8828); Iasdius (*CIL* 3.797–8 = *ILS* 2494; *CIL* 6.31651). There is a similar number of cases where men served in the same army as tribune and legionary legate, and as tribune and governor.

[3] See J. Morris, 'Leges annales. 1' *Listy filologické* vol. 87, 1964, pp. 316–337.

[4] Cf. A. R. Birley, 'The duration of provincial commands under Antoninus Pius' in *Corolla Memoriae E. Swoboda Dedicata,* Graz 1966, pp. 43–53.

[5] See the tabulation by W. Orth, *Die Provinzialpolitik des Tiberius,* Munich 1970, pp. 12ff. He overlooks the important case detected by J. Morris, 'Munatius Plancus Paulinus' *BJ* vol. 165, 1965, p. 88 ff.

[6] (Tac.,) *Agr.* 7.1 and (Tac.,) *Hist.* 2.13.1 (where Agricola's mother is not named). The Othonian troops involved went on to engage a Vitellian force despatched by Valens (2.14–15); news of their encounter reached Valens at Ticinum well before Bedriacum (14 April). See R. Syme, *Tacitus,* Oxford 1958, vol. 2, p. 676 f. K. Wellesley, *The Histories Book III,* Sydney 1972, p. 9, assigns this episode to March.

[7] G. E. F. Chilver, 'The army in politics, A.D. 68–70' *JRS* vol. 47, 1957, pp. 29–35, especially 34f., emphasises that Vespasian and Mucianus had been preparing for the coup for months, citing *Hist.* 2.5.2 and 5.10.2. As he points out, 'The penetration of Vespasian's agents into high circles is almost more extraordinary than that of Galba's'; but to say that Vespasian 'also succeeded in suborning . . . Vettius Bolanus and his young legionary legate Agricola in Britain' is peculiar, or at least proleptic. Agricola needed no suborning, and he was certainly neither a legionary legate, nor in Britain, when he joined the Flavians.

[8] *Hist.* 2.79.

[9] *Hist.* 2.86.4; 98.1. The first item is reported before

Vitellius' arrival at Rome (2.89.1, presumably 17 July, cf. 2.91.1). Primus: *PIR*[2] A 866; Fuscus: ibid. C 1365, R. Syme, *Tacitus*, vol. 2, p. 683 f.

[10] *Hist.* 3.43.

[11] Wellesley, op. cit., p. 9, states that Agricola 'did not join Antonius [Primus], for it was by Mucianus that he was appointed to his post as recruiting officer (probably in Northern Italy) and then to his legionary command in Britain. The interval between August and December A.D. 69 Agricola presumably spent at Intimilum or Forum Iulii.' R. M. Ogilvie and I. A. Richmond, *De vita Agricolae*, Oxford 1967, p. 154, likewise appear to assume that Mucianus appointed Agricola to the recruiting post as well as to the command of legion XX, and hence that the former appointment could not have been made until early 70. But even if the legionary command were not given until Mucianus arrived at Rome ('initia principatus ac statum urbis Mucianus regebat' [*Agr.* 7.2] strongly implies this, cf. *Hist.* 4.11.1, 39.2), Agricola's recruiting mission could have commenced in the summer. Note that Pompeius Silvanus had raised 6,000 men in Dalmatia, who were transferred to the Ravenna fleet (*Hist.* 3.50.2–3); thereupon 'e classicis Ravennatibus legionariam militiam poscentibus optumus quisque adsciti,' probably in early November (3.50.1).

[12] 8,000 men from the British legions were with Vitellius (April) (*Hist.* 2.57.1); 2.100.1; 3.22.2; perhaps 4.46.2.

[13] *Hist.* 1.60; *Agr.* 7.3 (he is not named in the latter place).

[14] Agricola's legion cannot be established; but it seems clear that he was appointed by Suetonius Paulinus.

[15] Agricola was born on 13 June, evidently in 40; 39 is possible, but see Ogilvie op. cit., pp. 141 ff., 301 f. Titus was born on 30 December 39 (*PIR*[2] F 309; Suet., *Tit.* 1 is wrong). The British tribunate is given by Suet., *Tit.* 4.1. (The story in Dio 60.30.1 is clearly an error.)

[16] *Ann.* 14.38.1.

[17] Cf. *ILS* 1025 (L. Roscius Aelianus): 'trib. mil. leg. IX Hispanae vexillarior. eiusdem in expeditione Germanica.' Titus served in Germania Inferior, together with the elder Pliny: see now R. Syme, 'Pliny the procurator' *HSCP* vol. 73, 1969, pp. 201–236, especially 206f., who puts Titus' arrival in Germany in 57 or 58. But I do not believe that Pliny need necessarily have been in Campania in person on 30 April 59, to observe the eclipse which he reports in *NH* 2.180. Hence Titus' arrival may be placed a little later. Titus doubtless served under the

governor Duvius Avitus (*cos.* 56), from Vasio, to whom he no doubt owed his commission. Avitus himself may be presumed to have owed his governorship to his fellow-townsman Burrus (likewise his predecessor Pompeius Paullinus to Seneca): Syme, *Tacitus,* vol. 2, p. 622 f.

[18] The legate of IX Hispana, Q. Petillius Cerialis, was to become a close kinsman of Titus, if he was not one already, probably the husband of his sister Domitilla: see G. Townend, 'Some Flavian connections' *JRS* vol. 51, 1961, pp. 54—61; A. R. Birley, 'Petillius Cerialis and the conquest of Brigantia' *Brit.* vol. 4, 1973, pp. 179—191.

[19] *Agr.* 6.1—2; Suet. *Tit.* 4.2—3.

[20] *Agr.* 6.2; presumably the daughter whose birth is here mentioned was to be the wife of Tacitus. A third child was born much later (29.1), but there may have been other children. Note the senator Velleius . . . Sertorius . . . [Ped]anius Fuscus Sa[linat]or Sallust[i]us Bla[esus] . . . Iulius Agricola . . . Caesonius, perhaps a descendant (W. Eck, *RE* Suppl. vol. 14, 1974, Velleius no. 12a). Titus may have had a daughter already, see n. 26, below.

[21] Ogilvie, op. cit., pp. 149, 317, following Furneaux and earlier commentators, suggests that Agricola may have also served under the upright Antistius Vetus. This will not do. See Mommsen, *St.* 2³, 1, p. 258. It may be pure coincidence that Agricola was quaestor under Otho's brother and had been tribune under a man who was to be one of Otho's generals (*Hist.* 2.37, etc.). He was presumably elected quaestor in 62, taking office on 5 December. This adds interest to Tacitus' comments on the elections for that year (*Ann.* 15.19): the *ius liberorum,* from which Agricola benefited, was being abused by fake adoptions.

[22] Agricola had a quiet tribunate (*Agr.* 6.3): 'gnarus sub Nerone temporum, quibus inertia pro sapientia fuit' — unlike a practitioner of *sapientia,* his colleague Arulenus Rusticus (*Ann.* 16.26.4: he was ready to use his veto).

[23] See H. Castritius, 'Zu den Frauen der Flavier' *Hist.* vol. 18, 1969, pp. 492—502, who demonstrates that Julia was much more probably the daughter of Arrecina than of Marcia.

[24] Suet., *Tit.* 4.2

[25] *Ann.* 16.21.1, 23, etc. Cf. *PIR²* B 55; A. Bergener, *Die führende Senatorenschicht im frühen Prinzipat (14—68 n. Chr.),* Bonn 1965, p. 194 ff.; R. Syme, *Ten Studies in Tacitus,* Oxford 1970, pp. 96, 98ff.

[26] *PIR²* A 678.

[27] The *coniuratio Viniciana* (*PIR²* A 700); Suet., *Nero* 36.

[28] *Hist.* 4.7.2.

[29] Suet., *Tit.* 4.2 See G. Townend, *JRS* vol. 51, 1961, p. 57, n. 10, for the date and reason. Bergener, op. cit., p. 195, places the marriage 'um 67', which must be wrong — Titus was already involved in the Jewish war by then.

[30] See E. M. Smallwood, *Documents . . . Gaius, Claudius and Nero,* Cambridge 1967, 26, for the date (*Acta Arvalium*); sometime in the summer after 19 June the Arvals had celebrated the detection of a conspiracy, presumably that of Vinicianus (ibid.).

[31] Suet., *Vesp.* 4.4.

[32] It is remarkable that Vespasian had his son as legionary legate: such appointments were abnormal, see E. Birley, 'Beförderungen und Versetzungen im römischen Heere' *Carnuntum Jahrbuch,* 1957, 5 f. Perhaps Titus' prudent divorce of Marcia emphasised their reliability in Nero's eyes.

[33] Frontinus is not mentioned in *Agr.* 8, recording Agricola's legionary command. Since Cerlialis was back at Rome by May 74, Frontinus had presumably already taken over, probably in 73: A. R. Birley, *Brit.* vol. 4, 1973, p. 189.

[34] *Agr.* 9.1.

[35] *Agr.* 9.5.

[36] *Agr.* 9.6.

[37] Suet., *Tit.* 6.1, followed by Aur. Victor, *de Caes.* 9.10; *Epit.* 10.4.

[38] Note also Philostratus, *Vit. Apoll.* 6.30: ἰσομοιρήσων τῆς ἀρχῆς τῷ πατρί.

[39] Suet., *Tit.* 1.1, 6.2, 7.1; Dio 66.8.1.

[40] Suet., *Tit.* 5.1, also has this story.

[41] *Historische Untersuchungen zum Domitianbild des Tacitus,* Munich 1971, especially p. 107 ff.

[42] Op. cit., p. 126 f.

[43] R. Urban, op. cit., p. 76 ff., discusses the treatment of Domitian in the *Histories.* I cannot follow him in every particular.

[44] My own view is that Helvidius and his friends wanted some kind of senatorial control over the *princeps*: see the brief remarks in *CR* N.S. vol. 12, 1962, p. 197 ff.

[45] Dio 66.12. Helvidius was praetor in 70: *Hist.* 4.53.3.

[46] *Vesp.* 25, a version also in Aur. Victor, *de Caes.* 9 and Eutopius 7.20. 'Sons' may represent an emendation made under Domitian.

[47] Dio 66.12.2. *Exc. Val.* 272 refers to Mucianus (66.2.4), 274 to Domitian as emperor (67.1). The scholiast on Juvenal 5.36 is reminiscent of Dio: '[Helvidius] postea Vespasianum ita studio libertatis offendit, ut putaret ... pristinum libertatis statum posse revocari.'

[48] M. I. Rostovtzeff, *Social and Economic History of the Roman Empire*, ed. 2, Oxford 1957, p. 586, n. 16.

[49] M. P. Charlesworth, *CAH* vol. 11, p. 9, cf. J. M. C. Toynbee, 'Dictators and philosophers in the first century A.D.' *G and R* vol. 13, 1944, pp. 43—58.

[50] C. Wirszubski, *Libertas as a Political Idea at Rome during the Late Republic and Early Empire*, Cambridge 1950, p. 147 ff.

[51] On 6 August 70, Titus' troops hailed him *imperator* (Jos., *BJ* 6.316, Suet., *Tit.* 5.2, etc.). If one may believe Philostratus, Titus had learned that this had been confirmed at Rome by February 71, at Tarsus (*Vit. Apoll.* 6.29). It is not unreasonable to suppose that the Senate met to confer *imperium* on Titus before the end of the year 70.

[52] Epictetus, *Diss.* 1.2.19—22.

[53] Suet., *Vesp.* 15: 'et servasset, nisi iam perisse falso renuntiatum esset'. Titus, who often boasted that he 'maximum falsarium esse potuisse' (*Tit.* 3.2), could have been responsible for the false report. For possible instances of such activities, cf. *Vesp.* 6.4; *Tit.* 6.2; *Domit.* 2.3. The phrase put into Helvidius' mouth in Epict., *Diss.* 1.2.19, that Vespasian could deprive him of his senatorial rank, suggests that the first stage in his removal may not have occurred until the censorship of 73—74. Syme, *Tacitus*, vol. 1, p. 212, puts his death in 74.

[54] Apart from a restored coin of Galba (*RIC* vol. 2, Titus 248). See A. U. Stylow, *Libertas und Liberalitas. Untersuchungen zu innenpolitischen Propaganda der Römer*, Munich 1972, p. 54.

[55] From his service with Paulinus in 60/61 and as legate of leg. XX.

[56] Cf. A. R. Birley, *Brit.* vol. 4, 1973, p. 190.

[57] *PIR*[2] F 398—9.

[58] *Agr.* 22; Dio 66.20.1—3. An achievement such as is ascribed to the third season by Tacitus makes the imperatorial acclamation and the prominence assigned to it by Dio more readily intelligible than would be the case if the year 79 were the second season. One may note in passing that a Caledonian bear, presumably supplied by Agricola, was included in the opening festivities at the Colosseum in June 80: Martial, *Spect.* 7.3.

[59] *Agr.* 23.

[60] Ogilvie, op. cit., p. 235; see further N. Reed, 'The fifth year of Agricola's campaigns' *Brit.* vol. 2, 1972, pp. 143—148.

[61] *PIR²* F 399.

[62] Dio 67.2.1—2. W. Eck, 'M. Pompeius Silvanus, consul designatus tertium — ein Vertrauter Vespasians und Domitians' *ZfPE* vol. 9, 1972, pp. 259—275, 271ff., casts doubt on this statement. But although, as he points out, several men honoured by Vespasian are likewise honoured by Domitian, a number of men in high places in the reign of Titus do not receive further advancement, e.g. Q. Corellius Rufus (*PIR²* C 1294); and see the cases which he himself cites in his *Senatoren von Vespasian bis Hadrian,* Munich 1970, p. 110.

[63] Dio 67.3.3¹.

[64] Cf. Juv. 2.159 ff.; 4.126 f.; 14.196; Statius, *Silvae* 5.1.90 ff.

[65] Cf. *Agr.* 27.1; 30.3; 33.3; 33.6.

[66] A. R. Birley, *Brit.* vol. 4, 1973, p. 187.

[67] Juv. 4.72 ff.

[68] Juv. 4.125 ff.

[69] Juv. 4.147.

[70] Juv. 4.109 f. see W. Eck, *ZfPE* vol. 9, 1972, p. 259 ff.

[71] A. R. Birley, *Brit.* vol. 4, 1973, p. 186 f.

[72] *PIR²* J 322.

[73] *ILS* 1025, cf. R. Saxer, *Untersuchungen zu den Vexillationen des römischen Kaiserheeres,* Bonn 1967, p. 22 f.

[74] A. R. Birley, *Brit.* vol. 4, 1973, p. 179 ff.

[75] *Agr.* 40.1, cf. Dio 66.20.3.

[76] Bolanus: Statius, *Silv.* 5.2.56 ff. Cerialis: *Brit.* vol. 4, 1973, p. 186f. Frontinus: Eck, *Senatoren,* p. 77ff.

[77] *Agr.* 45.5.

[78] *Agr.* 4.3; 24.3; 44.5.

[79] If one may believe Eusebius, S.A. 2105 = October 88—September 89, Domitian 'mathematicos et philosophos Romana urbe pepulit'; and Dio implies that the expulsion in 93 was the second (67.13.3).

[80] Herennius Senecio (Dio 67.13.2) and the younger Helvidius (Pliny, *Ep.* 9.13.2).

[81] *Agr.* 40.2, 41.1—4 and 42.1—2 seem to indicate this. The reference to the *alii* with whom Agricola was favourably compared (41.3) wins additional interest from the discovery that one of these men was the governor of Syria whose behaviour caused concern in 97; see G. Alföldy and H. Halfmann, 'M. Cornelius Nigrinus Curiatius Maternus, General Domitians und Rivale Trajans' *Chiron,* vol. 3, 1973, pp. 331—373.

The relationship of this remarkable figure to the interlocutor in the *Dialogus* creates something of a puzzle.

[82] I.e. II Adiutrix. E. Birley, *Roman Britain and the Roman Army,* Kendal 1953, p. 22, suggests that it was withdrawn 'slightly earlier' than winter 85/86.

[83] See e.g. B. Grenzheuser, *Kaiser und Senat in der Zeit von Nero bis Nerva,* Paderborn 1964; O. Murray, 'The "quinquennium Neronis" and the Stoics', *Hist.* vol. 14, 1965, pp. 41–61, especially 59 f.; H. B. Mattingly, 'Tacitus' *praenomen*: the politics of a moderate' *Riv. stor. dell'Ant.* vol. 2, 1972, pp. 169–185.

[84] Dio 68.1.3.

[85] Pliny, *Ep.* 9.13.2.

[86] *Agr.* 2.1: 'Legimus cum Aruleno Rustico Paetus Thrasea, Herennio Senecioni Priscus Helvidius laudati essent'.

[87] See on this passage above all R. Syme, *Tacitus,* vol. 1, p. 24 ff.

[88] *Hist.* 4.6.1.

[89] The term *odium* recurs in *Agr.* 39.3, 42.3, 43.3.

[90] As is done by T. A. Dorey, 'Tacitus, Agricola and Domitian' *G and R* N.S. vol. 7, 1960, p. 66 ff.

[91] B. R. Hartley, 'The Roman occupation of Scotland: the evidence of Samian ware' *Brit.* vol. 3, 1972, pp. 1–55, has, one hopes, put an end to controversy.

[92] See e.g. G. M. Streng, *Agricola. Das Vorbild römischer Statthalterschaft nach dem Urteil des Tacitus,* Bonn 1970, p. 136 ff., n. 444.

[93] See H. Nesselhauf, 'Tacitus und Domitian' *Herm.* vol. 80, 1952, pp. 222–245.

[94] *Agr.* 4.3.

[95] *PIR*[2] A 1410. His governorship is dated by *CIL* 16.43. He presumably gave a commision to Martial's elderly friend Q. Ovidius (10.44). One may note, finally, that the recent publication of Statius' *Silvae* 5.2, praising the achievements of Bolanus in Britain, may have been an added spur to Tacitus.

A. R. Birley,
School of History,
Leeds University.

CASSIO L F PAL CER E
FABRVM · VG O C CVRATORI
PVBLICOR ET L OCORVM PRIN
II VIRO QVINQ NO CVRATOR LA
VNIVERSA PLEPS CVM
CAESAR AVG IN AMPHITHE
CASSIA CATE CER VL F PIISSIMO

# 11

## Tacitus, Annals 13.48 and a New Inscription from Puteoli

Isdem consulibus auditae Puteolanorum legationes, quas diversas ordo plebs ad senatum miserant, illi vim multitudinis, hi magistratuum et primi cuiusque avaritiam increpantes. eaque seditio ad saxa et minas ignium progressa ne c⟨aed⟩em et arma proliceret, C. Cassius adhibendo remedio delectus. quia severitatem eius non tolerabant, precante ipso ad Scribonios fratres ea cura transfertur, data cohorte praetoria, cuius terrore et paucorum supplicio rediit oppidanis concordia.

I

Tacitean notices of historical events in the Italian municipalities are infrequent and cursory. When they do occur the specific episodes described may incidentally illuminate local social and economic developments; more often they are clues to Tacitus' special interest in particular Roman personalities. It is thus in the case of the present passage, an account of municipal turbulence in Puteoli in A.D. 58. Tacitus offers only the barest explanation of the causes of social friction, citing the violence of the populace and the fiscal niggardliness of the magistrates and certain other leading citizens. This brief glimpse is tantalising: Puteoli was Rome's chief harbour and principal centre for international trade before developments at Ostia under Trajan early in the second century, and there is independent evidence to suggest that the high proportion of *peregrini* and ex-slaves in the population, accompanied by the

155

rise to the local senate of an increasing number of descendants of ex-slaves, was indeed producing social tensions by late Julio-Claudian times.[1] Tacitus, however, shows little interest in these matters. As an acute historian he was certainly aware of the importance of Puteoli to the city of Rome, but he included the episode primarily, as Syme has suggested, because of the prominent rôle played in the dispute by C. Cassius Longinus (*suff.* 30), the famour jurist and exemplar of the stern virtues of an earlier age.[2]

A rapid review of the space accorded Longinus in the *Annals* will show this at once, and will reveal also the importance which Tacitus attaches to *severitas* as an ingredient of Longinus' character. The man's father, L. Cassius Longinus (*suff.* 11), appears but once in Tacitus (*Ann.* 6.15); he is there said to have practised *severa disciplina* in the upbringing of his children. C. Cassius Longinus is first introduced when serving as governor of Syria in A.D. 49 (*Ann.* 12.12). Tacitus testifies first to the man's pre-eminence as a jurist, then proceeds to portray his character through a description of the strict and old-fashioned discipline which he imposed upon his troops. Next, the episode at Puteoli, whose citizens found the *severitas* of Longinus insupportable; later in the same year, a firm stand in the senate against excessive offerings of thanksgiving to the gods for victory in the east (*Ann.* 13.41). All these episodes are preliminaries to a later event, the jurist's chief performance in the *Annals*: a famous and eloquent speech to the senate after the murder of Pedanius Secundus, the city prefect, by one of his slaves; Longinus, in accordance with ancient practice, advocated the execution of every slave in the *familia* (*Ann.* 14.42–45). Before the speech, Tacitus comments upon the division of opinion within the senate as to the appropriate reprisal: in summarising the basis of objection from Longinus' opponents to his position, the historian employs a word which he had last used in connection with Longinus' conduct at Puteoli: *severitas*.[3]

The characterisation of C. Cassius Longinus is thus sharply etched and entirely consistent; it culminates in an entry for the year 65 (*Ann.* 16.7.2 ff.) in which Tacitus asserts that the austerity of his character (*gravitas morum*), along with his large hereditary fortune, were the chief grounds for Nero's antipathy to Longinus, and for his eventual exile to Sardinia. Can Tacitus' characterisation of the man help to clarify the rôle played by Longinus in the dispute at Puteoli? Only in the sense, that the very consistency of Tacitus' emphasis upon the *severitas* of

Cassius Longinus is sufficient to raise questions as to its precise nature in a given situation. Doubts arise particularly in the case of the present passage, where the *severitas* of Longinus' *remedium* is noted, but the solution itself is not described: this prompts the inference that Tacitus included the incident primarily by way of preparation for his more lengthy and powerful presentation of Cassius Longinus in the later scene. Further examination of the Puteolan passage increases perplexity. For however harsh and intolerable the *remedium* of Cassius Longinus, that of his chosen successors, the Sulpicii Scribonii, was appreciably worse, involving a cohort of the praetorian guard, which brought with it armed conflict, terror and punishment. Surely there is irony in Tacitus' report of the methods by which social harmony was restored in the port city.[4]

It has been traditionally assumed that Longinus was chosen for this particular assignment owing to his eminence as a senior consular and jurist, and to his strictness as a disciplinarian.[5] These factors need not have been the only, or indeed the major, reason for his selection. The normal relationships between Roman senators and Italian cities suggest an additional motive: Dionysius of Halicarnassus, in remarks as pertinent to the Empire as they were to the Republic, observed that every city had its own protectors and patrons in the capital, adding that the Roman senate regularly referred the controversies of cities to their Roman patrons and regarded their decisions as binding.[6] It is clear that at least some of the earliest Imperial *curatores rei publicae*, officials sent out to check municipal mismanagement of finances, were closely affiliated with the cities to which they were assigned — as might, indeed, have been expected.[7] In fact, C. Cassius Longinus may have had connections in the city of Puteoli, and these local ties may have constituted a prime reason for his being the first choice of the senate as arbitrator of the dispute. New evidence lies in an inscription from Pozzuoli which has remained unpublished until now despite its discovery some years ago during excavations of an important sector of the ancient city.

## II

The stone (see plate 1), Luna marble with small-grained crystal, measures 1.18 x .58 x .15; it is damaged, with letters missing at top left and top right, and a jagged diagonal break divides the

panel into two portions.[8] The reverse reveals bash marks and
was left rough; the two side edges, the top and bottom have been
carefully and smoothly dressed. The lettering consists of well-
cut, deeply incised and serifed capitals of monumental character,
with a squarish appearance; this fact, taken together with the
long tailed Q's, partially open P's, and the axis of Q's and O's
on the diagonal rather than at the tops, conveys a strong overall impression of late Julio-Claudian workmanship.[9] Three factors
militate against a completely satisfactory restoration of the
text. First, the inscription is only partially preserved; while the
left hand margin is almost entirely intact, a considerable
portion of the text is missing on the right. At the end of the
second line, however, *o[perum]* must be restored, and must in
turn have been directly followed by *publicorum* at the
beginning of line 3.[10] This enables the dimensions of the
missing panel to be fixed precisely as .37 x .58 x .15; the
discrepancy in the size of the two sections is almost certainly to
be explained by the fact that the left hand portion, which
measures exactly 2 x 4 Roman feet, was acquired first, and the
second portion was cut to meet the specific spatial requirements
of the ordinator. Second, there has been erasure both at the
beginning and end of line 5, and before the word *Caesari* in line
6. Third, the letters of the final line convey a more crowded and
wiry appearance than the remainder of the text, and the E's
display a marked tendency towards the rustic style: they are
probably a slightly later addition by a different hand. It is my
intention to present and to comment briefly upon the text of
the inscription, and then to suggest the ways in which it may
relate to the historical events described by Tacitus.

[L.] Cassio L(uci) f(ilio) Pal(atina tribu) Cerea[li praef(ecto)]
[f] abrum Aug(uri) Q(uaestori) curatori o[perum]
publicor(um) et locorum prim[o facto]
IIvir(o) q(uinquiens) quin(quennali) curatori aq[uarum]
//// universa pleps cum ////////////////
//////// Caesari Aug(usto) in amphithea[t(ro)————]
Cassia Cale Cer[ea]li f(ilio) piissimo.[11]

The text, which elucidates the distinguished municipal career
of the Puteolan notable Cassius Cerealis, falls naturally into
three divisions. Lines 1—4 review the man's *cursus honorum*,
and reveal that, like many another municipal notable who held
the post of *praefectus fabrum* early in his career, Cerealis
subsequently concentrated solely upon local advancement; this

prefecture heads the list of offices and titles in order to emphasise Cerealis' *transitio in ordinem equestrem.*[12] More important, the succession of offices includes the first example in any municipality of a *curator operum publicorum et locorum.* The full title, *curator aedium sacrarum et operum locorumque publicorum*, was the creation of the emperor Augustus and occupation of the post at Rome was strictly a senatorial prerogative; in the municipalities the standard title is simply *curator operum publicorum* and, although the position was not formally regarded as a magistracy, it was invariably reserved for persons of the highest distinction, holders of the other major local offices and priesthoods — like Cassius Cerealis in this instance.[13]

The *cursus* is followed, in lines 5–6, by an *elogium*, largely unintelligible owing to its fragmentary condition and to multiple erasure. Certain details can, however, be established with a reasonable degree of uncertainty. First, the initial word in line 5 was *hunc.* Traces of the H, N, and C are still clearly visible in a raking light; for the stone has been more lightly erased here than at the end of the line or at the beginning of the next. One ought always to resist the tendency to blame the stonecutter for what may prove to be deficiencies in one's own understanding; it is nonetheless tempting to believe that in this instance the obliteration of *hunc*, which seems otherwise inexplicable, was an error of the cutter, who initially mistook the beginning of line 5 for the beginning of line 6 (his actual destination), and recognised his mistake too late to preserve the word. Second, *cum* (line 5) functions here as conjunction, rather than as preposition: in all but one example known to me of the familiar phrase *ordo et plebs* (or *populus*) and its variants, the position of *plebs* is secondary, not primary, and there is thus every likelihood that *universa pleps* serves here as single subject of the missing verb in a dependent clause.[14] Third, the name of an emperor in the dative must have occupied the space at the end of line 5 and the initial position, before the phrase *Caesari Aug(usto)*, in the following line. On the other hand, more than the emperor's name has been erased: a main verb (of which *hunc* is direct object), the subject and verb of the *cum* clause, and very probably the direct object of the latter. The lettering of the inscription seems inappropriate to the brief reign of Gaius; all things considered, Nero is the emperor most likely to have been the victim of this *damnatio memoriae*. But it is equally clear that the erasure was intended to obliterate not only his name, but reference also to the event associating Cassius Cerealis with him. More than one restoration of the erased portion of this text is of course possible: the following proposal is frankly speculative, based, however, upon careful measurement of the available space, and upon epigraphical parallels; further, it attempts to satisfy requirements of sense and the other conditions which have been outlined above: *[hunc] universa pleps cum [ludos fec(erit) Neroni]/[Claudio] Caesari Aug(usto) in amphithea[t(ro) acclamavit].*[15]

The third and final section of the inscription, line 7, is syntactically independent of the *elogium* and consists of a statement of dedication by the honorand's mother. The phrasing is most appropriate to a *titulus sepulchralis* and, as was suggested above, it seems to have been composed later than the body of the text, probably after the death of Cassius Cerealis.

## III

It remains to explore the possible implications of the new inscription for the Puteolan episode described by Tacitus. Nomenclature provides the first and most striking point of contact. The honorand in the text from Puteoli was the son of a L. Cassius, who was very probably a freedman: since the mother of Cerealis bears the same *nomen gentilicium* as his father, as well as a Greek *cognomen*, it is virtually certain that both parents of the magistrate were members of the *familia* of slaves of a L. Cassius, and were subsequently manumitted. And the tribe of Cerealis, Palatina, provides further confirmation of his freedman descent.[16] L. Cassius, *patronus* of the father of Cerealis, may have been the brother of C. Cassius Longinus, for there is evidence to suggest that the Cassii Longini possessed estates in or near the territory of Puteoli,[17] and numerous Cassii, almost all of whom bear the *praenomina* Lucius or Caius, are attested in the local inscriptions.[18]

Ties of *clientela*, I suggest, connected C. Cassius Longinus with Puteoli; these, and not merely his influence as consular and jurist, gave specificity and point to his being selected by the senate for arbitration in Puteoli's municipal dispute. The full scope and precise nature of his *remedium* is more difficult to assess. Was his arrival in the city the occasion for assigning to Cassius Cerealis the new responsibilities of *curator operum publicorum et locorum*? That would have been appropriate: we know that one of the Sulpicii Scribonii, to whom Longinus yielded his local responsibilities when his own solution failed, was sent to Luna at some point during the reign of Claudius or Nero in a comparable capacity as *curator aedium sacrarum et operum publicorum*.[19] Furthermore, from a slightly later period there are examples of distinguished local notables being assigned the duties of *curator operum publicorum* by specific authority of reigning emperors, Vespasian and Hadrian respectively;[20] since the senate rather than the emperor had jurisdiction in the Puteolan dispute, Cassius Longinus may have exercised his authority as the emperors later employed theirs, appointing Cassius Cerealis to the office in this instance. Perhaps Longinus hoped that social tension could be relieved by investing a distinguished local notable, himself of servile ancestry, with unusually broad and sweeping powers, and by providing also considerable financial backing; perhaps consummation of the new arrangements was publicised and celebrated with games, given by Cerealis in the local amphitheatre in the emperor's honour. An inscription, in which the unanimous approval of the city's populace (*universa plebs*) was emphasised, was prepared for prominent display in a public place to commemorate the settlement.

For whatever reasons, the settlement was not long enduring. If Longinus' support of Cerealis was in effect a confirmation of the local *status quo*, and the Roman senate was thus acting, as it so often acted, in the interests of a city's upper classes, the *plebs* might well complain of the *severitas* of Longinus' *remedium*, and might continue to complain as well of the *avaritia* of the magistrates and most influential citizens — in whose number, assuredly, Cassius Cerealis must be included. Sterner measures were required, and were put into effect by the Scribonii and by a cohort of the praetorian guard. Nero elevated Puteoli's status to that of a *colonia* two years later, an act upon which these earlier events doubtless had a bearing: Puteoli was too important to the Roman economy for her social problems to be left to the senate for resolution. Colonial status implies concrete recognition by Nero that the emperor himself must intervene and exercise control.[21] Later, when the name of Nero came to be erased from the inscription, the reference to Cerealis' games was obliterated with it: there was no need to preserve a reminder of a benefaction which, in the event, had proved fruitless, and a stimulant to further violence. It was Cassia Cale who, having outlived her son, undertook to excise portions of the epigraphical text and to add the final line — thereby altering the form of the inscription from municipal elogium to sepulchral monument.

## Notes

[1] For the importance and prosperity of Puteoli see in general Ch. Dubois, *Pouzzoles Antique,* Paris 1907, pp. 64—83; M. W. Frederiksen, *RE* vol. 23, cols. 2044—45. Social structure: J. H. D'Arms, 'Puteoli in the second century of the Roman Empire: a social and economic study', *JRS* vol. 64, 1974.

[2] R. Syme, *Tacitus,* Oxford 1958, pp. 447, 563—64, 761; cf. *PIR*² C 501.

[3] Tac. *Ann.* 14.42.2: '. . . erant studia nimiam severitatem aspernantium, pluribus nihil mutandum censentibus. Ex quis C. Cassius . . .'

[4] For Tacitus' awareness of the ambiguity inherent in such words as 'remedium' and 'severitas', cf. the speech of Otho, *Hist.* 1.37.4: 'nam quae alii scelera, hic remedia vocat, dum falsis nominibus severitatem pro saevitia, parsimoniam pro avaritia, supplicia et contumelias vestras disciplinam appellat.' A different sense of 'concordia' appears in the only other Tacitean reference to the brothers P. Sulpicius Scribonius Proculus and Sulpicius Scribonius Rufus; in *Hist.* 4.41.3 they are described as 'concordia opibusque insignes'.

[5] Cf. Syme, op. cit., p. 447; E. Koestermann, *Cornelius Tacitus: Annalen,* vol. 3, p. 331.

[6] Dion. Hal. 2.11; cf. Th. Mommsen, *Staatsrecht,* vol. 3, p. 1203, for examples. For early imperial instances of internal strife within cities in the provinces, see P. A. Brunt, *Hist.* vol. 10, 1961, pp. 213—14, with n. 76. Note also the almost precisely contemporary incident in another Campanian city: at Pompeii in 59 after rioting between Pompeians and Nucerians during games, the senate banned performances in the amphitheatre for a period of ten years (Tac., *Ann.* 14.7.1); but they seem to have been resumed in the 60's owing to the intercession of Poppaea Sabina, who had close local associations: A. W. Van Buren, *Studies Presented to D. M. Robinson,* vol. 2, St Louis 1953, pp. 970—74; J. H. D'Arms, *Romans on the Bay of Naples,* Cambridge, Mass., 1970, p. 97, n. 122.

[7] E.g., Curiatius Cosanus, *CIL* 11. 3614 (= *ILS* 5918a; Caere, A.D. 113). The first such officials must be dated to the reign of Nero: P. Garnsey, *Social Status and Legal Privilege in the Roman Empire*, Oxford 1970, 31 n.

[8] Heights of letters: line 1: .07; 2–3: .06; 4: .055; 5: .045; 6: .042; 7: .045. I am grateful to Prof. A. De Franciscis, Soprintendente per l'Antichità di Napoli, for permission to publish the inscription, and to M. W. Frederiksen, M. Torelli, and J. B. Ward-Perkins for helpful discussion of the problems presented by the text; responsibility for interpretations suggested here rests entirely with me.

[9] Despite the generally expert workmanship, the text is not without its inconsistencies: in line 4, *curatori* has two apices and small -i, in line 2 no apices and tall -i.

[10] This fact, in turn, proves that *praef(ecto)* in line one must have been written in the abbreviated form.

[11] The following observations on points of epigraphical detail may be found useful. Line 2: *Aug(uri)*: for the augurate at Puteoli, cf. *CIL* 10.1685 (Domitianic: H. G. Pflaum, *Les Carrières procuratoriennes équestres*, Paris 1960, pp. 126–128 (no. 55), 1785. *Q(uaestori)*: 10.1799; 1806; 1810. Line 3: *prim[o facto]*, definitely to be preferred to *prim[ipilo]* (for a local example, cf. 10.1711): aside from considerations of space, the military post is out of place in this strictly municipal context. Line 4: Cerealis will have held the office of duovir five times, and was *quinquennalis* during his fifth duovirate (cf. 10.838: *IIvir i(ure) d(icundo) quinquiens, iter(um) quinquennalis*). The alternative, *IIviro q(uinquennali) quinq(uiens)* is improbable in the extreme, and without parallel. C. Cartilius Poplicola of Ostia held the duovirate eight times, thrice with censorial powers; he is a unique example: S. Panciera, *Arch. Class.* vol. 18, 1966, p. 55 ff. *Curatori aq[uarum]* : the restoration is certain: in addition to the -a, a portion of the left-hand stroke of the -q survives on the stone; for another occupant of the post at Puteoli, cf. 10.1805 with Mommsen's addition, p. 1150, *s.v.*; for the Augustan aqueduct, see I. Sgobbo, *Not. d. Scavi* 1938, 75–97; Frederiksen, *RE* vol. 23, col. 2057, with other references *ad loc.* Line 6: *in amphithea[t(ro)]*. The reference must be to the small building, probably of Augustan date, which stood in Puteoli until the great Flavian amphitheatre was begun under Vespasian, cf. Frederiksen, art. cit., cols. 2057–2058.

[12] *Praefecti fabrum* and municipal careers: B. Dobson, 'The *Praefectus Fabrum* in the early Principate,' *Britain and Rome* (ed. M. G. Jarrett and B. Dobson), Kendal 1965, pp. 61–84; E. Kornemann, art. *fabri, RE* vol. 6, cols. 1922–1923; for Campanian examples cf. *CIL* 10.688 (Surrentum); 1081 (Nuceria); 1266 (Nola); 3909 (Capua). Other *praefecti fabrum* at Puteoli: 10.1685, 1806.

[13] *Curatores aedium sacrarum et operum locorumque publicorum:* A. E. Gordon, *Univ. of California Publications in Class. Arch.* vol. 2, 1952, pp. 279–83; G. Molisani, *Rend. Accad. Naz. Lincei* ser. 8, vol. 26, 1971, pp. 808–11. *Curatores operum publicorum* in the municipalities: Kornemann, art. *curatores, RE* vol. 4, col. 1802; A. Degrassi, *Scritti Vari di Antichità*, vol. 4, Rome 1971, p. 81. *Curator operum publicorum* at Puteoli: *CIL* 10.1799.

[14] *CIL* 10.4760: 'ordo decurionum et augustalium et pleps universa;' 9.3160: '. . . decurionibus. . . liberis eorum . . . sevir(is) august(alibus) . . . plebei universae;' 9.2860: 'huic plebs universa municipum Histonie(n)sium;' cf. 5.3341; 10.5058. The pattern is not contradicted by 'populus universus et ordo splendidissimus' (*AE* 1962, 184, Bulla Regia).

[15] The form of Nero's imperial titulature suggested here is precisely paralleled in another inscription from Puteoli in which the name has been partially erased: *CIL* 10.1574 (A.D. 56).

[16] As at Ostia, the heavy enrolment in Palatina at Puteoli seems a direct reflection of the numbers of men of servile descent who were present in the town; the old tribe of Puteoli was Falerna. Cf. *RE* vol. 23, col. 2042; *JRS* vol. 64, 1974, n. 100.

[17] C. Cassius Longinus (*pr.* 44 B.C.), a direct ancestor of the jurist, seems to have had property in or near Naples: Cic., *ad Att.* 16.3.6, on which see D'Arms, *Romans on the Bay of Naples*, p. 58.

[18] Nearly one third of the fifty-two Cassii listed in the index of *CIL* 10 must be assigned to Puteoli: 1901, 1978, 1997, 2018, 2205, 2234–2240, 2526.

[19] *CIL* 11.1340, on which see E. Groag, *RE* vol. 3A, col. 889, no. 26.

[20] *CIL* 10.1266 (Nola, Vespasian); 9.1260, 1419 (Venusia and Beneventum, Hadrian); cf. De Ruggiero, *Dizionario Epigrafico*, 2.1335; Kornemann, *RE* vol. 4, col. 1802.

[21] Colonia Claudia Neronensis: Tac., *Ann.* 14.27.2; *CIL* 10.5369; 4.2152; 3525. Cf. Frederiksen, art. cit., cols.

2041—2042; D'Arms, *Romans on the Bay of Naples*, p. 98, n. 126.

J. H. D'Arms,
Ann Arbor,
Michigan University.

# 12

# Descendants of Freedmen in Local Politics: some Criteria

Under the Principate membership of city councils passed down from father to son as long as a family survived, maintained its economic position, and did not advance into the senate or the equestrian service. In practice, however, the statutory number of councillors could not be maintained solely by the controlled introduction of young men from established families, having or lacking experience as minor magistrates. It was necessary for municipal authorities to turn to men from families with no record of political service in the community in order to retain an *ordo plenus.*

New recruits into the local governing class were drawn from among the following groups: descendants of freedmen, ex-soldiers, free immigrants and their descendants, indigenous peoples inhabiting dependent rural districts, and free plebeians of local origin.

That patterns of replacement within city aristocracies varied greatly from place to place and within individual cities at different periods is obvious. For example, descendants of freedmen are known to have held official positions in many cities in Italy and the western provinces, but are not, or not yet, attested in Africa or in cities of the eastern provinces, Athens excepted. In Athens[1] the intrusion of sons and grandsons of freedmen into organs of government is attested for the Antonine era, that is, for the middle of a period in which the influence of men of servile extraction reached its peak in the West. Again, under the Empire veterans played a prominent part in urban life and local politics in frontier provinces and the more backward areas, but are rarely recorded in positions of authority in the old-established Greek cities of the East or in the larger western cities and the more Romanised regions of the West in general.

There is little detailed documentation relating to the recruitment of new families into the local aristocracy. Most of the relevant information has to do with individuals and comes to us piecemeal through inscriptions: a freedman's son at Italian Suessa secured admission into the council without charge in consequence of his father's public benefactions; a veteran became decurion at Carnuntum in Pannonia; a member of the Chinithi, a tribe attributed to Gigthis in Africa, was perpetual flamen of Trajan and later served in the jury courts at Rome at Hadrian's invitation; a peasant attained the office of censor in Maktar, Africa.[2] The first problem we must face is how to draw inferences concerning the social origins of a city aristocracy as a whole from references to individuals.

Even a single inscription can serve to establish a negative point, such as that the order of decurions at Suessa at the end of the second century was not closed to sons of wealthy freedmen. As it happens there is no parallel inscription from this town — the other promotions cited above are unique in the same way. However, where an inscription does not stand alone, there may be material for a hypothesis of broader scope, and an investigation of greater depth may be in prospect. But clearly a pattern will emerge only insofar as evidence accumulates and converges.

Here we come up against a second problem. Anyone undertaking an investigation into social mobility will soon discover that status is not often explicitly indicated. How are the majority of cases to be handled? If we ignore them, we will produce a study which is relatively safe from criticism but severely restricted in scope. The alternative is to attempt to formulate hypotheses of more or less limited generality, making use of all the evidence that is to hand, direct or indirect. I opt for the second procedure without apology, as both the more adventurous and the more likely to lead to positive conclusions. In this I am confident I have the sympathetic support of that master of imaginative hypothesis to whom this paper is dedicated.

In what follows I propose to focus attention on the influx into the local aristocracy of men who traced their origins to a slave, and to deal only secondarily with the various categories of men of free descent with which they are liable to be confused.

Some new arrivals of slave background are easily identified. Libertine status may be indicated by the juxtaposition of *libertus* and patronal *praenomen*, both often in abbreviated form, where a freeborn citizen might show mark of filiation and patronymic. Other signs of freed status include tenure of the office of *sevir* or *sevir Augustalis* (or another local variant), except in a few cities where such officials were often freeborn,[3] and the award of some of the privileges of local councillors without the office. Even after the passage of the Visellian law of A.D. 23,[4] forbidding the participation of freedmen in local government, it is possible to identify a few freedman magistrates with the aid of these criteria. One who slipped through the net was C. Gabbius Messallae lib(ertus) Aequalis, *Augustalis* and adlected decurion at Larinum in Italy.[5] Inscriptions of this sort are a rarity; many more record the advancement of the son, where the father's freedman status is signalled in one of the ways just described.

There is reason to believe, however, that those inscriptions in turn are heavily outnumbered by others mentioning local officials whose servile origins are hidden from view. Descendants of freedmen bore no mark of status that set them apart from their colleagues of free descent. Moreover, as a class they had less reason than other new men to reveal their ancestry. The efforts of many of them to conceal their dubious origins (for example by discarding a servile or foreign name in favour of a respectable Latin *cognomen*) are only partly offset by the willingness of some freedman fathers to advertise the political success of their sons.

Some scholars have nonetheless held that the identification of descendants of freedmen is a feasible proposition, even in the absence of direct status-indications. Others, inevitably, have questioned the validity of the indexes of servile origin that they have advanced. I propose to evaluate some of these possible criteria afresh, and especially membership of the tribe Palatina and the bearing of a Greek name. I choose examples from a limited number of towns, and one in particular, Beneventum; I conclude by drawing together the evidence from this town. My choice of Beneventum is governed by two factors: first, the data are relatively plentiful, and second, scholars' estimates of the ratio of officials of freedman descent to those of free descent have been markedly disparate, ranging from 1:3 to 1:12.5.[6]

## II

A survey of the inscriptions of the Principate reveals that freedmen and their descendants frequently belonged to the tribe Palatina, that members of this tribe were represented among the municipal aristocracy, especially in Italy, and that they included some senior equestrian officials and senators. Palatina was the tribe of a few Roman senatorial families of the Late Republic, including some of patrician rank.

The distinction between Palatina and the local, rural tribes is most plausibly explained as one of status. It has been suggested[7] that at Ostia and Puteoli, the two towns where Palatina is most in evidence, the original tribes Voturia and Faleria were displaced by Palatina, perhaps by the agency of Trajan, in recognition of the close commercial and administrative connection of these ports with the capital. This argument can be seriously entertained only in the case of Ostia, for Puteoli was principally a local or regional port by the time Palatina had emerged as the dominant tribe there. But at Ostia no direct descendant of a family resident in the city in the early Empire can be uncovered among known members of Palatina. In contrast the Egrilii and Acilii who provided duovirs in A.D. 6 and 45 B.C. respectively were of tribe Voturia, while freedmen of the Egrilii are known as members of Palatina.[8]

Palatina, however, cannot be regarded as an infallible guide to freedman origin. Some families of free descent originating in Rome, and enrolled in Palatina on that account, may have become civic leaders elsewhere, or may have adopted members of indigenous municipal families prominent in local politics. (One would not, however, expect to find in this category blood descendants of senatorial nobles of the Republic.) This might in principle help to explain Palatina's strong representation in some regions adjacent to Rome, particularly Latium and Campania. On the other hand, a relatively high proportion of recorded members of Palatina in this area show signs of having been of foreign or servile descent, and in the city of Castrimoenium Palatina was the tribe assigned to one illegitimate.[9]

Illegitimates are regularly found in the tribe Collina, which was also the tribe allotted to a number of newly recruited legionaries of Asian origin. Pollia and other rural tribes were assigned to other soldiers of peregrine status.[10] The only identifiable class of newly enfranchised citizens who contributed to the membership of Palatina consisted of freedmen and their sons.

It has recently been suggested that Palatina was offered to local gentry as a mark of honour, as part of a deliberate policy of gaining their loyalty to Rome.[11] It is difficult to give any credence to this idea (which has never been expounded in any detail). The political battles fought in Republican times over whether freedmen and Italian allies should be spread among all the tribes or only the four city tribes tells against it. Morover, the distribution in time of the relevant inscriptions is just the opposite of what seems required by the theory: the heyday of Palatina was the second century A.D., not the period of the Republic and early Empire when the establishment of a *modus vivendi* with local aristocracies was a current problem. The earliest magistrates whose tribes are known were not in Palatina. In Pompeii, for instance, Menenia is the tribe of families of high social status such as the Clodii, who were prominent in the Augustan age. A freedman of this family was inscribed in Palatina.[12]

The size of the class of local aristocrats whose families were Rome-originating and enrolled in Palatina, or who were connected by adoption with such families, may be considered small. In contrast, the numbers of members of Palatina who were definitely freedmen or of freedman stock are considerable. If we did add those whose inscriptions appear to provide other signs of servile descent (however such clues are evaluated), the total number constitutes a majority of the relevant inscriptions in every region of Italy where Palatina is represented by more than one or two members.[13]

My provisional conclusion is that for the most part Palatina marks out families of servile origin.

At Beneventum known members of Palatina among the governing class include Nasellius Sabinus, son of the *Augustalis* Nasellius Sabinus who was certainly a freedman; Gavius Sabinus, whose occupation of scribe is regularly associated with slaves and freedmen, Afinius Hierax (see below, p. 177), Vibbius Proculus and Oclatius Modestus.[14]

Only a small minority of the inscriptions with which we are concerned give a tribal affiliation, and the tribe is not always Palatina. A magistrate of Aesernia, M. Celerius Corinthus, son of a freedman and *sevir Augustalis* of the same name and of the freedwoman Ovia Vitalis, was in Tromentina. If his brother Iustus had omitted to cite the names of their parents in the inscription set up in their honour, no clue to the origins of the magistrate would have survived, except perhaps his *cognomen*.[15] At any rate, in terms of the number of inscriptions involved, the issue of tribal affiliation is overshadowed by that of Greek or foreign names, and it is to this matter that we must now turn.

## III

The controversy over nomenclature has not been altogether productive. First, methodological shortcomings have hampered progress. For example, lists of 'suspect' Latin *cognomina*, and numerical calculations based on such lists, have sometimes been unashamedly impressionistic.[16] Kajanto placed the study of Latin names on a more scientific basis. But as he appears to have recognised as freedmen or slaves only those who are positively identified as such in the indexes of the *Corpus*, and to have classed all others as freeborn, his figures for the incidence of particular *cognomina* among the non-freeborn are much too low.[17] Secondly, no existing survey has systematically studied how differences of origin rather than status are reflected on nomenclature. Kajanto's analysis of Latin *cognomina*, which treats only the categories of senator, freeborn and slave/freed, is a case in point. Again, the debate over the significance of Greek names in Italy has focused on the question whether the prominent men who bore them were freedmen — a largely irrelevant issue in the case of local officials — without investigating in any depth the problem of their parentage and ancestry.[18] Similarly, no study has yet appeared of the frequency with which *honestiores* as distinct from plebeians retained Greek or 'suspect' Latin names through the generations.[19] Thirdly, arguments for the identification of descendants of freedmen from nomenclature have suffered from obvious deficiencies and have been undermined with relative ease by astute and cautious scholars. We are now told that the criteria that have been employed are not by themselves conclusive, that no rules have been established for interpreting the status of those who are not self-evidently of slave or free origin, and that progress can be made, if at all, only in individual cases.[20] Such negative formulations, if they gain the field, could force a premature closure on the investigation. I do not claim that a set of criteria can be arrived at which will be applicable in all cases. But there is point in trying to improve upon arguments that have proved unsatisfactory in the past, even if nothing more can be achieved — and this I would contest — than a clarification of the limits of our knowledge. In this paper there is room only for a preliminary investigation of one issue, that of the family origins of bearers of Greek or oriental names domiciled outside the Eastern part of the Empire.

I begin with the following proposition: a Greek or oriental name borne by a resident of a western city points to descent from either a free immigrant of the Eastern Mediterranean region or a slave.[21] This proposition steers clear of the problem of ethnic origins of slaves, which has provoked contradictory judgements ever since Tenney Frank enunciated the thesis that slaves with Greek names were of eastern origin.[22] Whether slaves of western as well as eastern origin were given Greek names is not a matter that needs to be investigated in the present context.

My proposition, is, I believe, relatively uncontroversial. It would be seriously undermined only by the demonstration that a significant number of local officials with Greek names were of free western descent. In fact, the incidence of Greek-named *ingenui* of any station, plebeian or curial, whose fathers had Latin *cognomina* is low.[23] Moreover, one may often suspect, and can sometimes demonstrate, that either the mother or a grandparent had a Greek name. I have indicated elsewhere the possible occurrence of reversion from Latin to Greek *cognomina* in some families who are represented in the album of decurions at Canusium of A.D. 223.[24] A more definite statement cannot be hazarded because of the difficulty of identifying blood relatives in the album. It is noteworthy that in most and perhaps all cases of reversion at Canusium the putative father has a 'suspect' Latin *cognomen* or imperial *nomen*.[25] We may be witnessing the discarding of suspect Latin for Greek names, or at most the integration of these two classes of names. Be that as it may, we are not entitled to state that 'respectable' Latin names and Greek names are used indiscriminately among surviving members of the indigenous aristocracy at Canusium.

Thus, while I consider it advisable to mention the possibility that a Greek name might be carried by a councillor of free, western origin because his father might have had a penchant for Greek names or regarded them as fashionable, I do so only for the sake of completeness, for the chance of this applying in any particular case is very small.

We have, then, in the *cognomen* a useful instrument for separating outsiders, whether of eastern immigrant or slave descent, from others who at least on the surface are western if not indigenous. This is a significant finding in itself, even if the task of distinguishing descendants of immigrants from those of slaves should prove insuperable. We can say, for example, that at least one-quarter of the 100 decurions at Canusium in A.D. 223 were in one or other of these categories; while at Beneventum we may count among 'outsiders' on the basis of *cognomina* (their own or an ancestor's) the following: Afinius Hierax (son of Acte), Concordius Syriacus, Adiectius Macedo (grandson of Narcissus), Staius Scrateius Manilianus (grandson of Eutyches), his father Manilius (whose brother Herodotus died young), C. Vibius Stephanus, and C. Umbrius Eudrastus.[26]

How then, are descendants of slaves to be identified? The case for servile descent is strongest where two or more criteria apply. C. Pettius C. f. Philtatus, equestrian and magistrate of Aquileia, was a member of Palatina. In this instance enrolment in a tribe rarely attested outside certain areas of the West, and specially associated with families founded by freedmen, seems incompatible with free immigrant descent. Philtatus belongs in the same company as his fellow Aquileian and magistrate C. Baebius C. f. Antiochianus, son of the *sevir Augustalis* C. Baebius Antiochus and clearly of servile stock.[27] Or there is Concordius Syriacus, the Beneventine equestrian. While the ethnic *cognomen* points to an oriental origin but is neutral as to status, the *nomen*, which recalls one of the names of Beneventum — the city's full title was Colonia Julia Concordia Augusta Beneventum — establishes that his father, or an ancestor, was a public slave. In his inscription he calls himself public recorder and Latin poet, not magistrate, and claims to have promoted in the city the *orchestopale*, a Greek wrestling-dance.[28] Again, we might cite N. Afinius N. f. Pal. Hierax decurion of the same town, already introduced. One commentator has assigned both him and Nasellius Sabinus a distinguished pedigree. Sabinus was son of an *Augustalis*; as for Hierax, the Greek name, the tribal affiliation, his parents' common *gentilicium*, and his mother's Greek name, confirm his servile origin beyond reasonable doubt.[29]

The situation is less promising where a Greek name does not occur in conjunction with any other possible index of servile (or immigrant) status. A reference to Cicero will highlight our dilemma. Cicero mentions several Avianii in his correspondence, among them C. Avianius Philoxenus, C. Avianius Evander, and C. Avianius Hammonius. If nothing but these names had come down to us, through whatever source, we would have been ignorant that Philoxenus was a free man who gained citizenship through a friend (who had access through Cicero to Caesar), while Evander and Hammonius were freedmen of another man.[30]

A way forward lies in the analysis of the Latin *nomina* with which Greek names are associated. They may be divided into four categories: imperial names, non-imperial names found frequently or occasionally in eastern provinces, names borne by Roman senators and found only, or with few exceptions, in the West, and non-senatorial names also largely or entirely restricted to the West.[31] For the moment I wish to concentrate on the first and fourth groups. My suggestion is that they were in large part made up of men servile origin.

A very substantial segment of the population of the Empire bore one imperial name or other. I am interested, however, in two sub-classes, one comprising men of free descent (who were made up of western immigrants and their descendants), the other men of servile origin. There is no doubt that the second category was greater numerically by a wide margin. It included not only descendants of imperial slaves and of their slaves (and so on), but also descendants of the slaves of those in the first category (and of their slaves and so on). But this is not the only consideration which should weigh with us in pondering any particular case. Relevant factors include the time-span between the creation of, for example, the first free CC. Julii and the date of the inscription under scrutiny, the approximate number of freedmen or descendants of freedmen likely to have borne a particular imperial name in relation to the approximate number of men of free ancestry, the scale of immigration of citizens of free ancestry who bear the name in question, the extent to which local officials of foreign origin in the city concerned and in other cities retain their foreign names, and the origins of other bearers of the *nomen* or *cognomen*, or both, in the city and region. Let us take the case of, for example, C. Iulius Agathopus, highest magistrate of Aquileia at some point in the Antonine or Severan period, applying only the first and last of the above tests. The bulk of the CC. Julii had been created by A.D. 41, and our inscription is at least a century later in date; Agathopus is a name carried by several freedmen of Aquileia, among them a *sevir* Julius Agathopus and an

175

imperial freedman C. Julius Agathopus.[32] The likelihood that our man was of pure descent from a C. Julius of free ancestry, civilian or military,[33] is very slim indeed.

The fourth group consists of those with a name in restricted circulation in the Greek-speaking provinces, if found there at all. The distribution pattern of these names implies that their bearers were not of citizen status if and when they were resident in an eastern province. The rarer the name and the more concentrated in the city or region where local office was achieved, the likelier it is that the family was enfranchised there. Both Afinius and Nasellius belonged to new families which had secured a double rise status, from (in their cases) slave to citizen, and from (plebeian) citizen to decurion. The case for local enfranchisement is even clearer where the person in question was a member of the tribe of the city concerned. At Beneventum, Staius Scrateius Manilianus, grandson of Eutyches, Umbrius Eudrastus, and Adiectius Macedo, grandson of Narcissus, were enrolled in the local tribe, Stellatina. This tribe is not found outside Italy. Staius (and cognates) is well-established in this part of Italy but otherwise uncommon, while Umbrii are prominent in local politics in Beneventum and nearby over several generations. It is exceedingly unlikely that any of these families acquired tribe and gentile name in the East.

Here, then, is a brand of *arriviste* whose rise in status was won through the initiative of private individuals to such a degree that they bore their names rather than those of emperors or functionaries. The assumption of a patron's name by his ex-slave was of course perfectly proper and exceedingly common. Promotions of this kind would surely have greatly outnumbered those of free clients of Eastern origin in the West, counterparts in the imperial age of Cicero's friend Avianius Philoxenus. It should not be assumed that such elevations were frequent, that emperors allowed a free choice of nomenclature, or that such beneficiences as there were inevitably took their local patron's name, rather than the emperor's or that of a noble intercessor (supposing patron and intercessor were not one and the same). Cicero finds it necessary to explain why Avianius did not become a Tullius. I regard the Staii, Umbrius, and Adiectius as 'prime suspects'. I note that the elder Staius was city-doctor — the medical profession was commonly practised by freedmen in the West[34] — and that Adiectius is not a true *gentilicium*, but a transformed *cognomen*, one moreover which is commonly borne by slaves and freedmen.

It is clear that only some of the considerations which applied in the case of the first group can be carried over to an analysis of the membership of the second and third groups. Their social composition is more problematic. Here I will simply explore one avenue of enquiry which is relevant to the origin of the one citizen of Beneventum of Greek name who awaits discussion. C. Vibius Stephanus of tribe unknown was a minor magistrate. The *nomen* is common, occurring in East and West and in all levels of society. However, there is a cluster of CC. Vibii in and around Beneventum, and at least one branch of the family provided city-leaders for several generations,[35] The chances are good that Stephanus, like the Staii and Umbrius, owed his acquisition of citizenship to a local family.

## IV

It remains to apply our results to the local aristocracy of Beneventum, taken as a whole.

I have singled out Nasellius Sabinus as son of an *Augustalis*. I add now Lollius Suavis, aedile and *praefectus fabrum*, whose father Orio was an *Augustalis Claudialis.*[36]

The four members of Palatina in addition to Nasellius were Afinius Hierax, Gavius Sabinus, Vibbius Proculus and Oclatius Modestus.

Afinius is one of seven bearers or descendants of bearers of Greek names. The others are Staius Rutilius Manilius and his son Adiectius Macedo, Umbrius Eudrastus, Vibius Stephanus, Concordius Syriacus. The first four were enrolled in Stellatina.

Concordius, public recorder and Latin poet, Gavius the scribe, and Staius the doctor form a group with a fourth man, Rutilius Aelianus, decurion and *grammaticus*, whose wife Primitiva shared his *nomen* and was probably with him an ex-slave from the same *familia.*[37] The occupations of the four are regularly associated with slaves and freedmen in the West.

Thus far we have thirteen persons, all of curial or equestrian rank, all or most of whom were of slave descent.

Twenty-one magistrates are recorded who held office in the late Republic or early Empire,[38] I omit them from the present survey which is restricted to the period extending roughly from the Flavian to the Severan period.

Our thirteen suspects amount to about two-fifths of known leading citizens of the city in this later period. This conclusion is not based on a survey of all the possible criteria of servile descent. Among those tests I have not attempted to evaluate or apply are, the 'suspect' Latin *cognomen* and the imperial *nomen* in combination with a Latin *cognomen*[39]. There is in fact little to be gained from pressing the matter to the bitter end. Certainly any attempt to produce an exact statistic for the proportion of freedman's descendants is doomed to failure. It will be clear that I consider Gordon's tally of 25 per cent much closer to the truth than Pleket's of 8 per cent.[40] However, my principal aim has been to show that the political success of the freedman's son and descendant is a profitable area of enquiry, and that progress can be made if the historian is prepared to consider the probable as well as the certain.

## Notes

[1]  J. H. Oliver, *Aspects of Civic and Cultural Policy in the East*, *Hesp.*, Suppl. vol. 13, 1970.

[2]  *ILS* 6296; *CIL* 3. 11223; *ILS* 9394; 7457,

[3]  G. E. F. Chilver, *Cisalpine Gaul*, Oxford 1939, p. 198 ff.

[4]  *Cod. Iust.* 9.21.1.

[5]  *AE* 1966, 75. Other candidates include *CIL* 3. 3497; 10.1209; 24.2466.

[6]  M. L. Gordon, 'The freedman's son in municipal life' *JRS* vol. 21, 1931, pp. 65–77, at 70; H. W. Pleket, 'Sociale Stratificatie en Sociale Mobiliteit in de Romeinse Keizertijd' *TG* vol. 84, 1970, pp. 215–51, at 244.

[7]  L. R. Taylor, *The Voting Districts of the Roman Republic*, Rome 1960, p. 322 ff.

[8]  R. Meiggs, *Roman Ostia* Oxford 1960, p. 190 ff.; *NS* 1953, p. 255 (Vot.); *CIL* 14. 155 (Vot.); 949, 4899 (Pal.).

[9]  *CIL* 14.2468.

[10]  Th. Mommsen, *St.* vol. 3, p. 443, n. 4; *EE* 5, pp. 260 ff.

[11]  P. Veyne, 'La table des Ligures Baebiani et l'institution alimentaire de Trajan', *MEFR* vol. 70, 1958, p. 209ff.; Pleket, op. cit., p. 243.

[12]  *ILS* 5053.

[13]  In cities where the sample is greater than one they are numerically inferior only in Ariminum (3), Ferentinum (4), and Pisaurum (5).

[14]  *CIL* 9. 1618; 1646; 1638; 1657; 1619.

[15]  *CIL* 9. 2658; a likely parallel in 2666.

[16] E.g. A. M. Duff, *Freedmen in the early Roman Empire*, Oxford 1928, pp. 56, 110; apparently followed by Gordon, art. cit. (n. 6).

[17] I. Kajanto, *The Latin Cognomina*, Helsinki 1965.

[18] E.g. L. F. Smith, *CP* vol. 39, 1934, pp. 145–7; H. Thylander, *Étude sur l'épigraphie latine*, Lund 1952, p. 144 ff.

[19] A shortcoming of A. Calderini, *Aquileia Romana*, Milano [1930], p. 417, and of I. Kajanto, 'The significance of non-latin cognomina', *Lat.* vol. 27, 1968, pp. 517–34.

[20] H. Chantraine, *Freigelassene und Sklaven im Dienst der römischen Kaiser*, Wiesbaden 1967, pp. 128–39, at 139; P. R. C. Weaver, *Familia Caesaris*, Cambridge 1972, p. 83 ff.

[21] Indigenous citizens of Greek cities in the West form a vestigial group and may be disregarded as anomalous.

[22] T. Frank, 'Race mixture in the Roman Empire', *AHR* vol. 21, 1916; I. Kajanto, op. cit. (n.19), pp. 519 ff.

[23] Ibid. p. 526; B. Rawson, *CP* vol. 63, 1968, p. 157, n.4 (figures for Rome).

[24] *CIL* 9. 338; P. Garnsey, 'Aspects of the decline of the urban aristocracy in the Empire', in *Aufstieg und Niedergang der römischen Welt*, ed. H. Temporini vol. 2, pp. 229–52, at 246–7 (forthcoming).

[25] E.g. Kanuleius Felicianus (cf. Onesimianus); L. Marcius Fortunatianus (Carpophorus); T. Aelius Rufus or Flavianus or Antonius (Nectareus), etc. I am assuming for the moment that the distinction between 'suspect' (Felicianus, etc.) and 'respectable' names (Victorinus, Pius, Vindex, Rusticus, etc.) is a genuine one.

[26] *CIL* 9. 1638; 1663; 1637; *AE* 1914, 164, cf. *CIL* 9. 1655; 1971; 1658; 1685.

[27] *CIL* 5. 8749; *Suppl. ital.*, ed. E. Pais, 169.

[28] *CIL* 9. 1663.

[29] *CIL* 9. 1638; 1618; Veyne, op. cit. (n. 11) p. 209. Veyne is impressed by the rarity of the *nomina*. That is to overlook the fact that no *nomen* was in principle inaccessible to freedmen.

[30] *Ad Fam.*, 13.35.1; 13.2. 21; 27. J. H. D'Arms. '*CILX*, 1792: a municipal Notable of the Augustan Age', *HSCP* vol. 76, 1972, pp. 207–16.

[31] The fourfold distinction is serviceable even though the boundaries between the categories are in some cases fluid and uncertain.

[32] *CIL* 5, *Suppl. ital.*, ed. E. Pais, 196; *CIL* 5. 744; 1251.

[33] Or from a family of free descent adopted by a free C. Julius.

[34] See H. Gummerus, *Der Arztestand im römischen Reich nach den Inscriften*, Helsinki 1932, especially p. 54 ff; K. H. Below, *Der Arzt im römischen Recht*, Munich 1953, ch. 1.

[35] *CIL* 10.1658; 1684.

[36] *CIL* 9. 1648; cf. 1695.

[37] *CIL* 9. 1654.

[38] To judge from absence of *cognomina*.

[39] Witness, e.g. Septimus Primitivus, augur and priest in A.D. 228, *CIL* 9. 1538.

[40] See n. 6. It must be said that Gordon does not support her figure with any argumentation, while Pleket's argument completely ignores the inscriptions of magistrates, and is at best indirect.

I wish to thank Professor M. I. Finley for reading and improving a draft of this paper.

Peter Garnsey,
Jesus College,
Cambridge

# *13*

# Forte an Dolo Principis (Tac., Ann. 15. 38)

## I

C. E. Stevens was at his best teaching unsolved problems in Roman history. His pupils will remember with affection and gratitude the tutorials dedicated to the mysterious death of Scipio Aemilianus, to the first Catilinarian conspiracy, or to the problem whether Clodius was nominated land commissioner of Caesar. His pupils will remember that it was precisely the paucity of sources or the scarcity of information on a certain topic that fired his imagination. They will remain grateful to him for having forced them to reread the texts from cover to cover before allowing them to dabble in wild conjectures.

I shall never forget a long winter evening at Magdalen College when with great enthusiasm he compared the burning of the Reichstag in Nazi Germany with the accusation of Cicero that the Catilinarians intended to set fire to Rome. It is therefore not out of place to dedicate to Stevens some thoughts concerning another fire at Rome depicted by Suetonius in Nero's biography (ch. 38), by Cassius Dio in book 62 (17–18), and by Tacitus ([*Ann.*] 15.38–44).

The latter sets the unsolved problem in his typical way: it is uncertain whether the fire was due to chance or to the malice of Nero, for each version has its sponsors. This question has not engaged scholars in recent years. Most of them dealt with the legal question of the libel against the Christians (15.44). And rightly so. But an impressive paper by T. D. Barnes[1] made me reconsider Nero's rôle in the burning of the city.

A summary of the basic approaches to the Christian problem will make it easier to tackle the question: how did the great fire break out? Three main responses have been evoked by the passage, 'Igitur primum correpti qui fatebantur[2] deinde indicio eorum multitudo ingens haud proinde in crimine incendii quam odio humani generis convicti sunt.'

1.   The Christians were accused under the *lex Iulia de maiestate,* not as Christians but as magicians, arsonists, murderers, adulterers -- and all these fall under the *lex Iulia de maiestate.*

2.   A second theory assumes that there was a law, amended in the days of Tiberius or Nero, according to which it was possible to punish Christians for being Christians. This is based on a passage in Suet. *Nero* 16.2: 'During his reign many abuses were severely punished and put down, and no fewer laws were made.' Although Christians are not being specifically referred to in this context, some scholars interpret it as a reference to a 'Neronian' statute that dealt with Christians. Tertullian (*Apol.* 5.2) contains a hint that the Emperor Tiberius was favourably impressed by Christianity, but the Senate feared the penetration of the religion and rejected Tiberius' moderate proposals (the Senate declared it a *religio illicita*). Hence, in 64, Nero based himself on this law in persecuting the Christians after the great fire.

3.   A third version explains all activities against the Christians in the Roman Empire as taking place outside the system of criminal law. There were clearly police actions within the powers of *coercitio*.

The debate that began in the days of Mommsen[3] still continues.[4] Barnes brilliantly analysed all the primary sources that deal with persecution of the Christians from Nero to Decius. In his opinion there was no legislation against the Christians prior to Trajan, and the correspondence between Pliny and Trajan on this subject proves the justice of his contention. Nevertheless, Christians were accused and persecuted throughout the empire. A dry legal approach will therefore not solve the problem: in 204 B.C., the black stone was brought to Rome from Pessinus in Asia Minor. Henceforward, the ritual of the Magna Mater was recognised as an official ritual of the Roman state. Nevertheless, there was a strong feeling that worship of the ancient Roman gods should be continued and fostered, and this according to the 'tradition of the fathers'. And in Barnes' words:

'Mos maiorum was the most important source of Roman law, and it was precisely mos maiorum in all its aspects that Christians urged men to repudiate. The theory of national apostasy fails as an explanation of the legal basis of the condemnation of Christians, but it comes close to the truth if it is applied, not to the law but to the attitudes of men. It is in the minds of men, not in the demands of Roman law, that the roots of the persecution of the Christians in the Roman Empire are to be sought.'

Barnes' approach will remain valid only until the publication of the next paper. The bibliography is continuously growing.[5] The dilemma has its source primarily in the notorious chapter 44 of Tacitus' 15th book. The chapter is indeed significant, and does not lack contradictions. Many years ago, Momigliano was convinced that the confusion in Tacitus is due to a blend of two different and contradictory versions within one chapter,[6] while Sir Ronald Syme contends that the confusion was not of Tacitus, but of the prevailing situation: 'Tacitus reproduces the mixed character of the situation itself — false charges of incendiarism and the genuine dislike incurred by the Christians (per flagitia invisos).'[7]

There is no point in trying to overcome the obvious contradictions in the chapter. It is stated in one place: 'In order to dispel the rumours (that the fire had taken place by order) Nero substituted as culprits and punished with the utmost refinements of cruelty a class of men loathed for their vices whom the mob styled Christians.' And a few lines further on: 'Vast numbers were convicted not so much on the count of arson as for hatred of the human race (odio humani generis convicti sunt).' Tacitus did not want to clarify the subject but to confuse the reader even more.[8] He hated both Nero and the Christians and if he could concoct a description which, if it didn't entirely place the blame on one side, would slightly incriminate both — so much the better. Yet everything was written according to the rules of a respectable sceptical point of view, and no one could accuse Tacitus of lying.

This brings us to the main subject of our discussion. First, a number of undisputed facts: the fire broke out on July 19 (15. 41). For how many days did it rage? Dio speaks superficially of a few days and a few nights (62.17.1). Suetonius notes an exact number: six days and seven nights (*Nero* 38). Tacitus' description seems even more reliable: he relates that the fire was stopped on the sixth day. However after a short lull, it broke out again, this time striking at the less congested parts of the city (15. 40). His description is also confirmed by independent, external evidence: two inscriptions speak of nine days: *CIL* 6.826): *quando urbs per novem dies arsit Neronianis temporibus*; cf. ibid., 837.

It can therefore be concluded that the second fire lasted for another three days. Which areas were damaged by the fire? There is no doubt that the Capitol, the Basilicas and the temples in the Forum were not damaged. The areas beyond the Tiber and the hills of Esquiline and Quirinal were apparently saved too. On the other hand, the area of the great Circus and the Subura were badly damaged by fire.[9] The information given by Dio that two thirds of the city was totally destroyed must therefore be taken with a grain of salt. There can be no doubt, however, that the shock that the fire caused the residents of the city cannot be easily dismissed. Tacitus says in chapter 41 that the fire broke out on the same day of the year in which the Gauls set fire to Rome (390 B.C.) and others went so far as to calculate the period of time that elapsed between the two fires as a round number of years, months and days.[10]

And so, who was to blame for the outbreak of the fire? A most interesting answer was given in 1900 by C. Pascal.[11] In his opinion, a group of Christians set fire to the city. The Christian community in Rome consisted of fanatics who were determined to establish their existence at any price. Pascal ignores the information that the Christians were in fact not persecuted at this period in Rome; Paul's activities in Rome took place without disturbance: *Acts* 28.30--31. Pascal relies on late and dubious evidence, the *First Epistle General of Peter*, 2.13--14. From this he concludes that there was a zealot Christian group engaged in terrorist activities, whom Peter tried to pacify. These men believed that no redemption would come to the world without the destruction of the Roman Empire (Tertullian, *Apol.* 32.1); this empire must be quickly burnt: 'I am come to send fire on the earth; and what will I, if it be already kindled?' (*Luke* 12.49). On what basis does Pascal conclude that the second fire of Rome was not the first conspiratorial activity of the Christians? The proof is this time philological. Tacitus (15.44) specifically states: 'Repressaque in praesens exittiabilis superstitio rursum erumpebat, non modo per Judaeam ...' 'Rursum erumpebat' implies (according to Pascal) that it was a repeated act. Had Tacitus wanted to make it clear that this was a one-time eruption he would probably have written 'eruperat'.[12] From this follows another conclusion (which has no evidence in the sources) that masses of Christian proselytes infiltrated the ranks of Nero's Praetorians; after the arson they appeared on the scene of the fire (as if sent by the authorities), pretended to help in extinguishing the flames -- but actually added only 'fuel to the fire'. There is an almost identical description in Dio (62.17.1--2) and in Tacitus (15.38), and Pascal's thesis is plausible. But the sharpness of Pascal's analysis loses by the lack of consistency in his use and scrutiny of sources. One sentence out of the Peter *Epistle*, one paragraph out of Tertullian, the absence of any information on the social composition of the early groups of Christians,[13] and a doubtful guess about Christians within the Praetorian Guard cannot be allowed to dictate the conclusion that it was the Christians who set fire to Rome. Few scholars followed Pascal, but the view that the Christians did indeed set fire to Rome has not been completely abandoned.[14]

As against these, there are many scholars who accept the version -- widespread in the sources -- that Nero set fire to the city. As for Nero's motives, Suetonius' version appears acceptable: 'As though he could not bear the ugliness of the buildings and the narrow crooked streets he set fire to the city in order to be able to build a more beautiful and better planned Rome' (*Nero* 38). Dio's version that Nero burnt the city in jealousy of Priam, who was privileged to see his city and reign destroyed simultaneously, seems strange in the eyes of a rational twentieth-century historian. Profumo[15] prefers to maintain that Nero planned all the details of the fire, and even took into account the sirocco wind that blows in July. It is no coincidence that the fire spread from the southern corner of the Palatine towards Valle Labicana -- between the Caelian and the Esquiline: it was exactly in this direction that Nero wanted to expand his notorious Domus Aurea.[16]

Huelsen attempts to refute Profumo's contention. On the night before July 19, there was a full moon in Rome. The citizens were in no hurry to go to sleep in the hot summer months. Outside there was light and in their dilapidated houses darkness and suffocation. Had it been Nero that planned the arson he would not have sent his incendiaries under a full moon, when thousands of Romans were wandering around the city. The fire broke out by chance (so one of Tacitus' versions), but the Christians saw in this the finger of God, and did not allow the firemen to extinguish the flames (this is the significance of the description of men who forbade the quenching of the fire 'crebris multorum minis restinguere prohibentium' -- 15.38) and therefore Nero made them responsible for the whole conflagration.[17]

Huelsen's last point is at best a guess -- for no one knows to which people Tacitus referred. And as for the first, it is doubtful whether the logic of a modern scholar conforms exactly to the logic of a Roman emperor 1900 years ago.

There could be a fourth theory, so far never forcibly argued: the fire was started by a group of conspirators against Nero. The Pisonian conspiracy did indeed break out only in 65, when the opposition was in its death throes; but that same group might have tried to undermine Nero's position earlier. To support this view, one may quote Tacitus, 15.50: it was asserted that Subrius Flavus had conceived an impulse to attack Nero while he was singing on the stage or while during the burning of the palace he was rushing unguarded from place to place in the night. From this sentence it is possible only to understand one thing: upon the outbreak of the fire Flavus conceived the idea of murdering Nero. It cannot be concluded that in order to murder Nero, a group of conspirators decided to set fire to the city.

After four unconvincing conjectures, there is no point in offering a fifth. And yet it seems a better understanding of the text proper would lead us closer to the truth. To this end the following lines are dedicated.

## II

Hätt Nero den der von ihm schrieb bezahlt
Er wäre wie Trajan der Nachwelt abgemahlt

(Friedrich Freiherr von der Trenck, 1788)

Unfortunately, no history sympathetic to Nero has been preserved, but Josephus testifies that 'many historians have written the story of Nero of whom some, because they were well treated by him, have out of gratitude been careless of truth, while others from hatred and enmity towards him have so shamelessly and recklessly revelled in falsehood as to merit censure' (*AJ* 20. 154). Tacitus, Suetonius, and Dio used material which derived from the days of Nero. However, all inquiries into their sources still remain unsatisfactory.

Dio's history of Nero's period is preserved only in a précis of

Xiphilinus from the second half of the eleventh century. It is therefore very difficult to establish Dio's sources. The fact that one piece of information is to be found both in Dio and in Tacitus does not prove that Dio relied on Tacitus.[18] There is the possibility of a source common to Tacitus and Dio, or perhaps two common sources. How did Dio use his sources? This we cannot say, apart from the assumption that he certainly preferred an anti-Neronian source to an anti-senatorial one.[19]

A comparison of the description of the fire in Dio and in Tacitus will immediately prove that these are two different descriptions and that Dio wrote independently of Tacitus. In a few details there is similarity (cf. Dio 62.16 with Tacitus 15.38), and the contradiction between Dio, 62.18.5, and Tacitus, 15.39, is imaginary: Tacitus contends that the price of grain was lowered to three *sestertii,* and that foodstuffs were brought from Ostia and the nearby cities. Dio specifically states: 'And as for the Romans themselves, he stopped the distribution of grain'. Van Berchem rightly explains that Nero cancelled the distribution of free grain to the citizens. The tragedy struck citizens and non-citizens equally. In order to level the burden Nero lowered the price of grain, and at the same time allowed non-citizens to enjoy the low prices.[20]

In many other details, the differences are greater than the similarities: Dio specifically accuses Nero of setting fire to the city; Tacitus only hints at such a possibility. Tacitus can relate that Nero returned from Antium immediately upon learning of the fire. Dio tells no such story. In Tacitus, there is a connection between the fire and the persecution of Christians. In Dio, the Christians are conspicuous by their absence. Tacitus tells of people who frustrated the extinguishing of the fire on the pretence that their authority came from above ('esse sibi auctorem vociferabantur'). Dio also accuses soldiers and looters of interfering with those who were fighting the fire, but does not contend that this was done by order of a higher authority ('iussu'). Dio does not know how long the fire raged; Tacitus gives the exact figure, and there is no similarity between the two historians on the description of the scope of the fire, and areas that were damaged.

One paragraph in Dio deserves special attention. It states that the common people did not accuse Nero of arson. It would be interesting to know from where the historian drew this information. Perhaps a contemporary source. But a contemporary source is not necessarily superior to others.

Suetonius does not contribute much to the clarification of the problem. He writes circa A.D. 120 and Tacitus' books were not available to him when he compiled his biography of Nero. It seems that Tacitus had almost the same material at his disposal but Suetonius dealt with it as a biographer writing 'neque per tempora sed per species.'[21] His version of the fire is clearly anti-Neronian.[22] The Tacitus description is the fullest and most detailed and the only problem is whether one understands him properly.

Tacitus was a historian of stature who checked sources and investigated their veracity. For the history of Nero, he made use of the *commentarii senatus* (15.74) and at least knew of the existence of *acta diurna urbis* (16.22; 13.31). Among his other primary sources, it is perhaps permissible to count the memoirs of Corbulo (on which there is a hint in 15.16) and the memoirs of Agrippina (4.53), which are of course irrelevant to the discussion here.

Tacitus made much use of the historians who preceded him and for the period of Nero he emphasised this fact more than once: in 12.67, 13.17, 14.2 and 16.6.

Tacitus made use of Fabius Rusticus, who wrote the chronicles of Nero's time, and did not spare his rod on the Emperor (see e.g. 14.2.2). In A.D. 108 Fabius was still alive, and from *Agricola* 10 we learn that Tacitus admired his style; he dubbed him the most eloquent among the recent writers, but never praised his reliability. In 14.2.2 he did not rule in Fabius' favour, for Tacitus was a critical historian who was not tempted by every piece of information that fell into his hands.

He did make use of Cluvius Rufus, who lived at Nero's court and wrote a more favourable account of the Emperor. Though Tacitus should not be suspected of sympathy for Nero there are certain cases in which he preferred Cluvius to Fabius Rusticus (e.g. 13.20; 14.2).

Tacitus also perused the works of the Elder Pliny (13.20), who wrote the history of Nero's period. Tacitus treated him with respect but did not automatically accept his views. In 15.53, dealing with the conspiracy of Piso, he stated explicitly: 'This is the statement of Pliny. For my own part, whatever his assertion may be worth, I was not inclined to suppress it, absurd as it may seem . . . etc. . . .' This is indeed Tacitus' method and he refers to it clearly in 13.20.[23]

As far as the history of Nero is concerned, Tacitus' *Annals* are more reliable than Suetonius' biography, or the abstracts from Cassius Dio. The question can therefore be posed: why was Tacitus not consistent in his method of work when he came to tell of the great fire? The opening words of 15.38 are: 'Sequitur clades, forte an dolo principis incertum (nam utrumque auctores prodidere)'. Why did not Tacitus record the names of the authors? Why did he not quote Cluvius Rufus and Fabius Rusticus explicitly? And why did he not record the version of the Elder Pliny, who was certainly an eye-witness and apparently put the blame on Nero? The text of Pliny is not clear, and the reading of the paragraph 17.1.5 (in which 'Nero's fire' appears) is not above suspicion: 'ad Neronis principis incendia' ('quibus cremavit urbem, annis postea.' secl. Detlefsen, Berlin 1866). But from the words 'Neronian fire' it is impossible to be sure that Nero did indeed set fire to the city. Another hint is to be found in the drama *Octavia* (lines 831–833), but it is doubtful whether conclusions may be drawn from the words placed in Nero's mouth by an unknown writer. Again, if Tacitus knew a univocal truth, why did he hide it from us? If he preferred one version over another why did he not say so in this case — as was his habit in many other cases?

The great fire of 65 became an 'affair', an event composed of complex stages in which the motives of the protagonists are obscured, giving rise to questions like 'who gave the order?' or 'was there an order given at all?' or 'who was pulling the strings behind the scenes?' These questions have more than one reasonable solution, though no single one has been convincingly established. Such an 'affair' is characterised by the presentation of each party's interest heatedly and in an extreme form, so that the third and apparently objective (or simply uninvolved) party remains with only two possibilities:

1.   To be sympathetically 'objective', i.e. to compromise between the parties and to describe the event as a miserable accident without placing heavy blame on the involved parties.

2.   To be unsympathetically 'objective'; to try and complicate the 'affair' even more, so that both parties will appear guilty. The real truth will never become clear. Therefore the unsympathetically 'objective' party makes use of the method of iniquitous hint, or of innuendo which blurs much more than it clarifies.

There seems to be no doubt that the burning of Rome became an 'affair' and Tacitus reported it with unsympathetic 'objectivity'. He was, however, a serious historian. He would not have thought of using the invalid *post hoc ergo propter hoc* argument. Though Nero built a more beautiful and better planned city, this is no proof that Nero started the fire.

Tacitus was well aware that he could not prove that Nero was the arsonist. I have described elsewhere a long series of conflagrations during the days of the Republic, in the context of their social background.[24] The negligence of contractors and lack of supervision by the authorities were among the main reasons for the outbreak of fires, and it was only after 64 that the legislator took care to prevent conflagrations by means of supervision of building. Is it an accident that the law has come down to us as *lex Neronis de modo aedificiorum*?

A brief glance at the sources will prove that fires frequently broke out in Rome in the days of Augustus and thereafter.[25] Just as nobody could blame Augustus for the fires, so it was impossible lightly to cast the guilt on Nero. Tacitus knew this well and therefore used his notorious innuendo which is on the face of it 'objective': 'The fire was due to chance, or to the malice of the Princeps.' It is unnecessary to repeat the arguments of Ryberg,[26] who has convincingly shown how he created certain impressions in his readers' minds which he could not give as certainties as a historian and that when he knew that his views were unsupported by clear-cut facts.[27] But in 1896 Leo said: 'Tacitus hat sicherlich nirgends absichtlich etwas Unwahres gesagt. Denn er dachte hoch von der Würde seiner Kunst. Aber er weiss so zu erzählen dass in allen Fällen in denen sein Gefühl mitspricht der Leser auch gegen die Tatsachen von demselben Gefühl ergriffen wird und das glaubt was Tacitus fast glauben möchte. Noch heute werden die meisten Leser des Tacitus meinen bei ihm gelesen zu haben, dass Tiberius den Germanicus habe durch Piso vergiften lassen. Und doch sagt Tacitus selbst dieser Teil der Anklage sei als grundlos nachgewiesen wordern.'[28] Leo's principle could easily be applied to the phrase 'forte an dolo principis'.

A detailed analysis of Tacitus' usage of the words *vel* or *an* would perhaps prove that the second 'or' was usually closest to his own view.[29] 'Coercendi imperium inter terminos' was Augustus' advice to his heirs (1. 11) but Tacitus added his own interpretation: 'incertum metu an per invidiam' (ibid.). There must have been some basis for the contention that Nero set fire to the city (and it is worth stressing again that Tacitus did not even raise the supposition that the Christians may have been the incendiaries). Hence the question -- what was the source of doubt in Tacitus' mind?

He was usually not excited when faced with two sources that contradicted each other. But Tacitus sometimes used oral tradition as well and integrated it into his history. In 3. 16 we read: 'Audire me memini ex senioribus. . .' In 14. 2: 'Sed quae Cluvius eadem ceteri quoque auctores prodidere, et fama huc inclinat' ('fama' should here be translated as 'hearsay' or 'rumour').

During the fire of 64 a wave of rumours and gossip swept through Rome, and Tacitus did not want to ignore this very significant fact. There is no doubt that 'people often struck (at Nero) with their tongues' (15. 73) and that the spreading of rumours was usually a major political weapon in the days of the early principate.[30] Nero was sensitive to men's talk, and fought against the many rumours that circulated in Rome after the banishment of Octavia (13. 15; 14. 60). After he got rid of Agrippina, Nero spread rumours of her evil nature, in order to dispel her public popularity. *Rumor vulgi* was Nero's greatest enemy. And it is not for nothing that Tacitus explicitly states in his *Histories* — that Nero was deposed more by rumours than by force of arms (*Hist.* 1. 89).

In our 'affair' too, Tacitus gave prominence to the wave of rumours: in 15. 39 he says: 'pervaserat rumor' and adds, that at the time when the fire was consuming Rome, Nero climbed on to his private stage and sang of the destruction of Troy — typifying the ills of the present by the calamities of the past. Tacitus knew that this was a rumour, and did not treat it seriously. In the same chapter, he admitted that when the fire broke out, Nero was in Antium, and returned to Rome when the fire was about to consume his house (15. 39). Nowhere did he with absolute certainty rule that Nero gave the order to set fire to the city.

Three questions therefore arise:

1. What gave rise to the rumours?
2. Who spread them?
3. Why did Tacitus bother to refer to them at all?

The first question can be answered simply: a broken lock cries out to the thief, and the weak one is vulnerable to attack on all sides. Such was Nero's standing after the death of Burrus and after the removal of Seneca in A.D. 62. Relations between him and the Senate had worsened. Tigellinus exerted a bad influence on the young emperor (14. 57), and incited him against men of high standing. Thus fell Plautus and Sulla (14. 59), and Nero's growing disdain of the Senate found expression in daily acts: in all major affairs, he would decide after conferring with his close associates; matters of little importance he would refer to the Senate and even then reject the advice of the Fathers (15. 36). Any man who appeared suspect in the eyes of the régime was eliminated, from freedmen (14. 65) to Torquatus Silanus, a descendant of Augustus (15. 35). At the same time, Nero made an effort to endear himself to the common people. He himself appeared as a singer, charioteer, dancer, and frequenter of inns and taverns.[31] In such circumstances a senatorial opposition might emerge. It might be satisfied with replacement of the present Princeps by a better one. However, as long as Nero continued to be popular in the Roman street, it was difficult for such an opposition to act. It would wait for an opportune moment, and would meanwhile try to reduce the Emperor's prestige and popularity. Encouraging signs were first visible when Octavia was banished. The common people were sympathetic to her, demonstrated their rejoicing when she was removed from danger — and later mourned her death.[32] Nero's enemies were more and more convinced that his image was close to being undermined, even among the common people. And it was precisely at that time that the fire broke out. Nero, who made it a habit to move among the common people, did not appear at a time of disaster. It must have seemed rather unusual. In the days of the Republic, it was customary for the consul to go to the people during fires, and personally to help the victims (cf. Cic., *in Pis.* 26: 'Equod in hac urbe maius umquam incendium fuit cui non consul subvenerit'). Livia made a personal appearance at the time of a fire near the temple of Vesta, and encouraged the people and the soldiers to increase their efforts (Suet., *Tib.* 50. 3). Drusus behaved the same way when a fire broke out in A.D. 15 and when citizens were in need of assistance (Dio, 57. 14. 10). Claudius surpassed them all. When a fire broke out in the Aemiliana, he remained in the Diribitorium for two nights, and when a body of soldiers and of his own slaves could not give sufficient help, he summoned the commons from all parts of the city and placing bags full of money before them urged them to the rescue, paying each man on the spot a suitable reward for his services (Suet., *Claud.* 18). Upon the eruption of Vesuvius, Titus hurried to Campania (Dio 66. 24. 1) but rushed back to Rome when he found out that a fire broke out in the city. This was not the case in A.D. 64.

Nero, the Princeps popular with the masses, was not with

them in the time of their sorrow.[33] This was probably an accident but to the urban plebs the presence of the Emperor in Rome was a matter of importance. They never forgave Tiberius for leaving the city.[34]

But Nero was in Antium and when he returned to Rome at the peak of the fire he did not go down to the scene but first tried apparently to survey the situation from a distance. He ascended the Palatine hill (or the roof of his house), perhaps in order to give appropriate instructions. It is a fact that extensive rescue operations were carried out after a short time (15. 39) — but the Emperor missed the big moment: to be with the people at the most critical time.

The stage was set for rumour-mongering — exacerbated by the Emperor's behaviour during the fire. And so rumour was given wings. It was no crude lie — but a series of half truths. It was a fact that Nero ascended a high place to look over the conflagration; there was only need to add a story that was particularly likely to conform to Nero's dramatic and theatrical personality — that he stood and sang of the burning of Troy. And the snowball began to roll; it was a fact that Nero did not personally participate in extinguishing the fire; a 'logical' conclusion was added: he wanted Rome to burn in order to build a more beautiful city. (And so he did.) Moreover, some did exploit the fire to loot and steal; why could not these men be 'emissaries'? The modern researcher will have no difficulty in reconstructing the emergence of a wave of rumours and Tacitus himself admits that a wave of rumours it was: 'pervaserat rumor'.

It is much harder to determine who spread the rumours: it is only possible to say that enemies of Nero did it but this is not much. It might be permissible to conjecture that some of them were people who, already in 64, were thinking of a conspiracy to overthrow the Princeps. Tacitus linked the beginnings of the conspiracy to the events of 62, and said: 'Romanus (probably a Caesarian freedman) had attacked Seneca as the associate of Gaius Piso, but was himself more surely struck down by Seneca on the same charge. The result was the alarm of Piso and the birth of an elaborate and luckless conspiracy against Nero' (14.65). It was therefore not surprising that there was a plan to murder Nero during a disturbance (15.50), a plan that was perhaps conceived by Subrius Flavus.

Yet, a rumour takes wings only when the time is right for it. Nero's prestige had, apparently, declined in the year 64. It was only after a special effort (particularly after the Pisonian conspiracy) that he succeeded in restoring his popularity.[35] Nero, however, did start a counter-attack immediately after the fire, to restore public sympathy: he opened the Field of Mars, the Agrippa monuments and even his own gardens to the dispossessed people; he hastily erected buildings to absorb the homeless masses; he lowered the price of grain to three *sestertii*; he brought foodstuffs from Ostia and elsewhere; he started to collect large sums from the people and from communities, and began extensive building and rehabilitation works.

But the public excitement did apparently continue. Nero decided to make the Christians a scapegoat. It is permissible to believe Tertullian's claim that Christians could be blamed for anything (*Apol.* 40.2). The common people in Rome never showed excessive sympathy for the fanatics who came from the East and believed in one God who was not born of woman. The Roman authorities saw the Christians as Jews in a minor variation, and Tacitus despised men who held superstitions (Christianity, like Judaism, was for him a superstition). In 64, there was an event likely to cast suspicion on both Nero and the Christians. Tacitus hated both equally, Nero perhaps a little more. He used every trick to denigrate him. He repeated unfounded rumours and denied them,[36] made his readers believe that Nero might have been capable of committing any crime, and made Subrius Flavius say: 'Odisse coepi postquam parricida matris et uxoris, auriga et histrio et incendiarius extitisti' (15.67). Chateaubriand was probably right: 'C'est en vain que Néron prospère. Tacite est déjà né dans l'empire.' Tacitus described the chain of events, without anger or pretence. There is not one absolute judgement in his description, while suspicion could be aroused at many points. On another occasion he disclosed his own credo. The death of Germanicus was 'an affair which, not only to the generation which witnessed it, but in the succeeding years, was a battleground of opposing rumours. So true it is that the great event is an obscure event: one school admits all hearsay evidence, whatever its character, as indisputable. Another perverts the truth into its contrary. And in each case posterity magnifies the error' (3.19).

Tacitus did not conceal the truth. He did not know it, and made no special attempt to pretend to it. With a malicious 'objective' smile he laughs at Nero and the Christians equally. And perhaps he also mocks those, who 2,000 years after the event are still trying to solve the riddle: 'Who really set fire to Rome?'

## Notes

[1] T. D. Barnes, 'Legislation against the Christians', *JRS* vol. 58 (1968), p. 32.

[2] On the significance of the concept *corripere,* cf. Tac., *Hist.* 2.84.2; *Ann.* 2.28.5; 3.49.1; 66.2; 4.19.2; 66.1; 6.46 4; 12.42.4; especially H. Fuchs, 'Tacitus über die Christen' *Vigiliae Christianae* vol. 4, (1950), pp. 65—93. See also P. Allard: *Histoire des persecutions pendant les deux premiers siècles,* Paris 1903; M. Dibelius: *Rom u. die Christ. im I. Jahrhundert, Sitzungsb. der Heidelberger Akademie der Wissenschaften,* Phil. Hist. Kl. vol. 32 (1941), p. 18.

[3] Th. Mommsen, 'Der Religionsfrevel nach römischem Recht' *Hist. Zeitschr.* vol. 64 (1890), pp. 389 ff. = *Ges. Schr.* vol. 3, pp. 389 ff.

[4] J. Beaujeu, *L'Incendie de Rome en 64 et les Chrétiens, Coll. Latomus* vol. 69, Brussels 1960 (the best summary). A. N. Sherwin-White, 'The early persecutions and Roman Law' *Journal of Theological Studies* N. S. vol. 3 (1952), p. 199 = *The letters of Pliny,* Oxford, 1966, p. 772. The author is not of the opinion that there was a general law, but the explanation of *coercitio* does not satisfy him either. A detailed analysis of Pliny's letters to Trajan leads him to the conclusion that the Christians were accused of *contumacia.* See also H. Last, 'The Study of the Persecutions' *JRS* vol. 27 (1937), pp. 80—92; G. E. M. de Ste. Croix, 'Why were the early Christians persecuted' *Past and Present* vols 26 (1963), pp. 6—38; 27 (1964), pp. 28—33.

[5] J. Molthagen, *Der römische Staat u. die Christen,* Göttingen 1970; A. H. Chroust, 'A Note on the persecution of the Christians in the Early Roman Empire' *C et M* vol. 18 (1970), p. 321; J. Plescia, 'On the persecution of the Christians in the Roman Empire' *Lat.* vol. 30 (1971), p. 119.

[6] *CAH* vol. 10, p. 887.

[7] R. Syme, *Tacitus,* Oxford 1958, p. 533, n.5.

[8] It is worthwhile mentioning here an article which has not received adequate attention and was not quoted in Syme's great work: F. W. Clayton, 'Tacitus and Nero's persecution of the Christians' *CQ* vol. 41 (1947), pp. 81—5. His reasonable analysis

appeals to me. I cannot accept R. Pöhlman's view: 'Was man gewöhnlich die Weltanschauung des Tacitus nennt, ist ein Chaos von unausgereiften Meinungen etc. . . .' (*Sitz. Ber. Kgl. Bayer. Akad. Wiss.*, Phil. Hist. Kl. (1910), p. 1.

[9] For a detailed summary of what was burnt and what remained intact, Furneaux ad loc. and recently the important article of Beaujeu, quoted in note no. 4 above.

[10] See Furneaux on 15.41.

[11] C. Pascal, 'L'incendio di Roma e i primi Christiani', Turin 1900 (French translation 1902).

[12] See Pascal, op. cit., p. 53 n. 1.

[13] From expressions such as 'ingens multitudo' (15.44), ὄχλος πολύς, or πολὺ πλῆθος one cannot learn much.

[14] P. Bonfante, *Storia del diritto Romano* 2.3, Milan 1923, p. 8; L. Hermann, 'Quels Chrétiens ont incendi Rome?' *Rev. Belge de Philol. et d'histoire* vol. 27 (1949), pp. 633–651. The latter contends that the Christians first tried to burn Rome in 57, and refers to 14.45.

[15] A. Profumo, *Le Fonti ed i tempori dell'incendio Neroniano*, Rome 1905,

[16] There is a vast literature on this subject, and the conclusions do not always derive from the sources. The present writer accepts the conclusion of Charlesworth that 'the House of Gold' was built for the extravagant taste of Nero and not as a matter of religious policy. See M. P. Charlesworth, 'Nero, Some Aspects' *JRS* vol. 40 (1950), p. 69, and Tacitus 15.42: 'incredibilium cupitor'.

[17] C. Huelsen, 'The Burning of Rome' *Amer. Journ. Arch.* vol. 13 (1909), p. 45. Y. Tresch, *Die Nerobücher in den Annalen das Tacitus,* Heidelberg 1965, does not deal with the problem.

[18] For detailed discussion, see F. Millar, *A study of Cassius Dio,* Oxford 1964, p. 34 ff.

[19] Dio puts all the guilt on Nero in the affairs of Britannicus (61.7.4), Agrippina (61.23.14) and Octavia. Tacitus at least tries to appear more objective.

[20] Van Berchem, *Distributions de Blé et d'Argent à la Plèbe romaine,* Geneva 1939. See also Z. Yavetz, *Plebs and Princeps,* Oxford 1969, p. 143.

[21] Suet., *Div. Aug. 9.*

[22] W. Steidle, *Sueton und die Antike Biographie,* Munich 1951.

[23] Cf. 4.53.3. Often Tacitus is less specific and contents

himself with 'diversa reperiuntur', e.g. 1.81; 3.19; 4.65; 12.24.

[24] Z. Yavetz, 'Living conditions of the urban Plebs' *Lat.* vol. 17 (1958), p. 512; M. Voight, *Die römischen Baugesetze. Berichte der Gesellschaft der Wissenschaften, Leipzig,* Phil. Hist. Kl. vol. 55 (1903), p. 175.

[25] See Z. Yavetz, *Plebs and Princeps,* p. 96.

[26] I. S. Ryberg, 'Tacitus' art of Innuendo' *TAPA* vol. 73 (1942), pp. 383–404.

[27] See also B. Walker, *The Annals of Tacitus,* Manchester 1952, pp. 83 ff.

[28] F. Leo, *Tacitus,* Göttingen 1896 = *Ausgewählte Kleine Schriften* vol. 2, Rome 1960, pp. 263–276 = *Tacitus,* Wege der Forschung vol. 97, ed. V. Pöschl, Darmstadt 1969, p. 1.

[29] For an example, see 15.73: 'whether because of envy or out of fear.'

[30] On rumours and gossip as a national epidemic, see details in my *Plebs and Princeps,* p. 135 ff.

[31] On Nero becoming the darling of the people, see ibid., p. 120.

[32] On the Octavia affair, ibid., p. 15.

[33] Ibid., p. 112 ff.

[34] Ibid., p. 112.

[35] Tac., *Hist.* 1.4.

[36] For spreading rumours and denying them see Cic., *pro Reg. Deiot.* 33–34. Cf. Z. Yavetz: 'Fama, Existimatio and the Ides of March' *HSCP* vol. 78 (1974), pp. 72 ff.

Z. Yavetz,
Department of History,
Tel Aviv University.

# 14

## Christianos ad Leonem

It is common ground that the attitude of Republican Rome towards foreign, un-Roman cults was non-repressive. There is no evidence that such worship was suppressed or that individuals, whether or not they were Roman citizens, were in any way prohibited from participation in 'alien' religious activities as such. When such cults were acted against by the authorities it was because they encouraged, or were believed to encourage, criminal behaviour. The best known instance is that of the Bacchanalians in 186 B.C., where Livy (39. 8 ff.) attests that the reason why the cult was proceeded against was that it was held to undermine public morality and incite its adherents to multifarious crimes. By the same token, there is no evidence of any kind to indicate that Roman citizens – still less, non-citizens – were under any formal obligation to worship the gods of the Roman state pantheon or to abjure the worship of other gods.

Even the monotheistic Jews could be brought beneath this umbrella. In 66 B.C. Cicero (*pro Flacco* 66 ff.) is a witness to their numbers and influence at Rome, and tells us that they were regularly permitted to send money from Italy and elsewhere to the Temple at Jerusalem: 'Cum aurum Iudaeorum nomine quotannis ex Italia et ex omnibus nostris provinciis Hierosolymam exportari soleret'. Yet many Romans no doubt shared Cicero's view that Judaism was a 'barbara superstitio', and the export of gold had often been frowned on by the Senate. Even Pompey, Cicero tells us, was restrained by *pudor* from despoiling the Temple when Jerusalem fell to his arms. The evidence for the marked consideration which Julius Caesar later accorded to the Jews has been conveniently collected by T. Rice Holmes (*The Roman Republic*, Oxford 1923, vol. 3, pp. 507—9), and Suetonius tells us that they were outstanding amongst the multitude who publicly mourned his death (*Div. Iul.* 84). Augustus proved as accommodating as his adoptive father, and allowed his name to be given to a synagogue at Rome[1]; Claudius confirmed the privileges and upheld the religious freedom of Jews throughout the Roman world[2]; and, even after the capture and destruction of Jerusalem in A.D. 70 as a consequence of the Jewish Revolt, the action of Vespasian in setting up a special *Fiscus Judaicus* into which should be paid the moneys previously subscribed by the Jews of the diaspora to the Temple indicates a continuing recognition of the right of the Jews to pursue their ancestral ways as a separate group[3]. Still later, toleration of the Jewish religion may be discerned in the licence Jews were allowed by Marcus Aurelius to circumcise their own children although they were forbidden to proselytise.[4]

Not that the Roman government never showed hostility to Judaism, but it did so only for special reasons, political or judicial. Revolts and obstructiveness had to be repressed. As for crimes, under Tiberius in A.D. 19 some Jews were dealt with for gross immorality and embezzlement; and under Claudius they were proceeded against for breach of the peace and riot on the famous occasion when that emperor expelled from the capital the Jews who were 'continuously rioting through the incitement of Chrestus': 'Iudaeos impulsore Chresto adsidue tumultuantis Roma expulit'[5] But there is no sign of persecution of the Jews 'for the Name', that is to say for the mere profession and practice of their faith. All in all, there is nothing in Rome's relations with the monotheistic Jews that can lend colour to any suggestion that Christianity was attacked merely because of its alien origin or because Christians as monotheists were hostile to other gods and debarred by their religion from certain acts of public worship which polytheists could accept. An accommodation was possible with the Jews. Why not with the Christians?

It seems likely enough that what lay behind Claudius' expulsion of the Jews of Rome was a continuing conflict between Christianising and non-Christianising Jews. The name 'Chrestus' is itself a clue, for to deny the possibility that it conceals 'Christus' is to strain coincidence very seriously. On top of that we can add the fact that the Pontic Jew Aquila and his wife Priscilla, who were among the Jews expelled from

Rome by Claudius, were plainly Christianising Jews, for they entertained Paul at Corinth and provided him with a base for his missionary work there: 'After these things Paul departed from Athens and came to Corinth; and found a certain Jew named Aquila, born in Pontus, lately come from Italy, with his wife Priscilla; (because that Claudius had commanded all Jews to depart from Rome:) and came unto them. And because he was of the same craft, he abode with them, and wrought: for by their occupation they were tentmakers. And he reasoned in the synagogue every sabbath' (*Acts* 18.1 ff.). All the same, it is evident that as yet the Roman government did not recognise a clear distinction between Jews and Christians — not surprisingly, since this was not yet recognised by the parties themselves. In *Acts* 10.28 we read of Peter's hesitation about entering the house of the centurion Cornelius because 'it is an unlawful thing for a man that is a Jew to keep company, or come unto one of another nation'. The disciples, after the martyrdom of Stephen, 'preached the word to none but unto Jews only' (*Acts* 11.19) and even after they acquired the specific name 'Christians' (11.26), their preaching was regularly carried on in the synagogues (13.15, etc.). The first Christians still saw themselves as Jews, albeit of a particular persuasion, and Paul was able to angle for the support of the Pharisees on that ground (23.6 ff.). Understandably the same confusion existed in the minds of the Roman authorities, as the action of the proconsul Junius Gallio demonstrates at Corinth: 'And when Gallio was the deputy of Achaia, the Jews made insurrection with one accord against Paul, and brought him to the judgement seat, saying, This fellow persuadeth men to worship God contrary to the law. And when Paul was now about to open his mouth, Gallio said unto the Jews, If it were a matter of wrong or wicked lewdness, O ye Jews, reason would that I should bear with you: But if it be a question of words and names, and of your law, look ye to it; for I will be no judge of such matters. And he drave them from the judgement seat. Then all the Greeks took Sosthenes, the chief ruler of the synagogue, and beat him before the judgement seat. And Gallio cared for none of these things' (18. 12–17).

Claudius was taking action against a civil crime: riot and breach of the peace ('adsidue tumultuantis'). There was no question of religious persecution. So too with the aftermath of the Great Fire at Rome in A.D. 64. Suetonius is unsatisfactory, for though he mentions both Nero's harshness to the Christians and the Fire (*Nero* 16 and 38) he fails to connect the two. Tacitus is much more helpful (*Annals* 15.44): Nero, anxious to divert suspicions that he had started the Fire to clear the way for his grandiose building schemes, had it bruited abroad that the culprits had been found in the Christians of the city, a group of people in any case so unpopular that any heinous crime could be laid at their door (and especially, if one reflects how much they must have talked of the Fiery Furnace, the crime of arson). So practising Christians were arrested, and a confession of Christianity was treated as tantamount to a confession of arson. Tacitus did not accept that the Christians were guilty of arson (*incendiarii*); but he had no sympathy for the adherents of this 'exitiabilis superstitio' (or 'superstitio nova ac malefica', as Suetonius terms it), and accepted that they were otherwise deserving of the severest punishment ('novissima exempla').

The Christians, Tacitus assures us, were widely unpopular with the common masses; and by now they were distinguishable from the Jews. Though not guilty of the crime for which they suffered savage penalties, they could be punished (it was expected) without protest and even with public approval because of their alleged *flagitia*, the abhorrent practices which their religion was widely held to enjoin on them, and their 'odium humani generis'. So, while in a loose sense of the word they were 'persecuted', this was not persecution in the strictest sense. Nero acted, not to suppress Christianity as such, but to persuade the inhabitants of Rome that those responsible for the conflagration had been arrested and suitably punished. It was the misfortune of the Christians that they chanced to be the group singled out as scapegoats. Understandably, later Christian writers saw this as 'persecution for the name', and described official oppression of their church as a practice initiated by Nero (*institutum Neronianum*).[6] But they must not be followed here, as they have been by some modern scholars.[7] In this, as in many other instances, Christian sources must be treated with suspicion; they may be good guides as to what happened, but they are unreliable as to the reasons which led the Romans to act as they did. It is evident that the affair was confined to Rome, and the belief that Nero issued a general edict against Christians everywhere (based on passages from the *Apocalypse*, *I Peter*, and *Hebrews*) is ill-founded.[8] And the Christians were convicted and punished as *incendiarii*, not for the *nomen ipsum* ('the Name').

For the next fifty years the picture is dark. There is no space here to go into detail, but suffice it to say that firm evidence is lacking until we come to the clear light of the reign of Trajan, and to the famous letter which the younger Pliny as consular legate of Bithynia wrote to that emperor and the reply which it received.[9] From these it is beyond dispute that by A.D. 112 (though for how long before we cannot say) it had become an accepted practice in certain circumstances to execute Christians who refused to abjure their faith, and to do so on the simple grounds that they were practising Christians.

Pliny writes as follows:

'I have never been present at any proceedings involving Christians, and so I do not know what the practice is as regards the nature and extent of the penalty or the inquiry. I have been considerably exercised whether any distinction is to be made in regard to age . . . ; whether a recantation may win pardon . . . ; whether it is the name itself, even if it involves no *flagitia*, or whether it is the abominations that cohere to the name ('flagitia cohaerentia nomini') which are to be penalised.

'For the present, in the case of those who have been brought before me as alleged Christians, I have adopted the following procedure. I have asked them themselves if they were Christians; if they admitted it, I asked the question again, and then a third time, having threatened them with execution; if they still persisted, I ordered them to be taken away and put to death. For I had no doubt that whatever it was that they were confessing to they assuredly deserved to be punished for their stubbornness and unbending obstinacy. . . .

'I was given an anonymous denunciation containing many names. Those named who denied being Christians or ever having been Christians I decided to dismiss after they had called on the names of the gods and had offered incense and wine to your image (which I had had brought in together with those of the gods for this express purpose) and had moreover cursed Christ -- none of which things, it is said, can true Christians be compelled to do. Others named by the informer said they were Christians, but soon denied it; they had been Christians, they said, but had now stopped, some for three years or more, some for longer, one or two even for over twenty years. All of them too venerated your image and the likeness of the gods, and cursed Christ.

'They asserted, however, that this was the sum of their guilt or error: that they had been in the habit of coming together on a fixed day before dawn and joining in singing a hymn to Christ as if to a god, and binding themselves to a vow, not to *commit* any crime, but to abstain from theft and robbery and adultery, not to bear false witness, not to refuse to give up anything entrusted to them when called upon for it. This done, they would break up and then reassemble for a meal, but a meal of an ordinary and harmless kind -- something they had in fact given up after the publication of my edict in which following your instructions I had banned all clubs. I accordingly deemed it necessary to inquire what the truth was from two female servants, called deaconesses, even using torture. I discovered nothing beyond a depraved and immoderate superstition.

'I therefore adjourned the inquiry and hastened to consult you. For it seemed to me a matter worth consulting you about, especially because of the number of those endangered. For many people of all ages and classes, and of both sexes, are being involved in danger and will be so involved. It is not only the towns but the villages too and the countryside which have been affected by the spread of this contagion, which it seems can be halted and put right. Certainly it is sure enough that the temples which have been all but deserted have begun to be thronged again, and sacred rites long neglected to be begun again, and sacrificial victims are everywhere on sale for which till now there had been few buyers. From this it is easy to judge what a host of people can be made to mend their ways if only clemency is allowed for repentance.'

Granted that in certain circumstances the mere profession of Christianity could be treated as a capital offence, it was a very odd offence. Let us turn here to Trajan's reply to Pliny. He begins by approving Pliny's action, and denies the possibility of laying down any universal rule applicable to all such cases; then he goes on to add that 'These people are not be specially sought out. If they are denounced and found guilty, they must be punished, provided however that if anyone denies that he is a Christian and gives practical proof that he is not (that is, by sacrificing to our gods) he is to be pardoned on the grounds of repentance even if he is suspected of having been a Christian in the past. As for anonymous informations, these ought not be admitted in any criminal matter.' So these criminals are in a curious category. A crime which the proper authorities are enjoined not to seek out but to ignore unless it is brought formally to their attention, a crime which though capital if persisted in can be rendered wholly venial by an assurance that it has been abandoned, is an unusual crime, to say the least. And so Tertullian thought, when he protested: 'What a decision! How essentially confused! Trajan says they are not to be sought out, implying their innocence: and he orders them to be punished, implying their guilt. He spares them and he savages them, he pretends not to see and he takes cognizance of them.'[10]

It is plainly ridiculous to imagine that a Roman emperor would ever order his subordinates to refrain from seeking out and punishing crimes of the nature of the *flagitia* popularly attributed to the Christians — cannibalism, incest, ritual murder, and so on — or that anyone guilty of such crimes in the past could win immunity by simply promising 'not to do it again'. It is evident that the offence was the practice and profession of Christianity itself, the *nomen ipsum.*

That Trajan was prepared to 'let sleeping dogs lie' suggests that official action was only to be taken if Christians provoked trouble in some way. That they often did is clear from Christian testimony itself. A few passages from the *Acts* will show this. At Antioch (13.50) 'the word of the Lord was published throughout all the region. But the Jews stirred up the devout and honourable women, and the chief men of the city, and raised persecution against Paul and Barnabas, and expelled them out of their coasts.' They moved on to Iconium, where (14.2) 'a great multitude both of the Jews and also of the Greeks believed. But the unbelieving Jews stirred up the gentiles and made their minds evil affected against the brethren. . . . the multitude of the city was divided, and part held with the Jews and part with the apostles.' At Thessalonica (17.5) 'the Jews which believed not, moved with envy, took unto them certain lewd fellows of the baser sort, and gathered a company, and set all the city on an uproar.' There are several other passages of a like nature[11] — Gallio at Corinth and the famous incident of the Ephesus silversmiths — which also go to show that the early spreaders of the gospel of this new religion could be a cause of tumult and riot and ill-will wherever they went. No authorities at any epoch welcome such men — the danger of civil commotion is one to which Trajan himself was sensitive enough.[12] And whatever we make of the detail of the information, civil commotion is in the background to the letter about Christians which Serennius Granianus sent from Asia to Trajan's successor Hadrian ('it was not just to put Christians to death to appease popular clamour'), and implied in Hadrian's own rescript to Granianus' successor.[13]

It is quite certain, as we have seen, that the offence for which Pliny convicted and executed Christians, with the approval of the emperor, was simply that of adherence to the Christian faith, regardless of any *flagitia* which might rightly or wrongly be believed to be an inescapable consequence of this. And Pliny was clearly not operating in a vacuum. Indeed, his letter is somewhat disingenuous, in that it suggests perhaps a greater uncertainty than Pliny in fact felt. We must accept that he had never personally been present at any 'proceedings involving Christians' ('cognitiones de Christianis'); but he knows of the existence of this special category of *cognitiones*, and it is only on points of detail that he seeks a ruling from Trajan — and that too after the event, for he did not adjourn the cases until Trajan replied but gave judgement before writing to the Emperor. Again, while he professes doubt about whether it is Christianity itself or the *flagitia* it carries in its train that are to be punished, he has none the less ordered Christians to be put to death although he had satisfied himself by personal investigation that no *flagitia* had in fact been perpetuated. All of which goes to show that, despite his lack of first-hand experience, this ex-consul and experienced lawyer and administrator and *amicus principis* had a very good grasp of what was involved and what the general practice was in such cases. And this indicates that for some time similar situations had been cropping up elsewhere, and that some sort of what we might very loosely call case-law had emerged from the application of general rules in comparable situations by other holders of *imperium*, some of whom at least surely also consulted the home government for guidance or confirmation.

Nevertheless, Pliny's hesitancy rules out certain answers which have been suggested to the question, under what head of Roman law did the offence of the Christians fall. *Maiestas* (very loosely, high treason) was long a popular answer, especially given that it was backed by the authority of Mommsen. This offence could certainly be laid at the door of anyone suspected of disloyalty to the Princeps or even of failing to pay him proper respect; and Christians were plausibly exposed to such charges on a number of grounds -- their professed allegiance to a heavenly king, their inability to take part in the imperial cult, and so on. But it is highly unlikely, to put it mildly, that Pliny would have expressed the sort of doubts he specifies about a straightforward case of *maiestas*, and even have failed so much as to mention the word in his letter. The act of pagan worship which he demanded was demanded simply as a sure test to distinguish true Christians from non-Christians: there is no suggestion that the refusal of such an act was itself the offence for which they were condemned. And this is fully corroborated by Trajan's reply that 'anyone who denies being a Christian and gives practical proof of this, i.e. by offering supplication to our gods, may regardless of any suspicions about his past obtain pardon on the score of repentance'. The inclusion of Trajan's effigy among those of the gods set up for the test-supplication was not more than a courtly gesture of Pliny's, and Trajan omits any reference to it in his own letter, specifying simply 'our gods' ('dis nostris'), among whom he certainly did not include himself. We have also to remember that Jews were as much inhibited as Christians from making sacrifice to 'di nostri' or to emperors, and yet they were not treated in the same way.

In fact, all attempts to bring the legal action against the Christians at this period under the head of any specific statute meet with no success on generally similar grounds. Persecutions were local and unsystematic and far from wholesale. Above all, we can point to an argument which I find conclusive: there is no mention in the abundant literature of the early Church, whatever its character, of any specific statute or legislative act which made the profession and practice of Christianity a criminal offence until we come to the Emperor Decius in the middle of the third century. In actual fact, of course, offences which would fall under the head of such statutes were often alleged against Christians, who were accused of ritual murder and cannibalism and incest and other such *flagitia*; naturally the apologists and defenders of Christianity used much ink in seeking to rebut these and similar charges, which were bandied about by their opponents in order to discredit them and their faith. But the fact that Christians denied being guilty of such crimes is no proof that they were formally accused and punished for them.

We have to distinguish clearly two questions: (a) why a Roman officer of state like Pliny took action against Christians, and took it in the way he did; and (b) under what rule of law did he take such action. Now, as regards the first question, it appears that Pliny took action only when others brought the Christians to his attention; and Trajan himself ruled that Christians were to be left alone unless they were the subject of a formal denunciation — indeed, he went further and forbade Pliny to pay attention to anonymous denunciations and specifically inhibited him from taking any initiative himself to seek out Christians and punish them ('conquirendi non sunt', he wrote). From which it seems that at this date, at any rate, Christians would be noticed and dealt with only if they offended local opinion or sensitivities. We saw earlier instances of how this occurred in apostolic times. If such complaints were made, if the activity of Christians led or was likely to lead to local disturbances and even rioting, then a Roman official, like the local magistrates of Asia Minor in the *Acts*, would investigate and take action; and, if he were satisfied as to the facts, he would then tell the Christians to cease their provocative behaviour. If they obeyed his order, and satisfied him of their sincerity, they could be let off with a warning, so to speak. If they refused, they had to be punished.

A magistrate's authority to act in this way lay in the *ius coercitionis* (the power of coercion) which was inherent in the *imperium* of a senior magistrate of the Roman state, the legal right to enforce obedience to his orders which involved a general right to take action against any individuals who might threaten the stability and good order of society, whether their offence was covered by formal statute law or not; for in matters of criminal as opposed to civil law the Roman legal system was characterised by an absence of settled form and a wide discretion and even arbitrariness on the part of its administrators.[14] It is the theory which lies at the bottom of Cicero's action in executing the Catilinarian conspirators in 63 B.C. without trial, perhaps the best known example of the exercise of *coercitio*. It left magistrates free to handle situations not specifically envisaged by or provided for in statute law. There is a good example too in Pliny's letter: the 'stubbornness and unbending obstinacy' ('pertinacia et inflexibilis obstinatio') which he detected in the non-apostate Christians he was faced with were not crimes under any act of legislation, yet Pliny held that they would have been worthy of punishment on this ground alone regardless of what crime they had or had not committed; and in so thinking he was contemplating the use of the simple power of *coercitio* at his own discretion to punish recalcitrants who persisted in a refusal to obey his reasonable orders.

A magistrate who was thinking of using his *ius coercitionis* could do so in summary style (*de plano*), especially if the offences and punishments were relatively trivial (*levia crimina*),[15] or he could proceed more formally by way of a regular hearing (*cognitio*). But there was nothing to stop him seeking advice or confirmation or support in his proposed action: Cicero had sought it from the Senate, Pliny looked to Trajan. I have suggested that such consultation of the emperor was not an isolated occurrence, and that the upshot would have been the emergence of a loose set of rules, rules lacking the precision and inexorability of a statute and leaving much to the individual judgement of individual holders of *imperium* to adapt them to the individual circumstances in which they found themselves.

We can turn now to the famous quotation from Tertullian about Christians and lions. We have seen the sort of local disorders that the activities of Christians could arouse, and it is easy to imagine others. The unpopularity of the sect in many places is abundantly documented. In times of danger and disaster, too, the inhabitants of the ancient world readily and understandably supposed that their tribulations were a mani-festation of the displeasure of the gods, or at least that an appeal to such superhuman powers might bring improvement or remedy. In their own societies there lived groups of people who practised a religion which either denied the very existence of these gods or denounced them as devils and forces for evil with no title to worship or respect. Unlike Judaism, Christianity did not have an ancient and national respectability capable of arousing a sense of *pudor* in others: it was not practised *more maiorum*; it was not a *patria religio*; and its increasing number of converts were themselves renegades and apostates from their own traditional ancestral or national beliefs — as Tertullian himself put it (*Apol.* 18.4), Christians were made, not born: 'fiunt, non nascuntur Christiani'. So the Christians, who were also popularly believed to be guilty of loathsome practices and hatred of their fellow-beings ('odium humani generis'), all to frequently became the focus of hatred or fear, and tolerance of their presence and activities in a particular community itself a cause of bitterness and suspicion or an obvious explanation for natural disasters and a bar to securing divine assistance and relief. Trouble arose, and unrest spread; the authorities soon became aware of the identity of the source of the trouble, and naturally ordered Christians to desist and start behaving like everybody else. Refusal to obey such a perfectly reasonable command (as indeed it must always have seemed to those who issued it) would mean a prolongation of public disturbances and would in effect constitute a refusal to recognise the authority of the magistrate concerned. So Christians who persisted in their faith had to be disciplined and brought to their senses. Which is in effect what Tertullian attests in his famous complaint (*Apol.* 40): 'If the Tiber floods, or if the Nile fails to flood; if there is drought or earthquake or famine or pestilence; then at once the cry goes up "To the lion with the Christians!" '; 'Si Tiberis ascendit in moenia, si Nilus non ascendit in arva; si caelum stetit, si terra movit; si fames, si lues, statim Christianos ad leonem! adclamatur.' (Tertullian did not lack for a sense of humour and at once went on to add: 'All those Christians, and only one lion?' — 'Tantos ad unum?')

I have concerned myself only with the early stages of the collision between the Roman government and Christianity. Like many others, I am happy to go along with G. E. M. de Ste. Croix so far as concerns the later history of the question.[16] But, like A. N. Sherwin-White,[17] I believe that in making 'godlessness' ($\dot\alpha\theta\epsilon\dot o\tau\eta\varsigma$) the essential crime for which Christians were punished in Pliny's day de Ste. Croix has read back too much from this later history, and I do not find his rejoinder to Sherwin-White[18] convincing on this score. In large measure, my reasons for disagreeing are contained in the account and arguments set out earlier: there simply is no evidence for 'godlessness' as the basic crime, and there is evidence against it — which is not to deny that in an important sense 'godlessness' was in fact a chief reason why the trouble arose in the first place, given that it was a proselytising 'godlessness'. I think that Sherwin-White has the better of the argument, although he could in my opinion have expressed his point better than he did. Clearly — as de Ste. Croix properly insisted — the Christians were not tried and found guilty of *contumacia; contumacia* is essentially a second-order crime or offence, and it arises only when an earlier order or decision has been flouted or disobeyed. But the offence of which the Christians were guilty was close to *contumacia*, and punishment (as is obvious from Pliny's letter) would not have been inflicted if the Christians had not behaved 'contumaciously'. The trouble with the Christians was that their belief positively *encouraged* contumacy (in the wide sense) since it promised the very highest rewards to those who were prepared to suffer martyrdom for the faith, 'for the Name'. This is what gave to Christianity, as far as officials like Pliny were concerned, its special flavour. What led to the trouble in which the earliest Christians found themselves was the peculiar novelty of their faith; the practices which it was believed to involve which incited horror and disapprobation; a missionary zeal to convert others from older and more settled and 'respectable' faiths; a denial of other gods and a hostile contempt for other 'established' religions; a particular 'otherness' or sectarianism, which might lead to the break-up of families; a conviction that Christians and Christians alone were right; a challenge to existing practices and beliefs and vested interests — crudely, and paradoxically, their 'godlessness' or ἀθεότης. They created situations which led the forces of authority to take action against them, and which by Pliny's day had brought into existence at least in certain areas a common set of loose rules for dealing with them as and when need arose. At this point the stubborn adherence to their faith of considerable numbers of Christians, their 'contumacious' refusal to fall into line, produced a predictable result. Their crime was neither 'godlessness' nor 'contumacy'; their crime was not even that of being Christians; their crime was that special blend of 'contumacious godlessness' which was involved, not just in being a Christian, but in *insisting on continuing to be a Christian* whatever the cost. Pliny and Trajan were prepared to overlook the former, but not the latter. But, for a true Christian, being a Christian and continuing to be a Christian, come what may, are and were and always will be one and the same thing — the Kingdom of God never was, and never can be, of this world. Which is why the crime of which the early Christians were guilty was Christianity.

### Notes

[1] See, for example, Th. Mommsen, *Provinces of the Roman Empire* vol. 2, p. 171 ff; Bormann, *WS* vol. 34, 1912, p. 362.
[2] Momigliano, *Claudius: the Emperor and his Achievement*, reissue, Cambridge 1961, p. 29 ff.

[3] Dio 66.7; Jos., *BJ* 7.218; Martial 7.55; Mommsen, loc. cit.

[4] *Digest* 48.8.11.

[5] Tac., *Ann.* 2.85; Jos., *AJ* 18.81 ff.; Suet., *Div. Claud.* 25.

[6] Tertullian, *ad Nat.* 1.7.

[7] E.g. de Ste. Croix 'Why were the early Christians persecuted?' *Past and Present* no. 26 (November 1963 pp. 6–38.

[8] De Ste. Croix, art. cit., p. 10 and notes.

[9] Pliny, *Ep.* 10.96 and 97.

[10] Tertullian *Apol.* 8 -- a good example of the failure of Christian writers to penetrate the mind of the Roman authorities, for nobody will lightly suppose that they were as stupid as Tertullian makes out.

[11] I see no good reason to put this emphasis on Jewish opposition down to 'propaganda'. It was only to be expected that, to begin with, Jews should have constituted the chief and most active opposition to Christianity.

[12] Pliny, *Ep.* 10.34 and 92, for example. Note too the reference to outlawing 'clubs' in Pliny's letter about the Christians. Such organisations were commonly regarded by the Roman authorities, republican and imperial alike, as potential sources of civil violence or 'covers' for illicit organisations.

[13] Eus., *HE* 4.8.6; 9.1. Pliny's reference to the transformation his own action had produced in attendance at temples and sales of sacrificial victims also indicates that this was one aspect at least of the trouble with which he had to deal.

[14] Sherwin-White, *Journ. of Theol. Stud.* N.S. vol. 3, 1952 pp. 199–213. De Ste. Croix (art. cit., p. 12) aptly cites Mommsen ('a legalised absence of settled form'), Schulz, and Jolowicz on this aspect of Roman criminal law.

[15] de Ste. Croix, art. cit., p. 12 and notes.

[16] See n. 7.

[17] *Past and Present* no. 27 (April 1964) pp. 23–27.

[18] Ibid., pp. 28–33.

D. L. Stockton,
Brasenose College,
Oxford.

# 15

## Culturae Mancianae: Field Patterns in the Albertini Tablets

With the publication in 1952 of the so-called Albertini Tablets[1] an important body of new material was made available to the student of legal and economic institutions in the later Roman Empire. The aim of this paper is to examine one aspect of these documents which has not hitherto been fully dealt with, namely the structure of the estates involved and in particular the question of field patterns, and to attempt an assessment of what appear to be its wider implications.

I

The Tablets appear to relate to an area on or near the modern frontier between Algeria and Tunisia, about a hundred kilometres south of Tebessa.[2] They are of wood, and are inscribed in ink with a series of documents in Latin. Of the thirty-four documents, partial or complete, which have been published, one is a description of a dowry, two are accounts or calculations of some kind, and the rest are deeds of sale — one of a slave, one of an olive press, and the remaining twenty-nine of plots of land.[3] How the documents came together is not clear, but it is perhaps significant that of the twenty-eight purchasers named all but three have the name Geminius, and it seems likely that what we have is part of a family archive.[4] Where complete, the documents are dated, and all the extant dates fall between March, A.D. 493, and April, A.D. 496; they belong, therefore, to the time when this part of Africa was under the Vandal king

213

Gunthamund, on whose regnal years the dating is normally based.[5]

The documents which concern us here are those recording sales of land, particularly those parts which hint at the distribution and organisation of individual holdings. Such hints as there are, however, are difficult to interpret without some knowledge of the immediate circumstances and of the wider historical background, and it is with this that the discussion has to begin.

The plots of land whose sale the documents record are under the *dominium* of someone other than the buyers and sellers themselves. Of the twenty-one documents in which the preamble is reasonably complete, nineteen ascribe the *dominium* to one Flavius Geminius Catullinus, who has the same family name as most of the purchasers and is presumably a local landowner. In six documents plots are said to be 'in fundo Tuletianensis', and in fifteen others the deed is recorded as 'actum Tuletianos'; the natural assumption is that all or most of the plots are linked in some way with this *fundus*, and that Geminius is its owner.[6] As far as it relates to the plots themselves, however, his *dominium* is clearly something rather less than ownership in any normal sense of the word. He takes no part in the sale itself, and once the price has been paid the purchaser takes over the plot without any obvious limitation of rights: 'ut h(a)b(eat) p(ossideat) utatur fruaturque ipse heredesbe eius in perpetuo',[7] terms which, had we not been told otherwise, we might have taken as implying full *dominium*. This is not in itself of major importance: the concept of *dominium* underwent considerable changes in the late Empire, and the situation here is not without parallel.[8] What *is* important is that in this case the Tablets provide us with an additional piece of information which can be linked, not only with references in contemporary sources, but with those of a much earlier period. The result is that we can provide an explanation of the tenure system of the *fundus Tuletianos* and at the same time fill in much of its detailed background.

The crucial item is that the plots of land in the Tablets are regularly referred to as *culturae Mancianae*; the phrase occurs in the preamble of thirteen deeds, and although there are at least eight in which it does not occur there is some justification for the view that it applies to all or most of them. There can be little doubt that these *culturae Mancianae* are the ultimate product of a *lex Manciana* of (perhaps) four centuries earlier, and since this appears in a series of detailed inscriptions relating to the imperial estates of the upper Bagradas valley a mass of supporting information becomes available.[9]

The *lex* or *consuetudo Manciana* appears first in an inscription from Henchir Mettich, dated to A.D. 115–117, in which it is cited as the basis for certain arrangements made on an estate called the *Villa Magna Variani* by two imperial procurators.[10] What the status of the *lex* was is not clear, and there is no obvious explanation of its name, but it was clearly well enough known in the area to be referred to.[11] The arrangements made, for which it is quoted as a precedent, are that people living on the estate shall have the right to cultivate the *agri subsecivi* subject to certain conditions.[12] They are to hand over a proportion of produce to the *dominus* or his agents, and (possibly) to perform certain services on his demesne.[13] Otherwise they are to use the land as they see fit, their rights being defined, without further explanation, as *usus proprius.*[14] The mention of *agri subsecivi* makes it clear that the estate itself is in a centuriated area, and that the provisions of the *lex Manciana* were applied to land not included in the original survey; presumably at some time or other the need was felt to cultivate these lands, and terms devised accordingly. That the arrangements applied to other estates as well is clear from an inscription of a few years later,[15] in which reference is made again to the *lex Manciana* 'condicione [s]altus Neroniani vicini nobis', suggesting perhaps that once it was found to be workable it was adopted for neighbouring estates as the need arose. This second inscription, from Ain-el-Djemala, a few miles south of Henchir Mettich, also provides the next stage in the law's development: the request for the *lex Manciana* to apply on this estate is met by the imperial procurators with the reply that its terms are now subsumed under the *lex Hadriana de rudibus agris*, a more general enactment covering not only the *agri subsecivi* but land within the centuries which had become derelict. The *usus proprius* of the *lex Manciana* is now replaced by the more precise and more regular *ius possidendi ac fruendi heredique suo relinquendi*, a right which is essentially that of the holders of *culturae Mancianae* in the Albertini Tablets.

What we may now call Manciane tenure is therefore revealed as a form of tenure arising from the clearing and cultivation of waste land, available primarily (if not exclusively) to *coloni* on estates already existing. In the two inscriptions so far considered it is associated with land on the margins of centuriated

215

areas, and in the absence of contrary indications we must assume that the plots in the Albertini Tablets are of this kind. The legal position, at any rate, is now clear: Geminius is *dominus* of the lands in question, not only in the sense that he had residual rights over them arising from the original grant, but probably also in the sense that the holders of these lands are *coloni* on his estate; whether he can still exact the payments in kind to which the *lex Manciana* would have entitled him is not indicated, but it may be that the mention of his *dominium* in the documents is a reference to this right.

For some reason, then, the notion of Manciane tenure continued. Perhaps it was not submerged in the *lex Hadriana* but remained as a special category within it; perhaps, as has been suggested,[16] it provided a convenient and readily understandable way of referring to a particular kind of person holding land by a rather cumbrous title. Whatever the explanation, one C. Aufidius Utilis, recording a dedication in an inscription of almost a century later,[17] is able to describe himself quite simply as *manciane cultor*, presumably confident that this will be intelligible to anyone likely to read it; and as we have seen, the writers of the Albertini Tablets apparently saw no reason to explain the similar phrase when it arose in their documents of sale. What this seems to imply is that at least in this part of Africa (let us say, the area of the Bagradas valley generally) the kind of tenure we have been describing not only persisted for several generations but was sufficiently widespread not to arouse comment when it occurred. If this is so, an attempt to discover something of its physical appearance may be of interest.

II

On the question of field patterns the editors of the Tablets have little to say. There is a short discussion of the words used for special kinds of plots, and a comment that individual holdings appear to be scattered, but further than this 'les régimes agraires ... nous échappent complètement'.[18] As they point out, the shape of the plots is not given, nor is there any indication of their size: all that distinguishes them, unless they have trees on them, is their price, and size alone is not likely to have been the criterion for this. More important, the lands with which the Tablets are concerned are not an integral part of the estate but are situated around its edges and perhaps in odd corners within it; whatever the system within the centuries may have been (assuming that the centuries were still in existence), the Mancian lands will not have been part of it and may not have borne any resemblance to it. Nevertheless, we are not so well informed on fields and field systems in the Roman period that we can afford to ignore a documented example simply because its application may turn out to be limited. What the Tablets contain is a system which can be examined at a particular known date; the reasons for its establishment are known, together with its approximate age and something of the process whereby it came into being. How typical it was is a question that will have to be faced in due course, but a close look at its workings is clearly a first requirement.

The main outlines are plain enough. What is usually sold in the documents is a *particella,* or parcel, though other words are occasionally used.[19] It is not usual for a parcel to have a name of its own, and so great care is taken to fix its position exactly and thus avoid confusion. This is done in two ways: first, the parcel is said to be in a certain named *ager,* or field; and second, its neighbouring parcels in several directions are specified by reference to their owners. This latter practice recalls the requirement in the *Digest* that in entering a *fundus* on a census return the names of its two nearest neighbours should be given,[20] the supplying of more than two neighbours in the Tablets presumably resulting from the smaller size of the parcels and a somewhat random layout.

The *agri* are clearly the largest units in the system. How large it is obviously impossible to say, but some appear to have sub-divisions, or areas within them large enough to merit a name of their own, while others have names suggesting a definite locality rather than an extensive area. Variations of spelling complicate the picture somewhat, but the following list is as accurate as we are likely to get:

*Aggarione* (III, VII; sub-division *Gemines tres,* III. 8)
*Aumas* (XV, XIX; sub-division *Gemio de riu,* XV. 8--9)
*Buresa* (X; sub-division *Sus aqua putei,* X. 4)
*Buinac* (XV, XX, XXI, XXII, XXIV; sub-division *Caput de Bucnac,* XV. 10)
*Post Centenarium* (VIII)
*Domos Veteres* (IX, XV)

*Gunfliones* (VI)
*Pullatis* (III, XIV, XXIV; sub-division *Sussanu,* XIV. 6)
*Sela* (XI, XVIII)
*Sicilliones* (V, VII, XII, XVI; sub-divisions *Gemio,* XII. 6;
    *Gunfliones,* V. 9; *Sub Quercu,* VII. 10; *Susanu,* V. 16)
*Pars de Susu* (XV)
*Tres Arbores* (XIII)
*In Valles* (XXIII)

Some of these are obviously more extensive than others. Names like *Tres Arbores* and *Domos Veteres* suggest land in the immediate neighbourhood of some prominent landmark and therefore, perhaps, of limited extent. Others, such as *Aumas* and *Gunfliones,* are used elsewhere in the Tablets to indicate types of parcels,[21] and it is likely that as proper names they refer simply to groups of these parcels rather than to *agri* in the normal sense; *Gunfliones* appears as a sub-division of *Sicilliones* in any case, which seems to bear this out. At the other end of the scale *Sicilliones* itself, with its four sub-divisions in the extant Tablets alone, was clearly a larger area. A count of the known holdings in each *ager* tends to confirm these impressions: our deeds are concerned with the disposal of forty-one separate lots,[22] and leaving aside those which are not assigned to an *ager* the distribution is as follows:

| | | | |
|---|---|---|---|
| *Buinac* | 9 | *Aggarione* | 4 |
| *Sicilliones* | 7 | *Domos Veteres, Sela, Aumas* | 2 each |
| *Pullatis* | 5 | and the rest | 1 each.[23] |

The picture, indeed, is what we might expect: the same reasons which led to these lands being omitted from the original survey will have led also to the establishment of blocks of unequal size, and the decision to call a block an *ager* rather than an area within an *ager* may not have rested on size alone. Taking the evidence we have it would seem that *Buinac, Sicilliones, Pullatis* and *Aggarione* are the main *agri,* and the others of less importance, though obviously this is not something to be insisted on.

Assuming, then, that the *culturae Mancianae* of the *fundus* are grouped primarily into a number of these fields, we can proceed to the crucial question of the distribution of individual holdings within the fields. Granted that the buying and selling may well distort the pattern, what is the likely distribution of a particular owner's parcels, and how far is the pattern consistent from one owner, or one field, to another? Two features can be established beyond reasonable doubt: first, the parcels of an individual owner are likely to be distributed between more than one field; and second, his parcels within a given field are likely to be dispersed and inter-mixed with those of other owners. Clearly, these are features with some potential significance, and before attempting to assess this a certain amount of detail will be necessary.

In what we have taken to be the four main fields of the estate, a total of twenty-six owners are known to us from the Tablets.[24] One of these has parcels in all four fields, three have parcels in three of them, ten have parcels in two, and the remaining twelve have parcels in only one. In addition, the list of owners in the other fields contains two who already hold parcels in the main four: oddly enough, both of them are in the group with holdings in three of these four. Indeed, it is generally true that the more parcels that we know of as belonging to a particular owner the wider the distribution of those parcels becomes: in fact, in every case where a person's holdings appear in more than one Tablet they are found in different fields, which suggests that if we had a more complete picture such a distribution would be seen to be the rule.[25]

The second feature, that of the dispersal of parcels within a given field, is obvious enough in general terms, but rather more difficult to illustrate in detail. That it existed is plain from the complicated formulae needed to fix the position of parcels, and from the simple fact that the neighbouring parcels are more often than not the property of other people. To draw any sort of map, however, is out of the question: even if we knew what shape the parcels were we would still be in the position of having isolated pieces of the jigsaw rather than anything like the complete puzzle. Nevertheless, the pieces in themselves are suggestive, and once we try to assemble them the degree of dispersal begins to become apparent. In the field called *Buinac* (see *Table 1*) there is evidence of both grouping and dispersal. The adjoining parcels of the 'heredes Belli' and the block belonging to Cresconius, occurring as they do in what are tiny fragments of the field, are enough to suggest that more groupings would be revealed if more fragments were available. It should, however, be noted that Cresconius, who is one of the Geminii, is one of the main buyers in the Tablets, so that his block of four may be the result of his purchases, though whether this could explain other groupings is obviously not in

## Table 1: Buinac

XV    (*a*)   *Vendor*: Sidinna relicta Processani
            *Neighbours*:    NE   Victorianus
                         S     Fortunatianus
                         (SW and NW irrigation works)
        (*b*)   *Vendor*: Sidinna relicta Processani
            *Neighbours*:    NE   Fortunatianus
                         S     Urbanianus
                         (SW and S irrigation works)

XX           *Vendors*: Victorinus et Fotta
              *Neighbours*:   (missing)

XXI         *Vendors*: Julius Lambus et Sidinna
              *Neighbours*:   S     Secundianus and heredes Belli
                         (SW and N irrigation works)
                         (NW road)

XXII        *Vendors*: Victorinus et Fotta
              *Neighbours*:   S     Felix (purchaser) and Preiecta
                               relicta Benenati
                         SW   Preiecta relicta Benenati and
                               Victorinus (vendor)
                         NE   Cresconius
                         E     Cresconius
                         NW   Cresconius
                         N     Cresconius

XXIV    (*a*)   *Vendor*: Fotta relicta Secuniani
            *Neighbours*:   N     heredes Belli
                         NE   heredes Belli
                         NW   Felix (purchaser)
                         (SW irrigation works)
        (*b*)   *Vendor*: Fotta relicta Secuniani
            *Neighbours*:   S     Victorinus
                         NW   Donatianus
                         (SW and NE irrigation works)
        (*c*)   *Vendor*: Fotta relicta Secuniani
            *Neighbours*:   S     Felix (purchaser)
                         NW   heredes Belli
                         N     Donatus

XXVII       *Vendor*: Preiecta relicta Benenati (?)
              *Neighbours*:   (missing)

our power to decide. Elsewhere in the field dispersal is clearly visible: if we consider, for example, the parcels of Sidinna in relation to those of Fortunatianus, there is no way of joining together the fragments of No. XV so as to unite the parcels of both owners. The same goes for the parcels of Fotta in relation to those of the 'heredes Belli' or of Felix. In the field called *Pullatis,* as shown in *Table 2,* the existence of both grouping and dispersal is again evident. Neither Donatianus nor Victorinus and Fotta is known to us as purchasers of land, so this explanation of their grouped parcels is not immediately available, but here also the dispersal of holdings is clear in several cases. Even if by some feat of contortion we could bring together all the known parcels of Victorinus and Fotta, for example, the parcels would have to be very oddly shaped indeed

## Table 2: Pullatis

| III | (*a*) | *Vendors*: Julius Leporius et Coia | | |
|-----|-------|------------------------------------|----|------------------|
|     |       | *Neighbours*: | E | Quintianus |
|     |       |               | S | Quintianus |
|     |       |               | SW | Victorinus |
|     |       |               | NW | Victorinus |
|     | (*b*) | *Vendors*: Julius Leporius et Coia | | |
|     |       | *Neighbours*: | E | Processanus |
|     |       |               | S | Victorinus |
|     |       |               | W | Paternus Iaderis |
|     |       |               | NW | Januarius |
| XIV | (*a*) | *Vendors*: Victorinus et Fotta | | |
|     |       | *Neighbours*: | NE | Victorinus (vendor) |
|     |       |               | N | Victorinus (vendor) |
|     |       |               | SW | Saturninus |
|     |       |               | NW | heredes Benenati |
|     | (*b*) | *Vendors*: Victorinus et Fotta | | |
|     |       | *Neighbours*: | NE | heredes Iaderis |
|     |       |               | NW | heredes Processani |
|     |       |               | SW | heredes Iaderis |
| XXIV |      | *Vendor*: Fotta relicta Secuniani | | |
|     |       | *Neighbours*: | SW | Donatianus |
|     |       |               | W | Donatianus |
|     |       |               | S | heredes Belli |
|     |       |  | | (NE and E irrigation works) |

for us to do the same for Leporius and Coia or for Processanus and his heirs. Whatever the reasons for it may have been, the existence of dispersal as a feature of these lands is surely indisputable.

The question of reasons is obviously an important one. The complicating factor, as we have already noted, is the systematic buying of parcels by the Geminii, the motive for which is not at all clear. The editors of the Tablets suggested that they were merely recovering lands which had passed out of their control in the troubled period during and after the Vandal occupation,[26] and on this view the dispersed holdings would simply be a recent and exceptional feature arising from confused conditions. There is, however, no real evidence that this is what happened, and it is not very likely in any case. The existence of the Tablets makes it clear that the possession and disposal of parcels was still subject to legal supervision and control, and there is no hint of dispute, or even of uncertainty, regarding ownership. We know, moreover, that the first beneficiaries of the Manciane scheme were *coloni* or people of similar status, and if in the 490's we find the same kind of people disposing of their holdings we have to assume, unless there is very strong evidence to the contrary, that they are doing so on this scale for the first time.[27]

There is, in fact, a real possibility that the pattern of distribution and dispersal was part of the original arrangements, or at least something that arose very early on in the process. In three of the Tablets[28] parcels are recorded as being sold 'cum transitis suis', that is, together with the right of access to them, and if we can take this as one of the regular formulae the implication would be that dispersal was part of the system rather than a temporary aberration. The point is well illustrated by a passage in Siculus Flaccus, in which dispersal and rights of access are explicitly connected:

> 'Praeterea et in multis regionibus comperimus quosdam possessores non continuas habere terras, sed particulas quasdam in diversis locis, intervenientibus complurium possessionibus, propter quod etiam complures vicinales viae sunt, ut unusquisque possit ad particulas suas iure pervenire.'[29]

The vocabulary of the passage is slightly reminiscent of that in the Albertini Tablets,[30] and it is just conceivable that Flaccus or his source had seen documents connected with

Manciane tenure or something similar. Even without such a link, however, the reference to dispersed holdings in a writer of (perhaps) the third century[31] is important.

The likelihood that Flaccus is referring to Italy[32] raises the question of how widely the system may have extended. If, as has so far been assumed, it applied only to land on the edges of centuriated areas it will have been primarily an African and Italian phenomenon with possible appearances as a peculiarity further north; and it is on such grounds that Mr Stevens has mentioned it in connection with known field systems at Ripe and West Blatchington in Sussex.[33] Such an assumption, however, could be too cautious if the *lex Manciana* was incorporated into the much wider *lex Hadriana de rudibus agris,* or equally too rash if, as may well have been the case, extensions of the Manciane practice were only local and piecemeal. Archaeology is probably the only source of further clarification, though it must be admitted that field systems are notoriously difficult to handle and any degree of certainty highly unlikely.

## III

The quotation from Siculus Flaccus brings us to the final question concerning the Albertini Tablets, that of their significance for the wider history of field patterns. To several writers the mention by Flaccus of dispersed holdings has suggested a rudimentary version of the open-field system of the Middle Ages,[34] and as will have become obvious the Tablets do go some way to reinforce this impression. Not only the basic dispersal pattern, but several of the details can be paralleled in later documents, and it would be only too easy to take the plunge and claim the *fundus Tuletianos* as an ancestor of, say, Seebohm's Hitchin, with all that this might imply. There are, however, far too many uncertainties, as well as positive difficulties. The Tablets deal with the bits and pieces on the edge of the estate and not with the estate itself. We know nothing in detail of the agricultural practices that existed here, such as the rotation of crops, the system for grazing, even the type of plough. Moreover, the notion of an open-field system becomes a little peculiar when we note that many of the parcels sold had trees on them, and that some may even have been enclosed by a wall.[35]

On the other hand, if we are interested in the origins of the open-field system, we cannot remove this evidence from the discussion entirely. There are obvious resemblances, which may or may not be significant, and we do have the great advantage, in the case of the Manciane system, of knowing a good deal about its context. It is valuable to know, for example, that it arose among small farmers in a fairly developed seigneurial situation, and in connection with the clearing of waste land, both of which points are relevant to the wider discussion. Readers of Marc Bloch,[36] for example, will be familiar with the 'régime des champs ouverts et irreguliers', a system which was basically open-field but composed of parcels which were less regular in both shape and distribution. It seemed to him to be a largely Mediterranean phenomenon, but he noted its occurrence on the edges of more regular systems in northern Europe also, and it was from this that he attributed it to the clearing of waste by individual efforts. To claim a system like this as the direct descendant of that on the *fundus Tuletianos* would plainly be going too far; to see it as an analogous system, arrived at by similar processes and for similar reasons, is still to go a long way, but it is along this kind of path that the answer to some of the more fundamental questions will probably have to be sought.

## Notes

[1] C. Courtois, L. Leschi, C. Perrat, C. Saumagne, *Tablettes Albertini, Actes privés de l'époque vandale*, Paris 1952 (hereafter referred to as *T.A.*).

[2] For their discovery, see *T.A.*, p. 2, and for the geographical features of the area, p. 189 ff.

[3] The land sales are nos. II—XXX and no. XXXII; each of the last seven (nos. XXV—XXX and no. XXXII) has only the latter part of the document surviving, but the rest are reasonably complete.

[4] See *T.A.*, pp. 12—13; the family tree of the Geminii is worked out on p. 208 ff.

[5] For the historical background, see C. Courtois, *Les Vandales et l'Afrique*, Paris 1955, and P. Courcelle, *Histoire littéraire des grandes invasions germaniques*, Paris 1948, especially p. 109 ff.

[6] Other estates are mentioned in the documents: the *fundus Gemiones* appears in no. XXIX as the place in which the deed

was enacted, and the *fundus Magula* in no. IV (cf. also nos. III, VIII and IX, in which the road leading to the place *Magula* is mentioned). Whether these estates were also under the dominium of Fl. Geminius Catullinus is not made clear.

[7] The wording is that of no. III; the same (or a very similar) form of words occurs throughout.

[8] See in particular E. Levy, *West Roman Vulgar Law*, Philadelphia 1951.

[9] In addition to the works referred to in notes 10 and 15 below, the following are of value: Th. Mommsen, *Herm.* vol. 15, 1880, pp. 385–411; A. Schulten, ibid. vol. 29, 1894, pp. 204–30; O. Hirschfeld, *Die Kaiserliche Verwaltungsbeamten bis auf Diocletian*, ed. 2., Berlin 1905, pp. 121–37; M. Rostowzew, *Studien zur Geschichte des römischen Kolonates*, Leipzig and Berlin 1910, p. 321 f.; J. J. van Nostrand, *The Imperial Domains of Africa Proconsularis,* Baltimore 1929, ch. 6; G. Charles-Picard, *La civilisation de l'Afrique romaine*, Paris 1959, p. 61 ff.

[10] *CIL* 8, 25902; the inscription is discussed by R. H. Haywood in *An Economic Survey of Ancient Rome*, ed. Tenney Frank, vol. 4, Baltimore 1938, p. 98 ff., by Tenney Frank himself in *AJP* vol. 47, 1926, pp. 153–70, by J. Toutain, *Mém. Acad. Inscr. et Belles-Lettres* Ser. 1, vol. 11, 1897, pp. 31–81, by E. Cuq, ibid., pp. 83–146, and by numerous others. See also *T.A.,* pp. 116–34.

[11] For the view that the *lex* was the work of, and owed its name to, the T. Curtilius Mancia of *PIR* C 1605, see *T.A.,* pp. 140–142.

[12] Lines 6 ff. of Column I.

[13] The services appear towards the end of the inscription (lines 24 f. of Column IV), where the stone is rather more damaged than in the earlier part, and it is possible that the reference is to the estate as a whole rather than to the *agri subsecivi* alone.

[14] For various suggestions as to what this implies, see the works referred to in note 10 above.

[15] *CIL* 8. 25943; see the commentary by J. Carcopino, *MEFR* vol. 26, 1906, pp. 365–481, and the discussions by Haywood, op. cit. (n. 10), p. 98 ff. and *T.A.,* pp. 99–113.

[16] *T.A.,* p. 113.

[17] A. Merlin, *Inscriptions latines de Tunisie* 629 (from Djenen-ez-Zitouna), quoted and discussed by *T.A.,* pp. 113–4.

[18] *T.A.,* pp. 196–200.

[19] See the discussion in *T.A.*, pp. 196 ff.

[20] *Digest* 50.15.4.

[21] *T.A.*, pp. 196 ff.

[22] That is, parcels or groups of parcels: the total number of individual parcels in the deeds is rather more than a hundred.

[23] Clearly, the list could be shortened if we could be sure that some of the places mentioned only once or twice were sub-divisions of the larger ones: e.g. that the Gunfliones of VI was the same as the Gunfliones of V.9. But there is little to be gained from pressing the material too far.

[24] For the purposes of this part of the discussion it has been assumed that all the deeds were enacted at the same moment of time. Obviously this will involve some inaccuracies, but since the deeds are spread over so short a period (March 493 to April 496, with the majority coming in 493 and 494) the overall picture is not likely to be affected.

[25] There is, of course, the additional point that the Geminii are *buying* in all the fields.

[26] *T.A.*, p. 208 ff.

[27] The effects of buying and selling in general are not easy to assess unless one knows the intentions of the buyers. The nearest one gets to an explanation of their motives is the fact that they frequently buy from widows and minors, but even this could be interpreted either favourably or unfavourably.

[28] Nos. VI. 11–12; VII. 13; and XXV. 1; it is restored by the editors in V. 20 and VIII. 9.

[29] *Gromatici Veteres*, ed. Blume, Lachmann, Rudorff, Berlin 1848, vol. 1, p. 152.

[30] E.g. the use of the word *particulae* to refer to the plots of land (*particellae* in the Tablets); these are said to be 'in diversis locis', a phrase which occurs in several of the deeds (III. 4–5; V. 4–5, etc.).

[31] O. A. W. Dilke, *The Roman Land Surveyors*, Newton Abbot 1971, p. 44.

[32] His work in general seems to relate to Italy, and the phrase 'in multis regionibus' would not on its own suggest one or more of the provinces.

[33] A. C. Thomas (ed.), *Rural Settlement in Roman Britain* (CBA Research Report No. 7), London 1966, pp. 109, 121.

[34] E.g. by F. Seebohm, *The English Village Community*, ed. 3, London 1884, p. 278; A. Dopsch, *The Economic and Social Foundations of European Civilization*, London 1937, pp. 138–9.

[35] *T.A.,* pp. 196 f.; the word *gemio,* which is not uncommon in the Tablets, is glossed elsewhere as *macheriae* (cf. Goetz, *Corpus Gloss. Lat.* p. 298), and could therefore be a walled plot. To be fair, one should perhaps point out that walled plots are not unknown in open-field contexts later, for example, in the ninth-century polyptychs of northern France.

[36] *Les caractères originaux de l'histoire rurale française,* Oslo 1931, reprinted Paris 1960, vol. 1, pp. 49–51, with Planches VII–IX, and vol. 2, pp. 60–64.

John Percival,
University College,
Cardiff.

# 16

## Modern India and Ancient Europe

In absorbing the improbable truth that Tom Stevens is nearing seventy, it seems high time to pay him back in his own coin. Tom's strength has above all been as a teacher. His written and spoken words again and again provoked his pupils and his colleagues, waving before them novel and puzzling questions that orthodox assumptions had been too discreet to raise. He did not always come up with definitive and satisfying answers. That is a virtue in a teacher, for it leaves the pupil with work to do, whereas the smooth and rounded answer tends to abash and dispirit him, contrasting his teacher's superior knowledge and wisdom with his own lesser learning and dimmer insight. Tom's work has embodied the dictum of his own exemplar, Robin Collingwood, that in all historical enquiry the important thing is to get the questions right; the answers are thereafter comparatively easy.

One of Tom's challenges was to draw the attention of his hearers and his readers to out-of-the-way sources that it had never occurred to them to consider. It is more than forty years since he first warned me that a study of the peoples of the western Roman provinces is incomplete without the evidence of Irish literature. That was a generation before Kenneth Jackson published his 1964 Rede Lecture, *The Oldest Irish Tradition; a Window on the Iron Age;* a generation before excavators began to make serious use of descriptions of fortified halls in heroic literature. Tom had neither time nor opportunity to explore such out-of-the-way sources himself in depth. All he could do was to rub our noses in their existence, and leave it to later generations to make what use they could of the stimulus he gave.

It therefore seems appropriate to mention observations that I have no chance to study. A few years ago I was the guest of the Indian University Grants Committee, visiting historians in a number of Indian universities. I was also able to stay for the best part of a week in a village in central India on the edge of the Forest; and spent one day as the guest of the king of a 'tribal people', who came under the notice of established authority a little over fifty years ago. The occasion was fruitful, both because it was the day of their annual assembly, held in what had been a forest grove until the woodland was recently cleared for agriculture, and because my business was to help him to draft in English a petition against the maltreatment of his people by government officials. Discussion therefore taught me somewhat more of current practices than a casual visitor might have learnt; and to avoid any possible embarrassment, I refer to these people simply as 'TP'. On the way to India, I was also able to spend the inside of a week in the Lebanon, visiting Tyre and Sidon, Baalbek and Byblos.

It is possible to report only what I noticed. What anyone notices in a brief visit to a land unknown is necessarily subjective, for the questions which thrust themselves into the visitor's mind are those that his own experience has prompted. I have therefore resisted the temptation to look up the relevant literature, for there is no half-way house between unadorned reportage and thorough study; attempts to dabble in unfamiliar disciplines are likely to be more misleading than confessed ignorance. So I point to no conclusions, and leave it to others to enquire whether or not any of my random observations have any significant connection.

One of the problems of the pre-Belgic Iron Age in Britain is the striking rarity of burials. Their absence does not figure largely in modern literature, for at present archaeological research concentrates chiefly on what has been found; as yet, scant attention is paid to what is not found, either because it did not exist, or because it has left little or no trace in durable or preserved materials that excavation can recognise. In much of France, and in Britain in the East Riding and elsewhere, the elaborate burials of important people hit the archaeological headlines; and in parts of south-western Britain and in Scotland the graves of lesser men are recorded. Their existence throws into relief the almost total absence of cemeteries, or even individual burials, in much of the Midlands and the south-east, in sharp contrast with the frequency of Belgic cemetries and tombs in the last centuries B.C. A map of Iron Age Britain now records the homes of scores of peoples who were the contempories of the men of Little Woodbury, All Cannings Cross and other type sites. But it does not mark their burial places. Archaeologically, these people were immortal; their bodies have left no discoverable traces. Some have even suggested that bodies were left exposed in the woodlands, for animals to devour and destroy. A more sober line of enquiry invites us to guess at a mode of burial which leaves no visible trace.

Normal Hindu burial leaves no trace. It is most strikingly and permanently to be seen on the banks of the Ganges, especially at the holy city of Benares, where many elderly people who can afford the journey repair in old age, that their funeral may be conducted within its sacred precincts. The river bank is low and is regularly flooded. The edge of the bank is lined with neatly constructed piles of timber, ready for cremation. When a body has been burnt, a pile of ash remains, and is altogether removed when the next winter's rains flood the bank's edge. The funerals of the poor are often perfunctory; the rite requires that mourners purify themselves by a ritual bathe; one memorable sight was a single mourner, perhaps a son, who had bathed, and stood holding his shirt to dry by the embers of the fire, making his father useful to the last.

Not everyone lives by rivers, and not everyone is Hindu; but distance makes no bar, and the observances of the dominant people and religion permeate the practices of subject neighbours. On the journey to the homeland of the TP, very many burial places of older peoples were visible from the road. Their surface indications were circles of small stones, up to ten or fifteen feet in diameter; occasionally one was marked by a tall standing stone, roughly squared and tapered, the twin of those that are occasionally to be seen in northern English churchyards. Frequently, in the centre of the circle, the top of a huge humped-back stone poked above the surface, its visible portion not unlike the top of a European trilith, though it may be doubted if the burial went deep enough to accommodate supporting stones beneath. When I asked the king of the TP about his present burial customs, I was told that graves were still surrounded by circles of small stones, but that the large stones were no longer placed in the centre. Present custom however required that when a body was cremated the ashes were carried in an urn to the nearest river, many miles away. They were left by its bank for a fortnight, and then half the

231

ashes were thrown into the river, the other half brought home for burial within a stone circle.

It appeared that this practice was a recent compromise between traditional burial and prevalent Hindu custom. I did not however observe modern stone circles, and the information needed to be accepted with some reserve, since politeness commonly requires that a questioner receives an answer which he is thought to wish to hear, and in putting my question I had imprudently described the circles I had seen. But the statement of the carrying of the urn to the river bank was unsolicited; and so was an additional unexpected piece of information. I was told that the difference between inhumation and cremation depended upon whether the person buried was married or single. It is not probable that this distinction can be applied directly to European cemeteries of mixed rite; but it is a salutary warning that the kind of differences which appear all-important to the modern excavator may often prove to have a quite simple and not very important cause, which no guess-work would consider . . . but in this case a question very simply resolved by separately sexing and ageing the bones from cremation and inhumation, a test that few excavators would undertake unless the query were in their minds.

It further transpired that royalty had recently adopted a burial practice quite different from that of their subjects. The king now lived in a well-built modern house. But he had been born in the Iron Age fort of his ancestors, whose existence is said to be attested as early as the twelfth century. It had been evacuated in his father's time, and was already a grass grown ancient monument. But in the garden of his royal house he had buried his father in a large monumental Muslim type tomb, and expected to rest himself in a similar tomb in the same garden. These royal tombs, distinguished in place and style from those of commoners, inevitably recalled the frequency in Britain of the round barrows of the Bronze Age, the graves of single burials of important persons, rarely matched by cemeteries of their poorer subjects. Their context is vividly documented by Homer's account of the funeral of Patroclus, whose bones were separated from those of his lesser companions, burnt on the same pyre, and were buried in a golden vase, surrounded by a ring of stones, within which the earth was piled to form a barrow, 'seemly but not large'; and his staunch horses were said to have stood 'as firm as a gravestone erected on a barrow'. But nothing was said of the others who died with him.

Lesser men were interred in domestic vessels. Some European Bronze Age cemetries commonly used 'collared urns', bucket-shaped pottery vessels, whose rims were thickened at an angle to the body of the pot. In many parts of India, the roads are thronged with women carrying water on their heads. Sometimes the pots were carried on a thick bun of hair, sometimes on a pad of soft material designed to maintain an upright balance. Frequently, the women carry two vessels, a bucket, and on top of it a spherical bowl, whose rounded base sits easily within the bucket top and helps to balance it. Now, nine-tenths of the vessels are of light metal. But in a forest village, the potter still made their earthenware predecessors. The process was in two stages. A large flat wheel was rotated by a stick, and its momentum enabled two or three vessels to be thrown at one movement of the stick. When thrown, these vessels had a remarkable resemblance to plain Belgic urns in France and Britain; but they were left to dry for two of three days in the sun before the second stage. Then the potter thrust his hand inside, and with his other hand beat the surface with a small wooden bat. The walls of the pot were thinned, and the interior enlarged to two or three times its original size, to give maximum capacity with the least weight; the pot was commonly globular, but might have a small flat base or foot, though the point where the bowl rested upon the bucket remained perfectly circular. The pottery bucket upon which the bowl rested was strengthened to support its weight by thickening its rim. Hindu burial custom casts the ashes into the river, and does not inter them in domestic vessels; but if urn burial in domestic vessels were the practice, such strengthened buckets were available. It may be that the European collared urn owes its origin to a water-carrying bucket designed to support a bowl.

Burial practices are rooted in the religion of any society. Modern Hindu religion seems at first sight infinitely remote from the religions of Europe, distinguished by uninhibited rococo decoration of its great temples. But its origins are less remote, and are well recorded, especially in the Vedic hymns, whose core is held to be preserved virtually unchanged in precise metre, credibly reported to have been composed not later than about 1000 B.C. In the earliest layer of Hindu mythology, the Father of all the Gods is the Sky, Dyaus Piter. He is the Greek God Father Zeus, the Latin Jupiter; but not long after the Hindus moved into India, he was superseded by warrior God Indra. The numerous characteristics common to

233

both the Indian Brahmin and the Celtic Druids have often enough been remarked. These are the most obvious among numerous pointers which suggest that the divinities and the priesthoods of Greece and Rome, of the Celts and the Indian, descend from a well-developed religion observed by their common ancestors before the migrations of the Indo-European peoples into their present homes, in and after the second millennium B.C.

The bare noticing of this apparent common origin does not get us very far by itself, for the religious beliefs of each people developed separately after they parted company, and each was deeply modified by the customs and traditions of the lands into which it moved. Moreover, they continued to influence each other. A few such modifications are well evidenced. Philo and other ancient authors believed, probably rightly, that the ascetics of the late centuries B.C. in Egypt and the Syrian provinces were inspired by the example of Indian asceticism; and it was from the Egyptian and Syrian ascetics that European monasticism received its original inspiration. Small puzzling details also obtrude upon the observer. The prevailing Indian gesture of respect to the Gods is, and apparently always has been, a slight bow, accompanied by pressing together the palms and closed fingers of the hand. That is the modern form of Christian prayer. But it was not so in the Roman period, when men prayed with arms raised outstreched above their heads. Despite the enormous bulk of Christian literature, no one has yet discovered when the modern form prevailed among Christians in different regions, except that it was some time after the fall of Western Rome; but it seems probable that its origin is Indian, though many Christians would be disturbed to acknowledge that their manner of prayer was devised for the worship of representations of the phallus and the vagina.

One of the common characteristics of early Indo-European religion was worship in a woodland grove rather than in a special building, temple or church. The dating and the reasons for the origin of the Greek, Roman, and Celtic temple building are not easily discovered, though doubtless they owed much to the practices of earlier eastern mediterranean peoples. But Indian record offers some evidence. The Indian temple is a comparatively late development, for the climate permits splendid statues of the Gods to survive in the open air. One striking instance lately came to light when a new village was established in a forest clearing. The educated landowner noticed large bumps in the ground, which proved to be statues of the Gods, carved not significantly later than the turn of B.C. and A.D. He re-erected those that were lifesize or larger, but wisely left smaller ones buried, for objects small enough to be carried invite looters.

The large statues were here re-erected on their original site. Testing established that it was unlikely that they had ever been housed in a permanent building; but within weeks of their re-erection, the villagers had surrounded them with slender uprights of bamboo or similar wood, with horizontal pieces lached to their tops, from which they hang the feet of goats sacrificed in honour of the Gods, and eaten for the nutriment of the villagers. There are powerful indications that these flimsy shrines were a good deal nearer to those which surrounded the Gods when they were first carved than to the later temple structures; a similar token of sanctity in another place consisted of no more than a rectangular outline of white paint, daubed round a small rock shelf, at shoulder height by the roadside, on which were deposited a number of small figurines

The social and political changes that underlay the introduction of the temple are well enough documented, though their interpretation is arguable. The earliest records divide Hindu society into four classes, termed *varna*, the warrior aristocracy (*rajanya*, later *kshatriya*), the learned (*brahmin*), non-agricultural workers, chiefly craftsmen and traders (*vaishya*), and cultivators (*shudra*). Later, the obligation of each son to follow his father's callin₁ imposed caste (*jati*) upon the lower orders, effectively preven ing them from making common cause against their betters. Modern understanding of this peculiarly Indian development had been bedevilled by the incautious habit of translating both *varna* and *jati* by the same English word, 'caste'. But the basic division into four classes closely matches the earliest accounts of Irish society, divided into *feni* (warrior aristocrats), the learned *druids* and *filid*, the craftsmen *seor*, and the subject client cultivators *celi*. Both societies encouraged the belief that the noble and learned classes descended from superior conquerors, the subject cultivators from inferior natives; and both honoured the craftsmen, assimilating them to the ruling classes, in sharp contrast with the inferior servile status of the Greek and Roman craftsmen, from the time of Socrates onward.

The earlier political history of India turns upon the authority of great kings, especially of those established on the middle and lower Ganges, whose empire at its greatest was even larger than the territory of modern India, and who ruled in alliance with the nobility, encouraging rationalist philosophy, notably that of the Upanishads and of the Buddha, to the displeasure of many ritualist *Brahmin*. It was in the early centuries A.D. that the rise of powerful and localised merchant interests coincided with the disintegration of the monarchy and a growing identity of interest between the aristocracy and the *Brahmin*, who now acquired something of the functions described by the Christian and English word 'priest', a word that remains a misleading translation of the earlier *Brahmin*, or of Irish *druid*. The new theology, based upon the Trinity of Brahma the Creator, Vishnu the Preserver, and Shiva the Destroyer of an evil world, superior to the multitude of lesser Gods, is the recognisable beginning of modern Hinduism. The new theology also gave prominence to the symbols and beliefs of the native, pre-Hindu population, that are attested on the reliefs of Monendjodaro, carved long before the Indians entered India, in particular the phallus (*lingam*) and the humped bull and cow, although the earlier Vedic texts had scornfully denounced their conquered native subjects as the filthy worshippers of the phallus and the bull.

The change is marked by a large number of inscriptions, recording gifts of land by noblemen to men of religion, whose wording is curiously akin to the land charters of early medieval Europe, the principal difference being that a grant recorded in durable stone stood less need of dubious recopying in later centuries.

Another innovation of the new order was the stone temple. The few surviving very early temples strongly suggest Sassanid Persian inspiration, with perhaps some debt to Egyptian architecture, but very soon the familiar concepts of the Hindu temple replaced these foreign influences. Politically, the decline of the monarchy weakened the guard that earlier kings had kept upon the north-west frontier, and exposed India to later conquest by the Mongols, and thereafter by the Persian Moghuls. But the memory of the long but distant unity of the sub-continent helped the Moghuls, and after them the British Raj, to revive and maintain its unity; and since independence, when Moghuls and the Raj are no longer popular memories, the name of Asoka, the greatest of the ancient kings, long forgotten, reappears as the frequent title of a restaurant or a street in a housing estate.

Temple buildings were a comparatively late import into India.

236

They reach back to the religous structures of the near east, in a climate that needed no roof, and behind them to the simpler structures of stone age religion. One noteworthy temple at Byblos, assigned to the Bronze Age, commands attention, though its modern aspect prompts caution, since it was 'moved intact ... and reconstructed' on another site, evidently to facilitate the investigation of structures beneath. It consists of a large central stone or altar, placed on a small raised platform surrounded by a double rectangle of standing stones. Individually, the stones are tapered obelisks, smaller versions of the great monoliths of Egypt; but collectively they made a surround of columns; if the climate had required a roof, the structure would have closely resembled a Roman-Celtic temple in northern Gaul or Britain.

A week later I visited Rajgir (Rajagriha), some 70 miles south of the Ganges, capital of the kingdom whose empire the Mauryan kings later extended to Afghanistan and almost all India. It was there that the Buddha lived and preached, about 500 B.C. The vast area is naturally protected by surrounding hills, their crest strengthened by a surrounding wall some 35 miles in circumference; the blocking fort that guarded the main gate is on the scale of a Roman legionary fortress. Some hundreds of yards inside the gate was a shrine consisting of a small raised platform surrounded by a double rectangle of standing stone. It too bore a warning, 'These stones have been moved', raised apparently to their original upright position. The structure might have been the twin of the Byblos temple, except that the individual columns did not taper like obelisks; instead, they were hammer-headed, each in the shape of a letter T, with a small cross piece. They looked like a stone imitation of a wooden structure, in which some kind of continuous cornice had once surmounted the columns.

Rectangular and circular buildings do not necessarily distinguish one religion from another; most Christian western churches are rectangular, but we need go no further than Cambridge to find a round Christian church; and the pre-Roman religion of Britain and Gaul constructed rectangular as well as circular shrines. In size and shape the shrines of Byblos and Rajgir, though a thousand years apart in date, had some affinities with Roman-Celtic temples. But the shape of the Rajgir columns forcibly recalled the grander architecture of Stonehenge, itself the successor, at least in typology, of the double circles of wood that recent archaeologists quaintly call 'Woodhenges'. Stonehenge is a unique sophisticated monument, indebted to the traditions and perhaps of the craftsmen of Mycenean Greece; but behind it lies the long tradition of circles of rough unhewn boulders, very numerous in Britain and France. These too were met in India; but, unlike their European counterparts, they were still in use, so that something of their purpose could be seen.

At the annual assembly of the TP, the most prominent feature on the ground was a large double circle of massive whitewashed boulders. The Indian officials disliked it. Some explained the stone circle as a traffic roundabout, though there was no traffic to be routed; others suggested that the farmer had piled away stones cleared from his land, though without explaining why he had arranged them neatly and white-washed them. On close examination it was evident that the inner circle stones had been there for a long time, and were deeply embedded into the ground, with the recent whitewash spilling on the surrounding grass, but the outer circle had been placed there quite recently, with gaps between the grass and the bottom edges, where the unwhitewashed bits that the brush could not reach were visible. The TP king said that the circle had been there when he first came to the site as a child forty years before, but that his people were not now allowed to use it.

The government had provided an alternative shrine a few hundred yards away, a tiny Hindu style temple, where the snake God was to reveal his presence at midnight, in the presene of TP alone. A band, led by traditional oxhorns, played beside it, while a chain of women hastily constructed a mud Hindu phallus; nearby was a walled compound wherein the women were to cook their evening meal. But, in the midst of the crowd of visitors who sold ochre, sweetmeats, or cigarettes, or showed films in tents advocating new agricultural techniques or the use of contraceptives, we noticed that the TP themselves were conspicuously absent. When asked, the king told us that they were down by the banyan trees. We arrived as the last of them left. The area beneath the trees contained some dozens of small scale replicas of the great stone circle, each stone a little larger than a human fist. In most of them, the embers were still glowing of a fire that had cooked a sacrificial ritual meal in honour of Agni, the God of Fire, in Latin *ignis.* The little family circles were used because the communal sacrifice in the great stone circle was no longer permitted; but for the TP it was still the principal purpose and ceremony of the gathering, and on most of the small stones mystic signs were painted in ochre.

Agni is one of the few of the greater Gods of the time of Dyaus Piter whose worship is still widespread. At a tea party in one village where electricity had recently been installed, our host switched on the light as dusk came on; one of the guests, an educated gentleman of wide learning, clasped his hands in prayer and bowed to the light bulb, as his ancestors for thousands of years before had bowed to Agni when the evening lamps were lit. But in much of the countryside, Agni and the old Hindu Gods are overshadowed by a still greater divinity.

There was no doubt about the prevailing countryside religion in the areas I visited. Everywhere there were shrines to Kali, the Black Mother, whom orthodox theology has assimilated and represents as the wife of Siva. But she is honoured where he is not. Her shrines are simple pieces of light timber, like those erected round the statues in the forest village; and commonly have the feet of sacrificed goats hung from them. The goat sacrifice is inescapable. In one village, a communal effort had dug a large well; as soon as water was reached, the entire work force knocked off for a day and a half to sacrifice its goats to Kali, and beside the well were the bamboos and the goats' feet. When I mentioned Kali to an eminent judge, he smiled and assured me that if he asked a country witness in his district to swear upon the name of Vishnu or Siva, he might as well ask for an oath on the Christian Bible; but if he required an oath in the name of Kali, he would be sure that he got the absolute truth from his witness.

Yet the name and worship of Kali is little spoken of before strangers. In one region, we noticed a number of corpses of goats stuck high in tree tops, and several times enquired the reason; the answers were varied, the commonest being the rational explanation that the animal had died of disease, and was put in the tree to prevent other animals from eating it and catching the disease. But in one remote spot we found a twelve year old boy beside a tree with a goat skin stuffed with straw, and at the tree foot a number of tall poles with small projections lashed to most of them. He told us that once a year the young men of the village walked a mile or more to this tree on stilts, with the two oldest villagers in front of them, tapping the ground with sticks and beseeching Kali to keep the village clear of flies and mosquitoes; they then cooked, ate and sacrificed the goat, putting its stuffed skin in the tree top, and piling the stilts and sticks against the tree. When we reached the village, we found that the magic worked. The village was remarkably free of flies; but we had no zoologist with us to tell us why.

The moral of the unadvertised worship of Kali is twofold. It illustrates the capacity of a dominant culture and religion to absorb, countenance and contain alien practices, with greater ease than, for example, Catholic acceptance of the Black Madonna in South America. But it also warns of the important elements in the life and thought of a simple rural economy that archaeological enquiry cannot hope to discover; for the flimsy shrines of Kali rarely contain anything more durable than a rag doll image, coloured black or blue, and can leave no more permanent traces than cremation on a low river bank.

These are all lightweight observations, a selection of subjective impressions accumulated in a rapid visit, not understood, and not deeply considered. They raise questions, but the questions are not answered.

But though the questions are light, they treat of major themes. Greek and Roman civilisation transformed Europe and the Mediterranean, and sired our modern society; but it thereby obliterated almost all memory of the pre-Roman past. Indian society experienced no such transformation, and until the coming of the Persians and the Europeans, it evolved by its own momentum, disturbed only slightly by external influence. Evolution involved much change, so that no modern practice can be simply transported into the remote antiquity of India itself, let alone to Europe by analogy. But because change was less, and free from dramatic oversets, the sensitive study of past and present Indian society suggests many fruitful questions which the European evidence does not pose of itself.

Above all, it warns against over-simple answers deduced from the sparse evidence of Europe. It formally disproves the common assumption that early societies were simple. On the contrary, it demonstrates that early societies are complicated, shot through with ingrained contradictions and variations, and that it is modern society which is relatively simple; much as modern western European languages have shed the involved inflexions and conjugations of the past. But Indian society is also simpler than the European past; it shows what actually happened when one branch diverged from the rest, and developed independently, when and how it influenced the alien peoples it conquered, and was influenced by them; and how it affected and was affected by its later resident Persian and its absentee English conquerors. The study is comparatively simple because the Indians undertook but one major migration, and succumbed to two major foreign conquests, both of them in well-documented and relatively recent times. But each region of early Europe experienced a whole series of migrations and conquests, a repeated process of division of old unities, of regrouping into new loyalties and new conventions, each of them interacting on their neighbours. The example of a society that suffered less violent disturbance may serve to guide the study of deeper and more frequent change.

All these are problems for the distant future. The serious study of ancient India is still hampered by the current prejudices of the nostalgic heirs of a Raj recently ended, and by the still raw resentments of a newly independent nation. The men and money that such study demands are still in short supply. The day when the Indian evidence can be fully and soberly exploited by students of early Europe will not come for several generations yet. In the meantime, it is possible only to fly a kite, to point to concealed riches, admitting that the twentieth century scholar is about as well equipped to interpret ancient Indo-European society as was a thirteenth century scholar to interpret the Greek and Roman past. It is evident that little of what has been said here is likely to be of immediate use to contemporary scholars; but to draw attention to evidence and lines of enquiry that may prove profitable to the future seems a fitting tribute to Tom Stevens.

John Morris,
University College,
London.

# Index

Latin names, except those of emperors, authors, and other well known or notorious persons, are indexed under *nomina*. For Iamnia, Iulius, etc. *see* Jamnia, Julius.

243

# Index

# Index

# Index